The Miracle Bridge

Let Go and Let God Heal

MIKE SIMPSON

Copyright © 2019 by Mike Simpson

All rights reserved. No part of this book may be used or reproduced by any means, graphic, electronic, or mechanical, including photocopying, recording, taping, or by any information storage retrieval system, without the written permission of the publisher except in the case of brief quotations embodied in critical articles and reviews.

FOREWORD

In the fall of 1999, I was a 20-year-old college student, a good kid with a loving upbringing. On my way to a catering job my car stalled out on a deserted road. Two men stopped, offered to help me but when my back was turned they attacked me and forced me down into a ravine at gunpoint. They made me play Russian roulette on myself and with another individual. That person didn't survive. My life was forever changed. I was able to escape physically but not mentally.

My life was out of control. I suffered from a major case of PTSD. I had continual nightmares, guilt, self-loathing, fear, depression, anger, and anxiety. I turned to alcohol. I got kicked out of college and couldn't hold a job. I had multiple run-ins with the law. I went on a 90 minute televised high-speed chase and ended up in L.A. county jail and Chino prison. I thought this low point in my life would make me change. But I couldn't.

After my time in jail I went back to school but I could not shake the memory of that night from my mind. PTSD and alcohol ruled my life. I got kicked out of school yet again. I went on weeks-long drinking binges. After a binge, many times I would pass out on a sidewalk or alleyway. People would leave food next to me sometimes. Once I got picked up and taken to the hospital. I couldn't live that way any more. I had destroyed myself and ruined relationships with everybody that loved me. I wanted to end it all. I checked into a motel room determined to kill myself. Thankfully I didn't succeed.

I was beyond desperate. Having tried multiple rehabs and therapists without success I really didn't know where to turn. Without looking for Mike, somehow I found him. After Mike heard my story, he was still confident that he could help me. I was skeptical because of failures with all of the treatments that I had tried but I didn't know what else to do. So I put my faith in Mike.

Mike had a specific plan for me. Along with all of the different machines that he has at his wellness center, he used NLP and hypnotherapy to get to the root of my problem. I didn't think that I could be hypnotized but my willingness to trust him allowed me to do so. He used an example of me having a big rock in my mental garden. The rock was preventing me from living a normal life. I had to get rid of that rock so I could plant new seeds to help me grow into a new and better version of myself. I spent 28 days at the center using the machines. I had eight one-on-one hypnotherapy sessions with Mike. The sessions that I had with him are what made a difference. In the very first session I had a real breakthrough. I saw a better version of myself. To get to that better version of myself I had to forgive myself and those evil men from that night. During the first session I was able to forgive them.

By the fourth session I was able to forgive myself and discovered that I had value and purpose. Mike's method truly works. After I left the center he gave me the tools to maintain my value and purpose. I've discovered that with maintenance you can find peace. After eighteen years of suffering Mike Simpson gave me my life back. I am forever grateful.

Thank you Mike!

Christopher Smyres

Hypnotherapy has long been misunderstood however the efficacy as a therapeutic intervention is recognized as a viable, versatile and powerful modality today. Hypnotherapy does not subject a person involuntarily to do or say things outside of their own will. The hypnotherapist however acts as a guide to coach the person into a relaxed brain wave state, deepening their connection to their subconscious mind. This state then provides an effective tool to access one's innate strengths to cope and produce the desired changes to improve one's emotional or physical well being.

I had a wonderful experience doing multiple sessions of hypnotherapy with Mike Simpson. I have been to many therapists in the past and I am also a psychotherapist. My hypnosis sessions with Mike were profoundly insightful. Mike's techniques provided a deeper way to address my concerns at the root. These experiences with Mike have made me realize that every psychotherapist should add brain stimulation and hypnotherapy to their practice for true, deep healing in their patients.

Hypnotherapy can be one of the most effective treatments for certain individuals and oftentimes it provides phenomenal results that can significantly change forever the quality of a person's life.

Dr. Danielle Daniel, PsyD., LCSW

Table of Contents

Acknowledgment 1

Chapter One: How It All Began 4

Chapter Two: Healing Perspectives from an Outsider 20

Chapter Three: The Bridge to JC 34

Chapter Four: The Subconscious Mind 56

Chapter Five: Follow the Path 91

Chapter Six: When a Limiting Belief Is Born 116

Chapter Seven: The Cave of Unbelief 137

Chapter Eight: The Victim Can Become The Martyr 158

Chapter Nine: Are You The Enabler? 180

Chapter Ten: What If I Don't Deserve To Be Happy? 192

Chapter Eleven: The Blended Family 218

Chapter Twelve: My Own Buried Pain 229

Chapter Thirteen: Be Careful What You Wish For 254

Chapter Fourteen: Spiritual Opposition PG-13 276

Chapter Fifteen: The Bridge 292

Appendix 309

Acknowledgment

I would have never guessed 30 years ago that my life would become a container to gather so many amazing stories of tragedy and healing. But here I am with an astonishing collection of true stories I am excited to share with you.

It has certainly been an interesting journey leading up to this book. I didn't ever plan on doing this type of work professionally. I found Neuro-linguistic Programming (NLP) and hypnosis during a difficult time in my life. After it transformed me, I found that this was my calling in life to use these to help others. For many years I donated my time to do NLP sessions in the front room of our home. My wife, Diana, would often take the kids and leave for activities when strangers would show up at the door. I'm at a stage in my life where I would like to share this information with anyone who is looking to find real healing.

I would like to personally thank all of you who have had the courage to allow me to share your stories for the benefit of others. Perhaps, through the grace of God, others will find this book and use it as inspiration to create their own miracles.

Some names have been changed for privacy, but many contributors have chosen to share their real names in order to join their voices with mine in joint collaborations pertaining to this important work. If you visit my website **TheMiracleBridge.com/Contributors**, you can learn more about their projects. My hope is that this website, along with **MikeSimpson.live**, will become healing portals where we can build a virtual community for support to help the many ailing souls walking alone in this world. It is time we all come together and forget about the fences. This book is not about religion, but rather about true healing modalities that include God. I am excited for you to learn some amazing new techniques I am using to transform the world, one person at a time! I am planning on doing free monthly podcasts to present some real-time follow-up to these stories. Watch these websites for more information pertaining to this movement.

For their editing contributions and technical feedback, thank you Anne Hill, Dahlen Downing, Rosalie Lines, Danny Quinney and Kate Anderson. Every little bit helped.

I would also like to personally acknowledge Wanda Cooper for her ongoing influence and guidance with this book. Single-handedly, Wanda weaned me from the many exclamation points I used in the past! I didn't realize I was *yell-writing* without her humorous feedback!!!!! Wanda is the author of *Broken Vessel Restored* which is a powerful book on healing that goes hand in hand with *The Miracle Bridge*. I encourage you to read it. Thank you, Wanda!

I would also like to thank each of my children for their influence in my life. This has been quite the ride! You have filled my life with meaning, purpose, fun and chaos! This book is for you.

Last but not least, I would like to thank my beautiful and loyal wife, Diana, for her undying belief and support to help me get here. Diana, you believed in me when no one else did. I literally would not be here without you. I wrote and recorded a song for Diana titled, "This is Me," that explains how I feel about you. I love you forever. You can hear this song on **MikeSimpson.live/Music**.

CHAPTER ONE

How It All Began

"Stop taking your medications! You have absolutely no sign of Graves' Disease. Even your antibodies are normal! Can I ask you what you did? Graves' does not just go away!"

Nearly two years prior to this after-hours call from our doctor, my wife, Diana, and I knew something was wrong. Both of us have always been physically active and love to go mountain biking, rock climbing, and hiking, but we knew something alarming was happening. One day we were mountain biking and I noticed that Diana was no longer close behind me. This was really out of the ordinary, so I stopped and waited for her. She normally beats me to the top of the mountain or is pushing me from close behind.

A few minutes later she caught up to me and I asked her what was wrong. She didn't really have an answer. We noticed over the next few months that her skin took on a gray pallor, and her energy was completely gone. She almost passed out anytime she stood up. She was also becoming adversely affected by eating any food, especially food that contained gluten. It was a frustrating and scary time for both of us.

We decided to go to our doctor for help. After meeting with two separate doctors, doing blood tests, and a radioactive iodine uptake test, Diana was officially diagnosed with Graves' Disease, which occurs when the thyroid becomes overactive and emits too much thyroid hormone. Diana was also severely anemic. Things were so bad she had to be placed on an IV at the hospital to supplement her iron levels. She received these treatments every week for two months. She was also immediately placed on other medications to help with the horrific symptoms of itching and exhaustion. We were deeply concerned because our lives were changing drastically.

The only medical solution we found was to put Diana on a medication that was designed to slow down her hyper-active thyroid, but this also caused her many painful and unhealthy side-effects that were not likely to subside. We learned that eventually her thyroid would die and she would have to remain on medication for the rest of her life. We were stuck between a rock and a hard place.

About two weeks before the after-hours call mentioned above, Diana and I were sitting in the car at the grocery store on a Saturday afternoon when I gingerly asked her if she wanted to talk about the Graves' Disease. She knew this was a loaded question. You see, I had spent the previous 22 years practicing Neuro-Linguistic Programming (NLP) and she knew I was inviting her to dig deeper into the issue. She agreed reluctantly, and the conversation began. After only a few minutes of poignant questions, Diana was in tears and talking about her father's massive stroke which happened few years prior.

We discussed the events and circumstances that led up to his stroke. In July of 2013 while Diana and her father, Don, were driving around looking for a home for him to purchase, he lost his balance on a steep driveway while getting out of the car. He fell and struck his head sharply on the cement curb. She helplessly witnessed the entire traumatic ordeal. We rushed Don to the Instacare where he received many stitches across his eyebrow and wrist. He was in really bad shape. The doctor opted not to do an MRI or a CT scan of his head, which turned out to be a tragic mistake. They released him, totally unaware of his internal bleeding of the brain.

After this devastating day at the Instacare, we drove Don to his home and finally got him into bed. We were exhausted as we made the drive to our own home. Diana was completely traumatized and emotionally drained from the events of the day.

Later that night, we got a 3 am wake-up call from Diana's mother telling us that Don had fallen out of bed and was immobile. We rushed over and found Don on the floor unable to speak or move. At the hospital, the news was bad. He had experienced a massive stroke and we were informed that it was a miracle he was still alive. We also sadly learned that too much time had expired since the stroke to allow him to have a certain injection that could have possibly reversed the effects of the stroke. There were no options. We felt completely helpless. That night in the hospital, Diana's deadly conflict began.

Back to the conversation in the car at the grocery store. Diana's regret and heartache was now surfacing in our conversation with great anguish. She was berating herself, "If only I would have done this!" or "If only I had done that!" She had and felt so many regrets, so much guilt. She just knew if she had insisted on an MRI or a CT scan, or slept next to his bed that tragic night, then maybe this wouldn't have happened. There were so many narratives in her head that proved it was her fault. Here in front of both of us (as I deeply suspected) her guilt and shame were literally taking Diana to the grave with her father. Literally taking her to Graves'. After identifying her core conflict, I asked her if she felt worthy to be alive and healthy, and the answer was exactly as you might suspect: "No."

Diana was punishing herself because she believed she should have known better. It wasn't fair that her father had to suffer. It was at that juncture where I presented Diana with the outcome of her self-proclaimed death sentence — our family would have to live without her while she was busy paying the price for something that was completely out of her control. Diana's amazing loyalty to her father was literally taking her down with the ship like a brave captain.

Yes, she was actually going down with her father. But that day the decision to denounce her misplaced self-punishment turned out to be a miraculous turning point in her life. And it actually put her back out in front of me on the mountain bike again, right where she belongs. This powerful conversation in the car literally stopped her Graves' right in its tracks.

Mountain Bike Mama/Hey, Hey! Get Out Of My Way!

Lest you think I'm exaggerating about Diana being as tough as nails, I need to share a true mountain biking story. We used to try and catch a ride every evening that I got home from work before dark.

When Diana was nine months pregnant with our youngest son, she decided we should go mountain biking. I knew better than to try to coddle her. When she wants to do something, she does it! So we loaded up the bikes and hauled them to our favorite evening trail.

From behind, Diana looked completely normal and you would have never been able to tell she was pregnant. But her profile view showed an obvious baby bump between her and the handlebars. It didn't matter. It was a mere inconvenience. I affectionately gave Diana a new nickname that day: *Mountain Bike Mama!*

Up the trail we climbed, and yes, she was out in front of me. There is one really sketchy downhill section of the trail that always takes our breath away. It honestly feels like we were falling off a cliff when we dropped in and the tires barely manage to stay on the trail because it is so steep. We always take this drop-in with a full head of steam from the previous downhill rush.

This particular day, when we arrived at this downhill section of the trail, there were a couple of young men frozen in fear, daring each other to go down first. Diana flew right past them and dropped in without hesitation. I was still riding right behind her. As I rode past them I heard one of the guys shriek, "THAT LADY IS PREGNANT!"

I didn't stop and ask them for their man cards, but we all knew they had just been shown up by Mountain Bike Mama! I had compassion for them because I knew all too well how they felt. Life can be so unfair.

Diana went into labor only a few days after that ride. But as you probably already guessed, she recovered quickly. Only six weeks to the day after giving birth, she announced she was ready to go mountain biking again. So, of course, we loaded up our bikes and headed back to the same trail. After the ride, while loading our bikes onto the car, Diana saw the same two men standing by their vehicle talking to a group of riders. She overheard their conversation as she was loading her bike. They were telling the other bikers about this crazy pregnant lady who flew past them down the hill of death.

Diana chimed in, "That was me!"

"No that wasn't you." They replied, "That lady was PREGNANT!"

Diana insisted again, "I had a baby six weeks ago! That was me!"

It took a little convincing but once they finally realized it was really her, they quickly loaded their bikes and peeled out of the parking lot!

A Little More About Don's Stroke

Don's tragic fall and its aftermath silenced a voice that had been such a dominant and powerful inspiration in Diana's life. He was a larger-than-life public speaker. Entire audiences hung on his words. He was dynamic, inspirational, intelligent, funny, and powerfully motivating. He had built a very good business by motivating people and lifting them above their own doubts and fears. Sadly, the aftermath of the stroke silenced Don's voice. It nearly silenced Diana's voice as well.

There were two victims when Don fell and hit the cement that day. But Diana finally chose to arise and reclaim her life and health by changing her story. Her decision to rise again honored her dad, and it honestly relieved him to see her quit punishing herself. Victory rose from tragedy.

Some of the side effects of Graves' Disease are rapid weight loss and a rapid and unhealthy heart rate. A week after our conversation in the car, Diana had gained back 10 healthy pounds, which she desperately needed. Then one morning she ran up the stairs and was shocked that she didn't have to lie down from exhaustion. She was also shocked that she felt so strong. Her healthy skin color magically returned. This stark turn-around with her health spurred us to rush her back into her doctor to get tested again. This visit and the new test results are what sparked the after-hours, weekend call from the doctor.

"Stop taking your medications! You have absolutely no sign of Graves' Disease. Even your antibodies are normal! Can I ask you what you did? Graves' does not just go away!"

Diana explained to her doctor that we had done an NLP session to address her deeply buried internal conflict, but the doctor simply couldn't comprehend or explain the drastic improvement. She just kept asking, "Yes, but what did you do?" The short answer? NLP.

We literally experienced a medically unexplainable miracle and Diana returned to healthy, active, and normal living. At the time of this writing, she has been medically free of Graves' Disease for nearly five years. Miracles such as this have become more common in our lives than I could have ever imagined. The purpose of this book is to share and teach you some of the life changing concepts and principles that I've learned and fine-tuned over the past two decades. I am going to share with you what I now call, "Let Go and Let God Heal."

Wikipedia defines "Neuro-linguistic programming (NLP) as an approach to communication, personal development, and psychotherapy created by Richard Bandler and John Grinder in California, United States in the 1970s. NLP's creators claim there is a connection between neurological processes (neuro-), language (linguistic) and behavioral patterns learned through experience (programming), and that these can be changed to achieve specific goals in life. Bandler and Grinder also claim that NLP methodology can 'model' the skills of exceptional people, allowing anyone to acquire those skills. They claim that, often in a single session, NLP can treat problems such as phobias, depression, tic disorders, psychosomatic illnesses, nearsightedness, allergy, common cold, and learning disorders."

Over the past 22+ years, I have personally witnessed that nearly all of these NLP claims by Bandler and Grinder, and many more not listed, have verifiable merit. In this book, I will share some miraculous stories of transformation and healing that I have personally witnessed in my journey. I will also share some of the insights and techniques that I have acquired and used to help some of my fellow-travelers climb above their own tragedies and heartache.

I found NLP during a desperate search in my life while going through a divorce at the age of 27. My life and marriage had gone off the rails, and there were no real answers to be found. It was at this paradoxical stage where NLP was divinely dropped onto my path.

This path started providing me with profound insights and understanding that would not only illuminate my own path out of darkness, but also light the trail for many others that I helped along the way. These healing encounters have provided more fulfilment and purpose than I could have ever imagined. There was something profoundly divine about God leading me from failure and humiliation to truth and understanding. He intimately acquainted me with the very principles I would later use to help others rise from tragedy.

Feeling trapped in a hopeless situation ended up lighting an unquenchable fire that would drive me to find answers that I am now sharing with the world. I have to acknowledge that my life is such an eclectic collection of experiences that it is hard to categorize me. God is as much at my core as NLP and hypnosis. It is impossible to separate me from my belief in God because He has been such a crucial part of my life's transformation. Combining God with NLP and hypnosis was a natural union because it is God that placed me on this healing path and mission.

While I was in the process of going through the separation that preceded my divorce, I was shocked to learn that a close friend of mine had taken his own life. I was completely devastated by the news because he had opened up to me a few times and shared some of his unfavorable marriage circumstances. His wife had been unfaithful and didn't want to stay married to him. He was betrayed and humiliated by her choices. He had trusted me with the circumstances that were ruining his marriage but I had no idea he would end up taking his life shortly after our last conversation.

He left behind children and friends who cared about him. He had reached out and trusted me with the pain he was feeling near the end of his life but it never entered my mind that he would take it that far. I prayed fervently to God and asked him why this happened. It was so unfair to him and his suffering children. He was devastated by his wife's choices and believed there was no reason to continue. I felt so deeply for his children who would never really understand his choices. He had left a void in their lives as deep as the void his wife's choices left in his.

One day as I was on my knees praying to God about this tragedy I pleaded with Him, "Please give me the gift to help people like this!" I begged, "Never let anyone within my reach ever take their own life again!" I promised, "If you will give me the ability to help the people within my reach then I covenant with you that I will give you my time, my energy, and my talents, anytime, anyplace."

God has taken me up on this promise, many times.

It's Good to be Strange

It was also around this time of my failing marriage that I had a conversation with my "strange" Uncle Ray about NLP. I had heard about this before, but the whole topic seemed a bit taboo to me. Perhaps my uncertain life and marriage left me open to see some things to which I had previously been blind. Ray made a living as an NLP practitioner. I had a lot of questions. Our conversation had me riveted. He had my full attention. For a more thorough overview of NLP, Ray recommended that I read Anthony Robbins' book *Unlimited Power*. That was it, I was hooked.

I read that book as fast as I could and savored every single word. Amazingly, a new world opened up before me. I honestly felt like a shark that had just caught the scent of blood.

Shortly after I read Anthony's book, I talked to my Aunt Diane from the other side of the family about NLP. She excitedly informed me about an NLP certification course that she and her husband were ironically starting the following week. It was a sign! There was no denying it. I signed up for the NLP practitioner course at Anchor Point Institute in Salt Lake City and jumped in with both feet.

The first time I walked into class, it felt as though everything was moving in slow motion. I was home. After the second month of training, the course instructors pulled me into their office to have a private conversation. I was concerned and wondered what I had done wrong, but instead they told me they had been watching me closely and acknowledged I was naturally gifted at NLP. They then offered me a partial scholarship to take the Master's certification course in parallel with this class. I gladly accepted and doubled up the classes.

As I passionately pursued mastering NLP, I found that many of my classmates would approach me for help with their issues after class. You see, I wasn't learning NLP because it was a hobby. I was learning NLP because it was providing me real answers about how the subconscious mind can sabotage life. NLP was now illuminating and changing my life. I originally pursued these NLP classes partly hoping to "fix" my ex-wife, but it ended up changing my life instead. I started building a new foundation upon which my future would be built.

One day, in one of my NLP classes, I found myself completely transfixed on a technique being taught. It was how to elicit a subconscious template from someone's mind over which you lay a person's dysfunctional thought process to dissolve it. It was complicated for me to learn and understand then and is even more complicated for me to explain it here. But suffice it to say, I just couldn't shake the idea that I needed to understand this technique thoroughly. Each time we had a break in class, I would ask the instructor for more help understanding this process.

That evening after class I was driving to my Aunt's home, where I would stay during the weeklong block of classes for NLP. I heard a voice telling me to turn left onto the freeway instead of right. Turning left would lead me to my parent's home where I was living while going through the divorce. I somehow just knew I needed to go to my parents' home. So I swerved into the left lane and took the longer drive home for the night. No more than 15 minutes after I arrived home, there was a knock on the door. I opened the door to a complete stranger. He asked, "Are you Mike Simpson?"

With a puzzled look, I told him that I was. I thought to myself, "How did you know I was going to be here?" He proceeded to say, "I realize you don't know me. I was going to kill myself today. I was told I needed to talk to you."

I couldn't believe my ears, but I knew instantly he was the reason why I had to turn left and come home that night. God was taking me up on my promise. I invited him in and took him into my mom's hair salon, where we proceeded to do an NLP session. It was in this session that I used the very process I had spent all day struggling to understand. And as I built a subconscious template for his issues, he suddenly broke into tears and cried out, "That's my Dad!"

I didn't understand. He again exclaimed, "That's my Dad!"

Somehow, the way we had organized his thoughts and perception had created some type of window or portal in his mind that allowed his deceased father to appear. His father had some profound things to tell him about his life. What transpired with this man was certainly much bigger than NLP. It was bigger than me. It was God working through us! This man left my home that night on top of the world, and I had an unshakable witness that God had just collected on the promise I had made with him only a few months earlier. I had somehow helped a complete stranger experience divine intervention and God had led him to me. This was the first of many such experiences where God guided people to this "strange" person, Mike Simpson.

It was my "great paradox of ruin before rebirth" that placed me on this path of becoming gifted at navigating the subconscious mind and soul. My own unsolvable puzzles led me to become somewhat of a puzzle master. In my first marriage, I had to learn how to read minds because my ex-wife refused to talk about the problems that I was relentlessly committed to understanding and solving. It drove her crazy, and it drove me crazy!

Coupled with my evolving "radar" skills, this NLP training provided me with crucial tools and abilities I would faithfully use throughout my life in helping my fellow suffering sojourners to find their own healing miracles. As outlined with Diana's release of Graves' Disease, most of these miracles were tied to others identifying and releasing their own buried emotional conflicts.

Let Go and Let God

This principle has governed and transformed my life, and I mention it often throughout this book. I always believed in God prior to my divorce and served Him the best I could. But it was in the depths of hopelessness and darkness that God made himself known to me in a whole new way. The demolition of my old life placed me onto a path of healing and understanding not only for myself, but for countless others that I was able to help along the way. I have found unspeakable peace and joy through this path of healing.

After my divorce, I was led to Diana, who became the divine answer and blessing to every hardship I ever faced. God tore down the shack that was my old life and rebuilt me into something better. It was this rebuilding process that taught me directly that I could transform just like a blazing phoenix rising from the ashes. This transformation taught me how to combine God, NLP, and hypnosis to dig deeply into any authentic truth-seeker's soul. Together, we find and release hidden darkness that always seems to be the source of pain, anguish, and sickness.

One day about 10 years after completing my NLP training, I was doing an NLP session with a heartbroken woman. Her family had been devastated by unspeakable physical and sexual abuse from her ex-husband as the children grew to adulthood. Even worse, it all happened without her knowledge and the perpetrator had not been caught in his crimes. Now as adults, most of her children had returned home in a broken state. One son had become dependent on drugs. Another son was completely antisocial and unwilling to leave his room. Pure injustice had shattered her beautiful family, and now, years later, she was trying to pick up the daunting shards that were too overwhelming for her to manage alone. Her heartache, resentment, and regret were so great that she was certain she was dying. She was terrified. It was as if she were committed to die in protest to the aftermath of her ex-husband's tyranny.

During this NLP session, I was profoundly amazed by the pure information and inspiration flowing from God. I was teaching her that the Lord was calling her to be His arms for these devastated children. He wasn't calling her to die, but to also rise from the ashes and become her children's bridge to the Savior. She was to represent HIM to her children. The outpouring was surreal. I acknowledged in my heart that God was with us in that room. While these healing words and spirit poured into the room, I suddenly experienced what felt like a conduit open up from heaven. Through it, I could somehow feel and see the Lord nodding in approval while reviewing the trials of my life. I was completely puzzled. It felt as if time stopped. I was profoundly amazed at the truth and energy flowing in the room while observing the Lord endorse my previous suffering. I honestly just sat there dismayed, inspired, and yet confused. "What am I to understand from this message interrupting our session?" Then the Lord spoke into my mind: "You would not have been able to help her today had you not been through these trials. This is the price you agreed to pay."

My suffering was the great tutor for healing. My descent acquainted me with hopelessness and despair that I would learn to transcend with God's divine intervention. Yes, my suffering was a prelude to healing. This healing was to begin with me and was meant to then to be shared with others, just as God designed. Who am I? Nobody really. Just another man who walks and lives on this earth who has struggled with trials and insecurity. What are my credentials? Formal NLP, hypnosis, and HeartMath training, experience helping thousands of people, my own personal pain and suffering, and most importantly — God's divine direction.

CHAPTER TWO

Healing Perspectives from an Outsider

In 2015, I received a divine nudge from God to leave the software industry permanently and purchase a wellness center in the pursuit of helping people. In the next chapter, I share some details about purchasing the wellness center and the miraculous events and signs that followed, but I acknowledge I never planned on doing this type of work professionally.

NLP is a passion of mine that has transformed my life. People sought my help through the years because of the miraculous results they heard about. It was an unexpected leap of faith to walk away from a stable career with good pay and benefits. However, my time as a software engineer was drawing to its conclusion, as I was now moving from programming computers to reprogramming minds.

Software programming certainly enhanced my ability to debug the human mind and heart. During the two decades I worked in the computer industry, I donated countless evenings counseling people in my home with NLP. Because my time was donated, the laws around counseling people with symptoms of mental illness were the furthest thing from my mind. I was simply trying to follow the Savior's admonition to love my neighbor as myself and striving to keep the promise I made to God after my friend took his life.

After my transition to running the wellness center, the number of miracles increased significantly. There was no shortage of desperate people crying out for real help. For many of them, nothing else had helped ease their suffering. Through repetition of this work, I started noticing powerful patterns around emotional healing as the Lord started guiding me deeper into understanding His ways. Our reputation and visibility grew quickly as word of our success began to spread. Now that I was officially doing this type of work in the public domain, I was on a collision course with the laws that would attempt to classify my work as practicing medicine.

It was in July of 2018 that I was approached by a representative from The Department of Public Licensing (DOPL). They gave me a conditional warning of being prosecuted for "Practicing Medicine Without a License" if I did not retract all public claims that I could lead people in overcoming the effects of depression, anxiety, PTSD, addiction, psychosomatic issues, etc.

After reviewing the comprehensive restrictions list with this gentleman, I was reminded that because I am not a recognized, licensed medical professional by state laws, the state claims I am only legally allowed to help people with lifestyle choices that pertain to smoking cessation and weight loss. The laws literally consider everything else as medical conditions, and therefore deemed that they should be restricted from myself or anyone working outside of the established medical narrative. After this meeting, I took many steps to further include medical professionals in my protocols and to comply with the laws. I also changed my vocabulary and sought legal and professional guidance, because I was determined to move forward in my work.

For the record, I don't consider myself to be practicing medicine. I have been using NLP and hypnosis to effectively assist people in identifying and releasing the root cause of their suffering with tremendous success for over two decades with legitimate and indisputable results. I remain affiliated with multiple medical professionals who oversee and recognize my work and highly value my skills in navigating the subconscious mind.

From my website, **MikeSimpson.live**, you can read my reviews written over the past few years. Some of these reviews are from medical professionals. These testimonials provide real evidence that hypnosis and NLP often exceed the results achieved in the established medical narrative *because* they are outside the bounds of practicing medicine. These testimonials may not be relevant in a court of law, but they are certainly relevant in the court of public opinion that can affect, influence, and hopefully update these laws.

The Official Disclaimer for Mike Simpson

I, Mike Simpson, declare that I am not a licensed medical professional. Therefore, I do not claim to practice medicine in any form. I do not diagnose, treat, cure, or heal anything. In fact, I don't like labels. I also acknowledge that I have no control over what others may claim about the profound results they have created for themselves with my help.

BUT, I declare with conviction that our bodies and minds can and do heal themselves by releasing our own damaging emotional baggage and aligning our lives with true healing principles outlined throughout this book.

In this book, I will present scholarly work and evidence of some noted medical professionals in conjunction with my own information and perspective. All of it highlights new science that is challenging the pervading pharmaceutical narrative of our day.

I love Tevya's statement in *Fiddler on the Roof when* he says, "God writes straight with crooked lines." Stated differently, true healing principles are often obscured by false traditions and even rigid and unreasonable laws that are slanted towards special interests. However, based on my extensive experience, it is not only my own right but also a responsibility to share this information with you and follow Tevya's inspired counsel about writing straight.

We must have the courage to change these crooked lines of limitation and with God's influence, report our successful modes of healing in a new story of triumph and miracles. Asking the right questions is a great place to start.

Limiting Beliefs, and a Math Problem with a Twist

While going through my first NLP certification courses in 1997, I learned an amazing true story that demonstrates how limiting beliefs and preconceived bias can restrict what we believe is possible and therefore limit what *is* possible. I elaborate more about limiting beliefs throughout the book, but I want to share this next story first because removing these limiting beliefs is a crucial step necessary to heal. In 1939, there was a young man named George Bernard Dantzig, who naively shattered the mathematical narrative of the day. We aren't sure of his reasons, but George missed a significant portion of a statistics lecture discussing two problems written on the blackboard. It isn't far-fetched to think that this stats lecture put him to sleep. When he awoke, George quickly copied these two mysterious math problems onto his paper before rushing out of the class.

George arrived early at his next statistics class to discuss some of his findings with his professor. Apologetically, he told his professor both problems were extremely difficult and that he was only able to solve one of them. The professor looked at him with a puzzled stare. "Didn't you listen to my lecture?"

The professor explained that these problems were simply written on the board to demonstrate what *wasn't* possible. These math problems were considered unsolvable!

"Didn't you realize that you can't do this?"

But since George missed the lecture, he was able to approach the math problems without any preconceived prejudice or bias. And voila! An unsolvable math problem was actually solved by an unsuspecting and "unqualified" student. The math solution was presented to the professor as evidence that he needed to rethink his old narrative. George not only solved that problem but introduced new information that significantly contributed to the science of mathematics.

Take from this what you will. Sometimes, we accomplish amazing things when we are gifted, naive, and "uneducated" enough to do something without the official narrative blinding us.

To Mask or Not to Mask? That is the Question

I have found that if you remove the pebble from your shoe, then the pain medication for your sore foot is unnecessary. I encounter many people who are wary of the dangerous effects of antidepressants, but feel there are no other options. There are. It has been gratifying for me to witness many of these emotion-related "illnesses" disappear with some thorough, and often simple, negotiation with the subconscious mind.

The term *depression* is overused and carries a hopeless stigma with it. It has been treated almost as a death sentence. The pharmaceutical industry is raking in outrageous sums of money and dominating the depression narrative. I will share many examples of "depressed" people who miraculously experienced permanent freedom from depression by identifying and releasing the source of their emotional pain. It is this rising consciousness and inspiration that convinced me to write this book, and share my own insights about the practical steps you can take to escape from your suffering.

I certainly acknowledge there are many compassionate, competent medical professionals in this world who do amazing work. I have met many of them and have been blessed many times by their work. In fact, I have had some of them refer their loved ones and patients to me when they were out of options. Because of our consistent, amazing results, these professionals are taking a closer look at NLP and hypnosis.

Healing occurs by resolving the root of suffering and moving away from symptom management. Formal educational institutions can certainly slant students toward whatever discipline is being taught. Yes, professionals can be both empowered *and* blinded by their discipline.

Good intentions and medication are not enough to resolve deep-seated emotional suffering, even if medication might temporarily suspend the symptoms. The medicine itself does not claim to heal or cure any of the underlying issues. Gaining an understanding of the true principles of emotional healing in the subconscious mind and heart in order to release buried heartache is the first step to true healing.

I am excited to convey the many principles and insights I have learned and developed through the years to contribute to the bridge that leads us to a new healing paradigm. The current narrative is outdated, and the new narrative certainly must include God.

"For my thoughts are not your thoughts, neither are your ways my ways, saith the LORD." (Isaiah 55:8, KJV)

I'm Going to Seek a Second Opinion

Back when Diana's life was upended by Graves' disease, we met with two different doctors. One was an integrated doctor who promotes lifestyle, supplements, and mindfulness and uses pharmaceuticals as a final resort. She is the doctor who called us on a Saturday evening to tell Diana to quit taking the medication because there was no sign of Graves' disease in her recent blood test results. But when Diana talked with her other doctor around this same time, he insisted that she keep taking her medication because it was working. He wanted nothing to do with stopping the medication and *insisted* that the only reason her symptoms had disappeared was because she was taking the medication. This is a clear example of how someone can be so blinded by their own narrative that they will not even take the time to look at the conclusive blood test results that proved Diana's Graves' Disease was completely gone.

Our integrated medical doctor has also been hassled by the establishment with claims she is deviating away from its rules and regulations by incorporating "questionable" protocols of integrating supplements and using pharmaceuticals as a last resort. We signed her petition to challenge the limitations being imposed by the state. I am now adding my own voice to hers from outside the medical narrative. These "crooked lines," or laws, that are heavily influenced and enforced by special interests need to be redrawn.

A Medical Hex?

It is possible for a medical doctor to unintentionally and unknowingly use hypnosis to install limiting beliefs into an unsuspecting patient's subconscious mind. I've heard this termed as a *medical hex* in the hypnosis field. This inadvertent installation of a false belief could potentially warp someone's perception causing an unwanted medical condition and even cause a crisis for life. If your trusted doctor tells you it is impossible to recover from a condition, then it is possible that your doctor's statement will also become the new undisputed "truth" that your body may unquestionably follow.

I am a specialist who can help you identify and remove these hidden, toxic, and limiting beliefs in your subconscious mind.

They can be corrected easily once you find them. However, you might be surprised at some of the reasons people won't let go of these limiting beliefs. I rarely discover an irrational problem in the subconscious mind that doesn't have a payoff or benefit. In NLP, we call this secondary gain.

I will be addressing these secondary gains at length throughout the book. But for now, I want to establish the fact that these hidden, limiting beliefs with benefits can be both installed carelessly and removed methodically. The opposite is also true. Removing these hidden, limiting beliefs is a crucial step in creating miracles. These undesirable beliefs must be replaced with the blueprint of possibility if permanent change is to be obtained. I will write more on this later.

Mesmerizing

Back in the 17th century, a medical doctor from Germany named Franz Mesmer put his own form of hypnosis on the map. He is considered the grandfather of hypnosis by many in the profession today. Franz practiced medicine in Vienna until moving to Paris in 1778, where he took hypnosis into the mainstream with tremendous but unconventional success. The term "mesmerizing" was actually named after Dr. Franz Mesmer. He had some strange ideas about magnetism and interesting theories as to *why* his techniques worked so well. But as strange as his ideas seemed, hypnosis started helping people in profound ways.

Mesmer became the celebrity, go-to doctor of the day in France. However, his unorthodox approach created a lot of controversy with the established medical narrative because his ideas were so unconventional. These opposing doctors were naturally *only* concerned for the welfare of their patients. The established medical narrative of the 17th century in France was bloodletting. This was the *groundbreaking* practice of the removal of blood by physician or leeches from a patient. This blood removal was believed to prevent or cure illness and disease.

So these professional bloodletters encouraged King Louie to investigate this "preposterous" hypnosis practice that was defying their medical narrative. King Louie established a decision board that ended up declaring hypnosis as invalid and to be considered nothing more than outrageous imagination. This decision ruined Mesmer's career and left the bloodletters in peace to continue draining their patient's blood. The committee had banished a "snake oil salesman" and the bloodletters were safe. Now 200+ years later, we are calling bloodletters the snake oil salesmen. This is an interesting turn of events, don't you think?

Today the stigma associated with hypnosis is changing, due to many professionals (including medical professionals) around the world who are doing amazing work and creating legitimate credibility and results that are exceeding the limitations of symptom-management. Let us now explore some perspectives shared by some medical professionals in the industry who also dare to deviate away from the narrative, and are making huge inroads in redefining the pharma narrative.

Meet Dr. Daniel Amen

I strongly encourage you to look into Dr. Amen's groundbreaking work. He has written many books that educate people on improving mental health through counseling, nutrition, and lifestyle instead of a medication centric approach.

Dr. Amen tells a story about how sophisticated and advanced he was at prescribing medication but eventually found it troubling that psychiatrists are the only medical professionals in the industry that don't perform any type of a scan or x-ray before prescribing medication. One particular case that Dr. Amen encountered felt like a slam dunk. He went ahead with his automatic prescription pattern but then had a concern flash in his mind. He felt impressed to have this man get a brain scan instead, and luckily, he did have the scan. This patient actually had a tumor and the medication that Dr. Amen was going to prescribe would have literally killed him! This started Dr. Amen down the path of adopting an entirely different approach to dealing with depression and anxiety.

Dr. Amen reported 10 percent of patients taking placebos for depression reported a benefit while only 11 percent of those actually taking antidepressants noticed a benefit.

It is even more mind-boggling that so many people choose to take medication with only a net gain of one percent over placebos, even with all of the additional associated risks.

Furthermore, after conducting over ten thousand brain scans, Dr. Amen confessed he was *unable* to distinguish the difference between the brain of an alcoholic versus the brain of someone taking antidepressants. This is astonishing!

In 2016, NBC News reported that one in six Americans take some kind of psychiatric drug — mostly antidepressants. One in SIX!

Yet the FDA has assigned a "black box" label warning indicating that antidepressants may increase the risk of suicidal thinking and behavior in some children and adolescents with Major Depression Disorder. A black-box warning is the most serious type of warning possible on prescription drug labeling.

I have been amazed at how few people actually understand these documented risks of antidepressants. Isn't the prescribing doctor supposed to inform and educate the patient on all of the inherent risks of this medication? The prescription protocol is designed for the medical professional to discuss all of the negative side effects and risks of taking the chemicals into your body.

Kelly Brogan MD, another revolutionary in the medical industry, wrote a helpful article on the dangers of taking antidepressants on her website: https://kellybroganmd.com/whats-the-harm-in-taking-an-antidepressant. I recommend you read Dr. Brogan's research along with research done by many other medical professionals who are challenging the rhetoric of the antidepressant echo chamber. In this article, Dr. Brogan lists some of her reasons for putting down the prescription pad permanently. After years of patient horror stories, Dr. Brogan concluded that psychiatric medications result in worse long-term outcomes. She explains that these medications are debilitatingly habit forming, and cause unpredictable *violence*. She also acknowledges the risk far outweighs the benefits, and that this is just the tip of an ominous iceberg.

Below is a list of the dangerous effects of antidepressants listed on Dr. Brogan's site. I've provided her full description of the symptoms that I would like to highlight:

Gut disturbance, Liver toxicity, Weight gain, Heart problems, Urinary problems, Sexual dysfunction, Salt imbalance, Osteoporosis/Bone weakening, Bleeding, Nervous system dysfunction, Sweating, Sleep disturbances, Eye disease, Hormonal imbalance;

Mood changes: "Many patients taking SSRIs have reported experiencing emotional blunting. They often describe their emotions as being 'damped down' or 'toned down', while some patients refer to a feeling of being in 'limbo' and just 'not caring' about issues that were significant to them before... Furthermore, an activation syndrome in which patients taking antidepressants may experience anxiety, agitation, panic attacks, insomnia, irritability, hostility, aggressiveness and impulsivity in the first 3 months of treatment may ensue."

Suicidality: "**The incidence of suicide and attempted suicide has been a frequently underreported adverse outcome across antidepressant RCTs.**"

Overdose toxicity: "Patients with MDD are at increased risk of suicide and overdosing of prescribed medications is a common method used to attempted suicide."

Withdrawal Syndrome: "These symptoms include flu-like symptoms, tremors, tachycardia, shock-like sensations, paresthesia, myalgia, tinnitus, neuralgia, ataxia, vertigo, sexual dysfunction, sleep disturbances, vivid dreams, nausea vomiting, diarrhea, worsening anxiety and mood Instability."

Cancer risk: "Preclinical studies have found that antidepressants can increase the growth of fibrosarcomas and melanomas, and may also promote mammary carcinogenesis."

To quote Dr. Brogan, "Silent Pause. How depressing."

These documented risks are terrifying and should be communicated thoroughly to patients before they start taking any medication. We are deeply concerned that these medications with such dangerous risks are so easily prescribed and embraced by desperate people. Suicidal thoughts as a potential effect given to the emotionally unstable is unthinkable. Especially if you factor in the growing epidemic of suicide among the depressed! Depressed people need legitimate and proven options available that are outlined in this book.

I am encouraged that many medical professionals such as Dr. Amen and Dr. Brogan are bravely challenging the Pharmaceutical narrative raising legitimate concerns to educate the public. I am also encouraged that medical professionals are taking a closer look at lifestyle, NLP, and hypnosis as healthy and effective alternatives to help their patients.

You Can't Argue With Results.

There was a time when I was content to help people quietly in my front room. But now is the time to speak up and let these profound principles of healing supplant the existing narrative. We need to get more visibility for these powerful modalities that are safe and effective in helping relieve the suffering. It's time for the outdated and special-interest laws to be revised.

Buckle up.

CHAPTER THREE

The Bridge to JC

After her dad's massive stroke, Diana and I felt directed to purchase a bigger home to take care of both Don and Diana's mother, who had been struggling with breast cancer. We started making arrangements to sell our home and began looking for something that would fit the needs for both families and a live-in nurse. We eventually found the ideal house for our needs, but it was going to require a lot of work because it had sat empty for several years. However, it was still a beautiful home with great potential. So, we purchased the new home on a very tight budget and in miraculous fashion. The stars lined up for us to be able to do so, but we still had the daunting job of liquidating most of our belongings, repairing and completing the new home, moving both families, and selling our existing home. It was a whirlwind — and incidentally, this was the time that Diana was suffering with Graves' disease. It was a serious struggle to generate the energy to make this all happen. In the middle of this ordeal, we took the advice from one of our live-in nurses, Bambie, to take Don to a local wellness center to see if some of their alternative technologies could help him overcome some of the horrible effects of his stroke. After Bambie suggested this wellness center multiple times, we decided to take a closer look.

After two weeks of brain stimulation treatments, Don made a noticeable improvement with his hand-eye coordination and his countenance was brighter. This exposure to the technology and our new connections quickly led to us purchasing a similar wellness center in Sandy, Utah. I am typically very conservative with life changes but we followed God's promptings even though the timing could not have been worse. It was a terrifying jump but we knew it was the right thing to do.

The first 18 months of running the wellness center was overwhelming. Learning the wellness business and technology felt like we were drinking water from a fire hose. Even though we were following God in these extreme changes, some things didn't seem to be working out. We were unable to sell our home for 18 months while I was juggling my software job and running the wellness center. I was overwhelmed and depleted. I became an expert at eating fast food while frantically driving between both jobs. I was literally working 7 days a week to keep up. My phone never stopped ringing. At the wellness center, I wore every hat. I was the director, the NLP counselor, the office manager, the salesman, the HR director, and the equipment expert. Diana ran the center when I was at my software job during regular business hours but she was really conflicted about this demand. According to the original plan, she was supposed to be at home taking care of her parents. Meanwhile, my time was in such demand that I rarely saw my family. Free-time was a thing of the past. Not being able to sell our empty home felt like a betrayal from God after following His will and making these big changes.

After 18 long months, we FINALLY sold our empty home for well-under market value. It was a huge relief. I then finally conceded to Diana's pleas to leave my software job permanently so I could put all of my energy into running the wellness center. She just knew that it would take-off if I was there full time and giving it all my attention. And as usual, she was right. It was exhilarating and terrifying to walk away from my stable job with benefits. We were now officially going to sink or swim, and sinking felt inevitable. However, with some faith and concerted effort, the wellness center started thriving and became so busy we could hardly keep up with the demand. We were seeing so many amazing miracles that it was hard to believe. After this whirlwind of transition into the wellness center, I had a dream where the Lord approached me and jokingly punched me in the arm and chuckled, "You didn't think this healing business was going to be free did you?" I woke up in a cold sweat, "Ouch! That hurt!"

A few weeks later I had another dream where Diana and I were kneeling in our old home praying for protection from a horrible hurricane raging outside. The home was shaking and cracking and barely holding together. Then suddenly, the storm lifted and was instantly gone. I acknowledged to Diana in the dream that the Lord had heard our prayers and we were safe. We got to our feet and walked outside. The view was completely different. Instead of a devastated landscape from the tumultuous storm, we were standing in a beautiful tropical paradise that was the unexpected aftermath of the storm. The storm of our transition was finally over and the Lord revealed that He had accepted our sacrifice. Many more miracles and signs followed. To learn more about our wellness center and the amazing technology, please visit **MikeSimpson.live/Technology**.

East Sandy and the JC Connection

The following true story brought Diana and I the most amazing confirmation following our transition to running the wellness center. Our new client Ciera's life-threatening addiction to heroin and the circumstances which led her to us was nothing short of amazing and prophetic. Ciera's mother wrote and recorded this story in her own words.

From Ciera's Mom, Robin

In the year of 1992, east of Wayne County, Utah, there was a wedding going on in the church. I was there listening to the DJ. My friend was standing with her new husband in a wedding line close to the front entry. The wedding reception was winding down and very few people were left to congratulate the new couple.

I was sitting on a chair at the other end of the room, listening to music, when I saw a strange-looking man enter the front doors. He didn't stop to greet the couple, or even glance at their line. He continued towards me as if he knew I would be sitting there waiting for him. The man seemed to be in his late 60's or early 70's and his appearance was that of a vagabond. He came toward me, stood in front of my chair and held his hand out, "Can I have this dance?" he asked. I answered back, "I would love to!" We danced a couple of dances, and then he stopped me in the middle of the dance floor. He said to me, "You sing and write, don't you?" I answered, "Yes I do!" He went on to tell me that I was supposed to write a song and title it JC. I asked him how he knew me. He just waved his hand and explained that none of that mattered. I just needed to write a song and title it JC. He told me how it needed to begin and how it needed to end. I asked him what JC was about. He said, "Jesus Christ." He told me to do it or someone else would. I was surprised that I didn't discern the meaning of JC, but I felt chills after he confirmed the initials back to me. After our conversation, he turned to leave the way he came in. Then he turned back around and quickly said that he had almost forgotten to tell me that I needed to invest in property on the east side of Sandy, Utah.

I was still in a daze, wondering how he knew me and where he came from. He asked again firmly, "Do you know where Sandy, Utah is?" I answered back that I did, but again asked how he knew me. I reassured him that I didn't have any money to invest in any property. He smiled and said, "You will in the far future." He reiterated his request and told me that if I did this, I would triple my investment. He turned and walked back out the door, without a word to anyone else. I walked behind him slowly, as the bride and groom came towards me, giggling, and asked, "Who is your new boyfriend?" I inquired if they knew the little man I had been talking with. They replied, "No, neither one of us know him. We thought you did." I quickly ran to the door and looked up both sides of the street. There were empty fields as far as I could see. No one was walking up the narrow sidewalk back into town and no one was walking along the empty country road.

That memory of my dance and conversation with the stranger stayed with me through the years. I struggled with the song, but finally pushed through the words and wrote JC. It was recorded with my first music CD. My thoughts still left me wondering about the property on the east side of Sandy, but I knew that if it was God's will, it would unfold when needed.

The years kept rolling along, and my four children grew up, got married, and had children of their own. My real trials began when my youngest daughter, Ciera, found herself mixed up in drugs. This was a new experience for me and I learned a lot of what families go through with drug-addicted children.

Ciera was an outspoken girl with a high intelligence that most people would pray for. However, attention from boys is a teenage girl's first taste of maturity. She kept company with the wrong boys and one ended up holding her down and forcing her to experience her first episode with drugs. After that first time, it is hard to walk away from the high and your world is at the mercy of GOD. Somehow the demons manage to weaken your soul by getting you to doubt God and this gives them more power. Ciera fought her way through good times, as well as the bad. The good times brought her a good husband and a second child. The bad times left her with a broken marriage and two children that were dragged through the healing process.

As a mother, I was willing to help my child succeed with almost any sacrifice required of me. I paid money I didn't have for programs I thought would help her, but I still stood firm to the tough love that is needed to help one wake up from their selfish choices. There wasn't a day or night I didn't pray for God to break her addictions and surround her with His angels of light and strength. The struggle weighed on my marriage and my heart, but I continued to believe in God's strength and love for all of us. Her siblings were worn down and lost for answers. In the middle of the battle, suicide attempts were rescued by 911 calls and we continued to watch Ciera change before our eyes. Prayers never stopped. Her siblings and I were praying continually, through the bad and limited good times.

One day I was fasting and had just prayed for God to answer my prayers and help us rescue Ciera's little body before it was too late. I had two different friends, each lose their child to a drug overdose. I felt blessed every day she survived. That day I was watching television and saw an advertisement for Mike's Wellness Center, which I usually would fast-forward through. The advertisement explained how theta waves can help break drug addiction and personality disorders. I mentioned it to Ciera and said, "Wouldn't it be funny if that wellness center was located on the east side of Sandy, Utah?" Ciera told me she had read about it, and that it WAS on the east side of Sandy!

Instantly my mind flashed back to the hobo I had met at my friend's wedding 25 years prior. I thought that maybe my investment was in helping my daughter and her two children. I called Mike's wellness center and Ciera was quickly brought in to start her road to recovery. Things fell into place and she eventually finished her program with excellent success. She loved the people at the office and felt a comfort and attachment with Mike Simpson, who was an owner and an employee.

My Thoughts on Ciera's Circumstances That Brought Her to Us

I was deeply moved and humbled when Ciera shared this story with me during our first conversation at the wellness center in East Sandy. Ciera and I both knew this was the place that angel-in-disguise had told her mother about nearly 25 years earlier. I felt a profound appreciation and commitment to dig into Ciera's soul and help her remove her addiction. Through our program and multiple hypnosis sessions we found deep anguish and resentment for tragic circumstances that came to Ciera as a young girl. She had become an addict by the age of 13 to mask the heartache and confusion of hidden abuse she suffered in childhood. To remove the full effects of Ciera's abuse, we had to petition JC himself to remove the pain, shame, and resentment from her soul to eliminate her need to self-medicate. Ciera had a few setbacks after she completed her program, but I am happy to report that she is now thoroughly clean and has gained full custody of two of her children and shared custody with her daughter. Ciera and her mother both feel the investment that was tripled from the East Sandy transaction was nothing other than Ciera's three beautiful children coming back home to a mother finally free from the clutches of addiction and depression. If you are interested in hearing Robin's song "JC," please visit **TheMiracleBridge.com/Contributors**.

Julie, Lee, and JC

In the same week that I met Ciera, I had another client by the name of Julie approach me for help with chronic neck pain. We had an instant connection because of our combined passion for NLP and hypnosis. Julie was referred to me by a muscle specialist who was unable to resolve her pain and believed her suffering was tied to unresolved emotions. Julie had spent a lot of money trying many different modalities for her neck pain but up until this time, nothing had helped. Julie was hopeful that hypnosis would be different. After our initial discussion, we proceeded and Julie went into a deep hypnosis quickly and with little effort. While there, we quickly identified the emotional reason for Julie's chronic neck pain. The pain was connected to a brother who created unending emotional trauma and conflict in her family. I suggested to Julie that her brother had placed a hook somewhere in her body and asked if she could find the location. Julie was shocked to discover that hook piercing directly in her chronically painful neck. Quite literally, Julie's brother had been a lingering pain in the neck! I invited Julie to remove the hook and hand it back to her brother who reluctantly took it. After a few well-placed suggestions about forgiving her brother and being permanently pain-free, Julie emerged from hypnosis. The neck pain *seemed* to have subsided significantly but Julie wasn't sure if she could trust it quite yet. However, Julie's pain was *completely* gone a few days later and she remains pain-free to this day. Julie was absolutely amazed and grateful that her neck pain and resentment vanished and she calls her relief from suffering a miracle.

After our session, Julie told me that my NLP and hypnosis background reminded her of a close friend and mentor of hers named Lee, who had recently passed away. Before Lee's death, Julie relied on him for guidance in the many challenges she was facing. Julie confided a story to me where Lee had actually recently visited her in a meaningful dream. Lee lived most of his life as a good-hearted, skeptical agnostic. When Lee came to Julie in the dream, he told her how amazing it is on the other side. Their reunion was meaningful but brief. When leaving, Julie thanked Lee and asked if he could come back and visit again. His response was coy and yet telling. Lee informed Julie that visiting her isn't that simple because he was busy working over there and he would have to get permission from JC. When Julie mentioned JC, a jolt of electricity shot through me as I chuckled out loud. This was the second time in a week where a new client had come in and spoken to me about the Savior using the initials, JC! I asked Julie if she knew what JC stood for and she shrugged her shoulders. I told her that JC stands for Jesus Christ. She smiled and felt the confirmation. How else would a light-hearted agnostic admit that Jesus Christ is REAL and that He is the very one one that grants permission to visit this world?

When Julie learned I was writing this book she was excited to include her story. I asked if she wouldn't mind sharing this with you in her own words.

Julie's Own Words:

I learned about Mike Simpson from an interview where he spoke about helping people tackle various issues through hypnosis. You see, I had developed a severe pain in my neck that had been going on for over a year. I was in search of anything that could bring relief. The neck pain was so disruptive that I wasn't able to turn my head without moving my entire upper body. This was especially annoying when I needed to back up my car! I tried acupuncture, massage therapy, chiropractic, spoke with a surgeon (who thought surgery was the answer), and a MAT therapist (muscle activation technique) who said, "I think your issue may be emotional." Emotional? Could a difficulty in your life actually lead to physical pain? I had, in fact, been struggling for years with a family problem. Could this have been the cause of my neck pain?

After I saw Mike's interview, I made an appointment and met with him on a snowy November day. He asked if I was open to hypnotherapy, and I said I would try anything to avoid surgery and, with that, we started our session. Prior to this, Mike and I had never met and he did not know anything about me.

In our session, he guided me into a very relaxed state and asked some questions. I was aware of our discussion and we didn't get into specifics about what had been going on in my life. Instead, Mike asked me to simply drop into the place that I thought might have some connection to my neck pain. I did this quickly. Mike listened and suggested that I had been "hooked" by a situation which had literally become a "pain in my neck!" He asked if I was ready to take the hook out. I understood this was a metaphorical hook and I said YES, it's time to get rid of it! In my creative mind, I saw myself removing a big, scary-looking black hook from my neck. We ended our session and I thought, could healing actually be this easy? By the third day, the neck pain was completely gone and I had regained full range of motion! This was truly a miraculous and profound experience.

It has now been three years since that transformative, healing session with Mike and I have not had any neck pain since! Mike has an amazing gift and I am very thankful to have found him and for his help.

A second amazing thing happened during our session. I spoke to Mike about a lifelong friend Lee, who had suddenly passed away a few months prior. I told him that I was grieving the loss of Lee when I had this incredible, vivid dream that felt like a visit from him! In my dream, I saw Lee looking fantastic and I only had a couple of minutes to ask him the questions I had been wondering about since his passing. He answered all, in his usual comical style, with a laugh and a big grin. When I had to say goodbye to him, I asked if he could come back to visit again. He told me he didn't think so, but he would ask JC. Mike quickly asked, "JC? You know who Lee is referring to, right? That is Jesus Christ!" I told Mike this had crossed my mind, but that JC didn't make sense because Lee was a self-proclaimed agnostic. Over the years, Lee and I had many spirited discussions about God and we never saw eye-to-eye on our differing beliefs. But I now agree with Mike that Lee acknowledged that JC is real! I think JC was there to guide Lee, just like he will be there for us all!

JC Was Helping Me

It is fitting that I am discussing the Savior in this chapter. He has played a significant role in my life and in shaping my ideas around healing. One challenging dynamic of running the wellness center has been the extreme demand of desperate people looking for healing where nothing else has worked for them. Many of these individuals were suicidal and without hope. I really started to understand deeply that for many of these individuals, our wellness center might be the end of the line, the last stop. I felt the heavy but sacred responsibility of doing my best to provide them with hope and the path of healing. I started relying upon the Lord so heavily because I really had no other person to which I could turn. I was humbled and amazed to learn firsthand how much the Lord loves each individual he was sending and entrusting to me. I had a clear understanding that He was sending them to me, and it is He who was healing them as I helped them identify and remove their own internal obstacles that reinforced their suffering.

My job is that of a facilitator. The Lord started teaching me the finer points of faith and how to create miracles by identifying and eliminating the obstacles that were preventing them. Often, when working with a desperate case, the Lord will speak into my mind at the very moment I need His guidance. My workday is a continuous prayer, pleading for guidance and help. I cannot afford to make mistakes with their lives that are hanging in the balance. So it was out of necessity that I built a stronger connection with the Lord and it was through this line of faith that He started guiding me in a way that is even difficult for me to comprehend. He visits me in dreams from time to time and offers me guidance on the particulars of running the business. He even weighs in on who would be best to use as employees. I understand that the wellness center belongs to Him and that I work for Him. He is multiplying my talents out of necessity and my love for those who come. I am learning how to use discernment and look through the walls and stories that are blinding my clients. I am literally learning how to identify and eliminate the very stories that are preventing divine healing from taking place. Often people say that they know the Lord is real and He helps other people, but they just know it won't work for them. They build a story around not being worthy or good enough. Often these desperate souls are offended at the thought of letting go and letting God because they are angry and resentful toward Him for abandoning them in their darkest hour. Throughout this book, I will share many examples of these stories and what we did in order to create a viable path to the Savior. But not all of my cases end with miracles. We lost a few along the way. And that broke our hearts.

There was one particular alcoholic that came to me for a few individual meetings, but he would not commit to doing a program at the wellness center. The biggest reason he would not commit is because of the deep shame and disappointment he felt for letting his parents down. He couldn't stand the thought of them spending more money on him. They begged him to do a program with us but he refused. He was such a kind and gentle soul. I considered him a friend. A year after I met with him the final time, he was killed in an accident where his truck collided with a tree while he was driving under the influence of alcohol. I was heartbroken to hear the news. I prayed for his parents and for strength and an increase of talents and gifts to make sure this wouldn't happen again. But as deeply committed as I am to helping others, it will never be enough to overpower someone else's free will. I can imagine how difficult it is for the Lord to sit back and wait for those who have locked Him out of their lives, and either refuse, or don't know how to gain His divine help.

It is crucial to understand the nuances of free will in creating miracles. The Lord can only provide divine intervention IF we identify and remove the internal barriers and attitudes that keep Him locked out. And herein lies my gift to help others. The Lord has blessed me to discern and communicate with the willing seeker about what is preventing divine healing.

Humility, accountability, desire, and faith are all necessary ingredients if you want a healing miracle. A friend once explained it to me like this: "You can mix chemicals to create the perfect compound but without the flame of the Lord being applied to the flask, it will never create the chemical reaction you are seeking."

Prophecy And Josh

One of the biggest personal losses in my life and at the wellness center was the heroin overdose of my 28 year-old nephew, Josh. This loss jolted me and my family profoundly. The irony of his loss challenged my very existence at the wellness center. Josh had a horrible addiction to heroin. He eventually ended up in jail for seven months because of his lying and cheating that always accompany a desperate addict who will do anything for his next fix. When Josh went to jail, we were all thankful that he was off the streets. He was forced to get clean and we slept better at night knowing he was safely indoors through a long, cold winter. Josh had often come to me for counsel and help, but he could never turn the corner of being fully committed to quitting. He needed to suffer the consequences of his actions, and going to jail was literally an answer to our prayers. While Josh was incarcerated, I had a dream where I saw him smiling and standing in the wellness center. I just knew that I was finally going to be able to help him when he got out of jail. In fact, Josh was a huge factor when we decided to purchase the wellness center. I had members of my own family who could really benefit from this amazing work.

The first day Josh got out of jail, he came straight to the wellness center. I walked out of an appointment to see him standing in front of me exactly as I had seen him in my dream. That image of him standing there and smiling is frozen in my mind. He was so excited to see me and loved everything about the wellness center. I spoke to him about starting on our addiction program immediately. He readily agreed. While in jail, Josh thought constantly about the wellness center. He was actually released early for being a model inmate with a specific plan to become clean. That day at the center as I spoke to Josh about the addiction program, a foreboding prophecy came over me. I proceeded to warn him: "If you use heroin again, you will be dead." He agreed and said, "I know." I repeated, "Josh, I am serious. If you use heroin again, you will be dead." He promised me that he would not use it ever again. I then repeated to him the exact line one last time.

The timing of Josh getting out of jail had caught me by surprise. My wife and I had made arrangements for a short weekend getaway in Southern Utah. We left Josh with instructions and details of his program to follow while we would be gone. I received a call from my mother while we were out of town. She was sobbing uncontrollably and uttered the words: "Josh is dead. Josh is dead." He had used heroin one last time, and that foreboding prophecy that I had spoken to him was ringing in my ears. I could barely take it in. I was absolutely heartbroken. My family was devastated. The paradox of this loss is that I had been instrumental in helping strangers find their own healing from addiction, and yet my own flesh and blood could not be saved.

I am dedicated to my ongoing cause and mission in honor of Josh. I have shared his story with every addict I interview for our program. I tell each addict how serious and life-threatening their addiction is. They listen intently. Recently, I was working with an addict and had a flash of that dream of Josh standing in my Wellness Center. It was given me to understand that Josh is *still* standing with me in the great cause of rescuing lost souls. And of course, I also know that JC is standing with me and with every single person that walks through my door.

*The Dried Broken Petals Fall From His Hand
And Back To The Dust, Where the Caretaker Stands*

— **Mike Simpson**

Meet Kelley

I will conclude this chapter with the true story of Kelley. She was a desperate heroin addict who had lost custody of both of her children, and had been in prison twice. Although coming from ideal circumstances, she fell into addiction that ruined her life. When she arrived at the center she was skeptical, terrified and suicidal. No program had yet worked for her, and this visit was one last desperate attempt before giving up for good. As always, I took Kelley's words seriously. Kelley explained that she could not go more than three minutes without a body tremor screaming out for heroin. Kelley was absolutely committed to changing, and it was going to require every ounce of faith to get her through. I taught Kelley the principle of Let Go and Let God. I not only discussed with her what this means, but taught her how to do it through her subconscious mind where addiction and God meet in the middle.

Kelley's story is told in her own words below, but before you read it, I would like to share a sacred experience with the Savior which Kelley had while in hypnosis. Kelley's biggest trigger for heroin was the shame from the seemingly countless poor choices and compromises she made that led to losing custody of her children and devastating her family. While I had Kelley in hypnosis, we were exploring what it would take for Kelley to be willing to forgive herself for causing deep pain for her loved ones.

While discussing forgiveness, the Savior literally appeared to Kelley. He announced joyfully and powerfully: "I don't care about the details of your past. What matters most to me is your future. My grace is more powerful than your mistakes." A divine healing happened in front of both of us as Kelley exhibited the humility and faith to simply put the past behind her. Kelley has been clean for over two years at the time of this writing, and has received full custody of her children. She is engaged to be married and is living a model life. Here is her story:

Kelley's Story

I wasn't your everyday kind of addict. I grew up in an amazingly good home. My parents love each other very much and are still married. I was on the national honors list in high school and graduated with top honors in my class. I was also captain of the dance team my senior year. I had so much going for me in an ideal life. I went on an overseas trip to Germany after high school. I was on top of the world. Then one night it all changed in a moment. I attended a party and someone passed me an Oxycontin pill. I took it. My life snowballed downward. I instantly became addicted. Once a person becomes addicted to opiates, their goal is to try to not be sick. The withdrawals are horrible. I was an addict throughout college. I missed so many classes because I couldn't find a pill. It got to the point where I had to drop out. I finally came to the realization that I needed help. My parents enrolled me in the 12-step program. This may seem unbelievable, but it was in that program that I was introduced to heroin and at that moment I was hooked. I was already addicted so I thought, "What the heck." Being addicted to heroin also pulled me in with the heroin crowd. I then learned to steal, lie, and cheat to get my next fix. I would do anything for that next fix. I ended up meeting up with a heroin dealer where I got busted in a huge heroin sting operation the very first night I met her. Facing loaded weapons from the police was surreal. I had never been in trouble and now I was in the middle of it. This was where I had to tell my parents what was going on with heroin. They were shocked because I had pretended to be over my addiction. They thought the 12-step program had worked for me, and they were completely blindsided when contacted by the authorities. I admitted to my parents about the heroin. They sent me to a different rehab based on Scientology. While in this new program, the county police came to arrest me from the previous drug bust. I had never been in trouble in my life, and now I was facing 13 felonies and countless misdemeanor warrants for my arrest. Long story short, Sheriff Joe came and picked me up at my addiction program and flew me back to Phoenix. I had never been in trouble before this. I was still in good graces with the authorities because I had been at the rehab center. My dad borrowed $75,000 from his 401(k) to bail me out of jail. He hired a high-power attorney to defend me, but I was sentenced to jail anyway. While incarcerated, I met more dealers and users. My ability to find what I wanted became much easier.

After nine months in the Tent City facility, I was released and able to go back and finish the addiction program in Nevada. While in this program, I met my daughter's father and got pregnant. When I found out I was expecting a child, I had the thought that this baby was going to be my saving grace. I was committed to doing everything I could to be the best mother I could be. But even after giving birth to my daughter, it wasn't enough to keep me clean.

At this point, I was in the system. I was on probation and a whole whirlwind of jail time and probation ensued. Eventually I was sent to prison when my daughter was two. It is all a blur, but one heartbreaking thing that stands out to me is that when I got out and came home, my daughter did not know who I was. That was the hardest thing I had ever been through, because it was all my fault.

Even after getting out of prison, I went into another whirlwind of parole violations and heavy usage. I was stealing again. I found myself with guns being put to my head. I stole purses in grocery carts from old ladies. At one point I was even homeless. Honestly, it is by the grace of God that I am not dead and don't have some horrible disease.

After getting out of prison the second term, I actually met and fell in love with a man who, along with my father's help, made it possible for me to go to Sandy, Utah, to do an addiction program with Mike Simpson. From a friend, my father had heard reports of miracles happening there.

I was skeptical because I had tried everything under the sun with no success. When I got to Sandy, Utah, it was amazing how relaxing the program was. I expected strict routines. But instead I felt like I was in a safe haven where I could actually slow down and look at myself.

It is important to recognize that what Mike and I did in hypnosis was to break down the wall between my conscious and subconscious thinking. Now when the thought of drugs pops into my head, there is something fighting against it. One of the biggest turning points in my sessions with Mike was learning that God forgave me. That allowed me to finally forgive myself and release the shame and guilt from making so many bad choices. My addiction wouldn't go away originally, because I needed to numb my shame and embarrassment. Once my shame and guilt was taken by the Savior, He replaced it with love and forgiveness and a clean slate. That clean slate gave me a new chance at claiming my life back.

I can't explain the feeling of being clean for two years. All of a sudden, I woke up one day and the addiction was completely gone. My mom told me that I am suddenly a grown-up, and the light switched on. It is unreal how I am at this point, but it is really true.

I don't have words to explain my life. I now have a great job. I've been promoted several times. I've had multiple raises. I also have both of my children back and am getting married this spring! The difference between these past two years and the ten previous years is like night and day. I am not the same person.

I know deep in my soul that if I had not gone to see Mike I would be dead. And, my children would have to live on without knowing who their mother was. I would have been the one who left her children for the heroin addiction. I am so thankful they have me back. I was gone from my daughter's life twice while in prison. She is now eight years old. I was incarcerated for half her life. She remembers me coming and going. She now trusts me and knows I am here to stay. I'm not going anywhere anymore.

If I can do it, anyone can! I was so far down the rabbit hole that I just knew I would never get out of it alive. But miraculously, here I am, alive. God kept me alive and led me to Mike. I know this was God. How else was this change possible?

CHAPTER FOUR

The Subconscious Mind

In this book, I address many concepts that will likely push you to the edge of what you believe is possible. One of these concepts is limiting beliefs in our perception. These self-imposed limitations actually cap what we *think* is possible and therefore they limit what *is* possible. I have encountered many miracles that defy expectations simply because I believed they were achievable, and because I have learned how to identify and replace limitations that prevent miracles.

If we believe it, then we expect it.

And if we expect it, then it happens.

If we don't believe it, but it still happens, then we call it luck.

There is a phenomenon we call selective perception, or confirmation bias, that basically means that we see what we look for and are blind to anything outside of that filter or perspective.

Start Seeing Motorcycles

I read this very phrase quoted on the bumper sticker of a car one day. It really caught my attention because I ride a motorcycle. I found it extremely clever because it is actually a hypnotic suggestion. Little did I know the profound impact this bumper sticker would have on me in the near future.

A few days later I was driving through some back roads at night. I was getting ready to pull forward through the stop sign when I instantly caught a glimpse of a small motorcycle approaching the intersection without any headlights. I hit the brakes, just barely avoiding impact.

The rider was driving at night while wearing dark clothing and without a headlight. But I still saw him, and just in the nick of time! That bumper sticker flashed in my mind as I hit the brakes. Without a doubt, that hypnotic suggestion had expanded and influenced my awareness sufficiently to prevent a horrible accident!

The power in this suggestion to "Start Seeing Motorcycles" opened my scanning strategy while pulling through the intersection. While at an intersection, an inexperienced driver will typically ask themselves: "Are there any cars coming?"

Notice this limiting filter omits everything BUT cars. What about motorcycles, pedestrians, trucks, bicycles, or animals? The mind actually has the ability to delete or filter out anything but that for which we are specifically filtering. I know this personally because I got deleted by plenty of the ladies at dances when I was single.

We want to learn to open our perception to see everything, as opposed to ignoring everything that doesn't match our filter. Looking beyond our limiting filters and beliefs is where we find new insights, possibilities, and truths that will lead us to miracles.

Start Seeing Miracles

Once we truly believe something is possible, we tend to filter evidence to reinforce that our belief is true. This explains why it can be difficult to teach an old dog new tricks. Conversely, I propose that miracles can and will happen if we start looking for them. When we dig up and rethink our hidden, limiting beliefs we start seeing miracles happen. Miracles require you to suspend doubt to allow your mind to consider and entertain new possibilities.

You Can Be be Blinded By Your Focus

Be The Wall

For our anniversary one year, Diana and I hired a professional rock climber to take us for some rock climbing lessons. It was a really fun day, except for one major exception. Diana was making it up to the top every single time while I kept falling off the same part of the wall.

I was frustrated and humiliated. I was supposed to be showing off for Diana, but instead she was, as usual, beating me to the top. Luckily, I had an old football injury I pulled out to explain why my right elbow was bothering me that day. But Diana knew better because really, I didn't play football. It's hard to fool somebody when they know all of your background.

After about ten failed attempts *in a row* the instructor finally approached me to offer what turned out to be some Yoda-type wisdom. While trying to offer me his feedback, I interrupted him with a little quip: "Be the Wall."

He didn't think I was funny and he didn't laugh. But Diana gave me a complimentary chuckle to save me from double-humble pie. Stinking at rock climbing and not being funny would have been a blow that I may not have recovered from. To add insult to injury, Diana would just simply glide up the wall with ease while distracted by the butterflies and the hawk and all of the beautiful scenery everywhere around her. It was actually really annoying!

"Oh look! A butterfly!" she would exclaim as she ascended the daunting face with the grace of a dancer.

I reached down for the old football injury… was that my left ankle or my right?

The instruction began. He asked me if I knew the difference between focus and awareness. After stumping me, he explained that I was being blinded by *my focus*. He also observed that I would follow the exact same route, get stuck on the same part of the wall, and I would stop breathing. By the time I was out of breath, I would simply fall off the wall.

He explained that my focus was so intense that I wasn't seeing any of the many options that were being presented to me as I attempted to climb higher. He told me to open up my peripheral vision, keep breathing, and choose to be aware of all options around me, instead of being blinded by that single route that kept failing me. In other words, start seeing options.

I had failed so many times on this wall that my forearms were completely blown out. Yes, another excuse, but they actually were exhausted. However, I shocked myself, Diana, and my instructor by making it right to the top on the very next try! The whole way up I simply kept my peripheral vision and awareness open and remembered to breathe.

Then I climbed it again. Success! And again. Success! I couldn't believe it. All of my previous failures and exhausted forearms seemed irrelevant now as I was scaling up the wall with ease and even finding different ways to climb the wall each time.

The zenful lesson that I learned that day turned out to be profound. And since then, I have used it in many **NLP** sessions to train people how to identify and release old limiting beliefs that produce failure. If what you are doing does not work, try anything else such as being aware and breathing!

My climbing improvement was instant. My humor, unfortunately, is still a work in progress.

Deriving the Truth is No Accident

When policemen are trying to arrive at the truth of what happened at the scene of an accident, they interview each eyewitness separately. And naturally, each witness has a different version of the event. With so many contradictions to the story, how do they arrive at the truth? Well, unfortunately, they try to fill in the blanks by combining the information that each account has in common, and voila! The Truth. Sort of.

So the truth is obtained, deduced, and predisposed to human error while further distorted and skewed by emotion. Luckily for us, God knows the truth beyond our own biased opinions and warped perspectives. I want to reiterate that we can be prejudiced and flat-out blinded against true principles through life's conditioning and our own ignorance. Hence, it is my goal to teach some new principles in this book that I have dubbed **The Miracle Bridge**.

> **If You Want Something Different, Then You Need to Do Something Different**
>
> **If You Always Think What You Always Thought, You'll Always Get What You Always Got**
>
> **So, What Exactly Happens When You Combine Hypnosis, NLP, And God?**

When I went through my hypnosis certification course, my instructor made it very clear to me that NLP was not to be used with hypnosis. I rejected that proposed limitation. My NLP background is the very thing that contributed to my unique approach. I had been doing NLP for so long I knew it would be impossible to *not* use my NLP skills with hypnosis. And besides, why wouldn't I combine them?

In reality, I use NLP in every aspect of my life. It has morphed into the way I think, navigate, and problem-solve everything I come across. In addition, I have carried such a deep trust and conviction of God throughout my life, that it is just as impossible for me to separate God from my filters. So, naturally, or unnaturally — as you decide to perceive it — I found a way to combine God, NLP, and hypnosis. The results were profound and electric, and, I admit, out of the box.

Hypnosis can be perceived taboo by some people, and I get it. Hollywood has played a big role in painting hypnosis as sinister, mysterious, and magical. And I will admit, hypnosis is pretty magical!

Who has ever heard of NLP? Not many of us. But it is becoming more mainstream because of the many positive results being reported, including the stories in this book. It is not uncommon that the mention of God can polarize an audience. So yes, these sometimes charged, but life-transforming topics I discuss, may require you to rethink your narrative. Perhaps some of these unorthodox approaches are not so different than what Christ required of the true believers when He walked the earth.

The Blind Man Healed On The Sabbath

What a perfect example from the Savior's life, to illustrate an unconventional approach to create a miracle that brought Josiah, a man who had been blind since birth, vision to see clearly for the first time ever. The Jews had become so blinded by their embellished laws, that they ultimately conspired and crucified their King because His approach did not conform to their rigid guidelines and rules. The Savior broke two of the Jewish laws to heal Josiah's vision. First, he created a mud ball with saliva and, second, he had the "audacity" to heal on the Sabbath! I always wondered why the Savior healed Josiah's sight in such an unusual fashion until one day it occurred to me that Jesus was mocking the ridiculous guidelines that were blinding the Jews. He defied the existing limitations and narrative of the day so that perhaps not only Josiah might see but the Jews, also. Truly, Jesus was the master teacher. Unfortunately, the only thing the Jewish leaders chose to see from Josiah's miracle was blasphemy. They couldn't erase the indisputable miracle, but they did excommunicate Josiah from their midst because he would not denounce the Savior. For Josiah, the price to pay for claiming a true disciple's vision was to be rejected by God's own chosen people. Josiah was given sight, but the Jews remained blinded by their cherished traditions. How sadly ironic.

I've been making the case that a miracle isn't possible unless you believe. A good friend of mine once suggested that the mission of John the Baptist was absolutely crucial to the Savior's miracles. John was a forerunner to Christ who opened and prepared the minds of his followers for the greater things that were coming. John was a bridge to greater things. Unbelief and spiritual blindness had to be removed as a first step.

Moses was instructed to remove his shoes while in God's presence, because he was standing on Holy ground. And recently, I came across another layer of understanding of the necessity of removing your shoes in His presence. Are not your shoes under your standing? Is the Lord perhaps asking us to remove our previous *understanding*? Is He asking us to unlearn our old ideas and limitations so that more can be given?

Perhaps removing your old understanding is no different than a rocket releasing the fuselage once it has pierced through the atmosphere. The very thing the rocket *relied* upon to reach such heights is now required to be released so as to allow a new form of travel to be experienced. Flight in space is without turbulence and a new narrative must be embraced. This metaphor can also lead to a better understanding of the principle Let Go and Let God. What do we have to let go of to allow God to send us a miracle? If you don't have an answer to this question, I suggest you start asking God to show you. And perhaps dig a little deeper into the hidden recesses of your subconscious mind.

So, What Is Hypnosis?

Hypnosis is a consent state. Hypnosis is not sleep. It is a heightened state of awareness. A pure hypnosis state will make you twenty times more aware than normal. Think about it — twenty times more aware!

The average person goes into hypnosis nearly thirty times a day on their own. If you are driving on a long road trip and suddenly wonder where the last few hours went, you can rest assured you have been in hypnosis. When you are watching television, you are in hypnosis. When you are daydreaming, you are in hypnosis. When you read a page in a book and have no idea what you just read, hypnosis. Hypnosis is a natural state of mind where your conscious mind becomes more passive and a clear path to your subconscious mind opens up. Think of the conscious mind as a cute little circus monkey and the subconscious mind as a thousand pound gorilla. Who is going to win in a tug-of-war? You can use hypnosis to train the gorilla instead of fighting against it.

Dr. David Spiegel is a currently noted psychiatrist who understands and includes hypnosis as one of his recognized protocols. By his own admission on a Ted Talk appearance, he humorously likens hypnosis to "the oldest profession in the world that everyone seems to be interested in, but no one wants to be seen with in public."

Breaking Down a Few Mechanics of the Mind

I have spent many years working in the subconscious mind. I will share a simplified model of the brain to convey some simple concepts.

I want you to consider two backyards separated by a wall. The backyard on your left represents the conscious mind, and the backyard on the right represents the subconscious mind. Each half is separated by the wall and each half of the mind functions differently.

It is the conscious mind that houses rational thought and willpower. We spend most of our waking day navigating our lives with our conscious, rational mind. You can liken the conscious mind to the processor on a computer. This is where our calculations and evaluations are performed. But please understand that "rational" is a relative term here. Simply stated, "rational" means something different to each one of us. This conscious realm is where we decide what is "normal" and this is where we measure events in the world against this "rational" standard we have spent a lifetime defining. Your normal and my normal are likely entirely different. And, of course, I am weird if I don't see things your way. Yes, we tend to call things weird that don't match our own version of normal.

Take note: rational thought is *only* a component of the conscious mind. The wall that separates the conscious from the subconscious is called the Critical Factor. And this wall guarantees that rational thought *only* operates in the backyard to the left, in the conscious mind. Allow me to underscore here that rational thought is NOT present or active in the subconscious mind.

The subconscious half of the mind can be likened unto a video camera that not only records every single event in our lives, but also all of the emotions and perceptions associated with those memories. If you were comparing the mind to a computer, then the subconscious mind serves as the hard drive. This is simply where life's data and clutter gets stored. The subconscious mind does not decide when something should be rejected. Can you imagine a hard drive refusing to save your document because it disapproves of what you just typed on the screen? The hard drive simply stores what it is told to store.

Time does not exist in the subconscious mind. And because rational thought only lives and operates in the conscious half of the mind, this means we all have irrational ideas, fears, and beliefs that are often hidden from the conscious mind and rational perspective.

These hidden irrational fears can be likened unto an undertow or rip-tide in the ocean that is elusive but has the power to drag you out to sea and drown you. It can be really confusing because the waves appear to be pushing you to shore, but that invisible river running beneath the surface has the profound ability to undermine and sabotage your life in unexpected ways.

The phenomenon of the wall hiding things from us explains how we can become double-minded about something. We can unequivocally denounce or believe an idea consciously, while at the same time feel exactly the opposite on the other side of the wall. And when these irrational fears are hidden in the subconscious mind, we can be completely controlled by them unknowingly. An example of this principle might be the subconscious mind pushing you to fill an emotional black-hole by mindlessly eating and creating weight-gain to discourage you from socializing in a desperate attempt to protect you from risking rejection. You may consciously despise how you look in the mirror while the subconscious mind is happy to be free from the pressures of socializing.

The Savior taught this principal when He stated that a house divided cannot stand.

That Really Takes Me Back!

Have you ever been driving in the car and a song from the past comes on the radio and suddenly you are singing and smiling and laughing? This song on the radio is an external stimulus or trigger that is connected to a cluster of happy memories of your past. The fact that your mood just completely transformed is evidence that positive emotions are attached to the associated memories. And voila! Singing, laughing, and tears of joy are on full display in an instant. With a few familiar notes from the radio, minivan mama's mood has just transformed from the mundane and stressful to reliving drill team glory.

The point here is we can relive magical memories in an instant by encountering any associated external stimulus. But this principle of "that really takes me back" also applies to negative memories. Minivan mama had a magical transformation, but what about those negative triggers that inadvertently transform happiness into anxiety or despondency? These negative associations can get triggered just as easily and the results can be life-destroying.

These pesky negative transformations just might be the reason you are reading this book in the first place. Some of these negative triggers connect to pure terror and anguish from the past, and they can be triggered accidentally, in the same way as being zapped by an electric fence while on a pleasant evening stroll.

But Why the Wall?

Recall that the wall between the two backyards is called the Critical Factor. This Critical Factor is a barrier that separates the conscious mind from the subconscious mind. This wall is usually fully formed by five or six years of age. Once formed, this wall will attempt to protect you in some really strange ways. You can think of this wall as having the attitude of a picky two-year-old child that does not like to learn new things.

This wall rejects nearly everything. It tries to protect the subconscious mind from bad things by blocking out as much as possible. Both the good and the bad.

The wall makes it difficult for positive messages to get into the subconscious mind. Consider the smoker who keeps telling himself to quit but the wall won't allow the suggestion through. Now imagine the sound of a buzzer going off while rejecting the proposal. The message gets rejected over and over again. And it can be extremely frustrating!

This wall also protects you from dark elements in your past by actually hiding the painful and unresolved memories. For instance, it is very common for me to work with someone who has been through extreme child abuse but strangely has no recollection of anything from their childhood. It is common that this person would come to me and claim they have very few childhood memories. But I simply instruct them that it is not their memory that has failed them. Instead it is the Critical Factor that has been busy protecting them! Even though the Critical Factor will attempt to hide negative memories, it does not have the ability to hide the emotions connected to those memories. This can create a really puzzling effect for someone who mysteriously suffers from panic attacks or anxiety. The hidden alarm goes off abruptly and the negative emotions and stress hormones are quickly launched into the body, but the lights go out in a desperate attempt to protect you. It can be terrifying and downright puzzling. You could liken this wall to the enclosure at the junkyard. It can be a beautiful wall with aesthetic design and craftsmanship. And rest assured, this wall can hide the view of the garbage, but it cannot hide the associated emotions or stench to the triggers.

I worked with a woman who had a terrifying panic attack occur when she was driving on a busy freeway during rush hour traffic. Her body seized up as she was driving and she felt as though she were having a heart attack. Traffic was stalled and the emergency vehicles raced to get her to the hospital. After this terrifying ordeal, the doctors informed her that tests showed that nothing was wrong with her heart and that she had probably just experienced a panic attack. A what?

Let's now use the model of the wall separating the two backyards to explain what really happened here. While she was driving and talking on her phone, she started discussing something that really upset her and instantly she was physically incapacitated on the freeway with an emotional reaction that happened outside of her conscious awareness. From the conscious, rational side of the mind, she was asking the wall, "What's happening here?"

The Wall responded, "None of your business! I'm protecting you! Oh! And have a nice day!"

Thus we see how sometimes the wall "gets it wrong" and the outcome can be horrifying.

But this dynamic poses an interesting question. If the wall is hiding the very reason for your suffering then exactly how do you solve this problem? You can't solve a puzzle if you don't have the pieces! This explains why NLP and hypnosis can be so effective digging to the core of their issues and bypassing the symptoms.

Some Real Life Examples

I would like to share with you a few simple examples of people who came to me suffering from "hopeless depression" who left with some really simple, permanent solutions.

Meet Julia

Julia has given me permission to use her story in the hopes of helping others by learning from her desperate circumstances. Her story perfectly illustrates this "masking" phenomenon.

Julia came to me bewildered and in urgent need of a dramatic "Hail Mary" before giving up on happiness for good. Her medication was no longer helping her depression. Deep hopelessness kept her from getting up and out of bed in the mornings. Before coming to me in one last desperate attempt, she visited a psychologist who changed her medication *yet again* but told her there was nothing more that could be done and she even asked Julia not to come back.

That felt like the final nail in the coffin for Julia. The "expert" believed there was no hope for her and nothing more could be done. How tragic.

I wasn't there to witness this exchange between Julia and her psychologist, but suffice it to say that Julia left that meeting dejected and ready to accept her dismal fate. During our first 90-minute session, we uncovered a *complete* collection of puzzle pieces that would solve her mystery.

I was absolutely astounded that no one had ever sat down with Julia to examine the obvious clues, shallowly buried, beneath Julia's "depression."

Julia was raised in extreme poverty in Brazil. She grew up in a large family that had been abandoned by her father. She grew up being hungry and afraid, and was often shamed by her mother if she ate a piece of bread. Because her father was nowhere to be found, Julia's mother did her best to raise the kids alone. But the environment was bleak, both emotionally and temporally. Julia was reminded daily by her mother that she was worthless, just like her deadbeat father, if she didn't earn money and provide for the family.

Well, of course Julia wanted to have worth, so she became a hard worker. She became *the* provider. When circumstances finally permitted, when she was an adult, Julia moved to America where she found a good-paying job. She worked diligently and desperately to earn money, most of which she sent home to her ailing family. Her perceived sense of self-worth increased as she diligently labored to protect her nieces and nephews from living the nightmare of her own childhood. Julia worked her way to the top and found great satisfaction in becoming the family provider, as she was raised to be.

However, one day she started feeling extremely sick. She went to a doctor, only to find that she had a life-threatening condition that would require some intense medication to save her life. The medication was necessary and did work to save her life. But, just as the doctor predicted, one of the horrible side effects was that she would likely gain over a hundred pounds. And she did. Julia suffered through the recovery and weight gain, grateful to have recovered from her deadly condition. When Julia was finally feeling well enough to travel, she flew back to Brazil to meet with her loving family, but the visit turned out to be very painful. Julia was mocked and ridiculed by family members for being so overweight. The very loved ones she labored to support, the very ones who had never gone without a meal, were mean-spirited and judgmental towards Julia. It truly devastated her. It is a sad reality that some people become so blinded by entitlement that they become insensitive and oblivious to the personal sacrifice of their providers. Julia traveled back to America heartsick and dejected, but still devoutly committed to providing for those cute little monsters.

Julia's depression began when she retired. Her body was old and tired and she was unable to keep up the rigorous standard she had honored throughout her adult life as a provider. Now, she was actually having to be provided for by her own own children. Can you guess what conflict emerged?

Julia now believed herself to be worthless because she could no longer provide. Her strategy of providing was counterfeit self-esteem and was now on the top shelf, just out of reach.

Julia was raised believing that she would only be valued if she earned money. She heard that on a daily basis as an impressionable child, and it was seared into her soul with fear and shame. It was set in stone, or so it seemed.

Now, Julia had officially lost her ability to provide. Providing had been the answer to her childhood problems of scarcity and worthlessness, and now she was facing the same old haunts which returned for some unfinished business. But, this time she had to face her nightmare without youthful energy to meet her mother's heavy demands.

It was time for Julia's limiting beliefs from her childhood to be reworked. Julia needed to unlearn her childhood strategies and "remove her shoes." She now needed to base her personal value on an eternal principle: that she is a daughter of God. Through hypnosis, we revisited her childhood and let that scared and dejected little girl escape from the past, rewrite her story of worth and value, and come home to be provided for by her own children. This was the first time in her entire life that someone else had provided for her. The whole experience was beautiful and simple and, of course, it was healing!

This is Not Rocket Science

I want to share with you an amazing breakthrough that Julia had after we met together several times. One evening after our session, Julia found herself surprisingly filled with energy and wanting to go out to celebrate instead of going to bed early. This was a radical contradiction to her usual, depressed behavior.

She didn't have anyone to go out with, but instead of being discouraged, she chose not to let that stop her. She picked up the phone and called a restaurant and asked if they had a VIP section. She explained to me that a restaurant VIP section is a place where you can go eat alone, and not feel uncomfortable.

Julia went to dinner alone and found herself seated next to a few other VIP women who soon pulled her into their conversation. She became engaged in a fascinating exchange about everything under the sun. She felt included and valued.

Before long, one of the women (who was previously a complete stranger) asked her if she would be interested in attending a concert that her husband would be performing the following evening. Julia agreed to go. This experience completely contradicted anything she had previously believed possible.

When Julia arrived the next evening at the concert, she had a wonderful time. She talked with her new friend and enjoyed the beautiful music. Julia was just so pleased and happy to have something to do and someone with whom to spend time.

At the end of the concert, an elderly woman who was a complete stranger walked up to Julia, took her by the face with both hands, and said, "I hope you don't mind, but I want to tell you that I have been watching you all evening. I just needed to tell you that you are a beautiful angel!"

They both broke into tears and hugged. Again, this happened with another complete stranger!

Please remember that we are talking about a woman who had recently been so depressed that she couldn't get out of bed. She was simply trying to learn to accept life without purpose as a non-provider. By removing Julia's beliefs that her performance defined her value, she had just magically stumbled into a brand new life that she would have never believed possible.

Julia was never going to find those new friends and make those meaningful connections, if she was at home, hiding in her bed, punishing herself for not being the provider she was raised to become. Instead, Julia rejected those old limitations and was now living in a different world and measuring herself with an updated, inspired standard.

Julia Did Not Always Play Nicely with Others

As we went through some of our sessions, Julia discovered how her old provider-proves-value beliefs blinded her to the dynamic of alienating some of her past co-workers. Because Julia believed that providing was necessary to feel value, she admitted to me that she tended to be competitive and defensive with many of her previous co-workers, where contention and isolation was commonplace. So, with an adjusted perspective about Julia's distorted past motivations, we were able to explore the dynamics of interacting kindly with others instead of trying to desperately prove her value by outperforming them. When Julia decided to acknowledge her fear of others and put away her "porcupine quills," she was delighted to have her goodness recognized and reciprocated so quickly, even by strangers. Remember, porcupines love to be hugged, too.

Over her lifetime of providing, Julia had lost perspective of what it felt like on the other side of the fear and suspicion that she often reflected to unsuspecting coworkers. For her to move forward in a new productive life, she had to recognize that people would respond to her with the same energy that she projected to them. That old exhausting belief system had worn the tread from Julia's emotional tires, and thank goodness for that! Because of Julia's temporary depression, she was now being forced to confront her old programming which was ready to be released like the fuselage of a rocket piercing the atmosphere. And yes, pun intended here: It was really time for Julia to retire since the tread of her emotional tires was worn out.

The world had not changed, Julia had. The depression? What depression? Julia no longer needed a psychologist or medication. She was a new person with a new perspective.

Meet Annie

Annie came to me for help after her husband found my website while researching holistic solutions for Annie's ongoing depression. We had an amazing first session and decided she needed to do a comprehensive program at the wellness center to repattern some negative subconscious programming from her past. Discovering Annie's cause for depression was pretty simple, but rewiring her patterns of thought and perception was going to take some practical work. In fact, it was going to take a rototiller.

It was in my second meeting with Annie that we discovered the core reason for her sense of hopelessness. It is frustrating to encounter cases that have such simple solutions, but yet no former counselor ever took the time to dig beneath the symptoms and resolve the real issue.

Annie's husband Jim was deeply frustrated and tired. He was working a full-time job supporting Annie and his two young children while preparing for the birth of their third, unplanned child. This little surprise was adding extra fuel to the fire. The thought of this third child was sending Annie into a case of pure panic because she could barely handle the stress and pressure from the two children she was already raising. Jim would work all day only to come home to find Annie despondent and unable to function. So Jim would take care of the kids while she went to bed, depressed. This dynamic was certainly not improving the quality of their relationship.

Annie was raised by her grandparents while her parents worked full-time away from home. Annie spoke English, but her grandparents only spoke Chinese. She grew up feeling frustrated, misunderstood, overlooked, and neglected because of the language barrier and the sense of abandonment from her parents. Her grandparents were kind, but Annie's needs were mostly unspoken and unmet.

Through repetition as a child, Annie learned to "shut down" instead of communicating her needs. Annie's "normal" as a child was to wait helplessly for her uncommunicated needs to be met. Annie developed frustration when attempting to communicate and eventually just quit trying. And, of course, she felt alone and neglected. What if she was hungry? What if she was scared? What if she wanted a hug? She could not speak Chinese.

Annie, now a wife and mother of two children, suddenly mysteriously found herself shutting down and feeling invisible and neglected again. Her husband's biggest complaint was that Annie was unreachable, emotionally. She would just close down when he came home from work. It was the perfect storm. She spent all day with young children who couldn't speak, and then Jim had the audacity to come home from work and ignore and neglect Annie while attending to the children. She would sulk and punish him for neglecting her. But isn't it interesting that he *neglected* her because he was busy taking care of the kids? She was recreating the childhood pattern. The language barrier of her childhood repeated. Except, this time it was with a husband that spoke her language. Annie punished Jim by not speaking to him. Annie's childhood conditioning of being invisible and not having a voice was now sabotaging her marriage while she sank helplessly into the old comfortable hiding place she knew so well. Ironically, the guilt and shame she felt for not being a good mother was reinforcing her worthless narrative and inspiring despondency. She was becoming an absent mother while being physically present in the home!

The bulk of the work we did with Annie was to simply teach her that she *does* have a voice, and to communicate her needs instead of expecting Jim to read her mind when he was preoccupied. She realized that instead of being a martyr and feeling sorry for herself, she could be responsible for her own needs. She had to learn how to communicate her needs instead of having them silently ignored and building a silo of resentment towards her unsuspecting and "neglectful" husband. Remember that communicating is something she didn't learn how to do as a child and therefore didn't know how to do as an adult. But the point is, with some simple coaching she was able to recognize that she had a voice. Suddenly she felt empowered to speak about how she felt before she climbed down into the hole of resentment, worthlessness, and depression.

I came up with a funny analogy one day when I suggested to Annie that if she kept diving into the sewer like a rat, then nobody will be able to meet her unspoken and mysterious needs! She laughed at the analogy, sort of. Her husband became amazed that Annie was choosing to stop punishing him for her uncommunicated and unmet needs. He had many skills as a father, but ESP was certainly not one of them.

Annie also learned that if she would proactively communicate her needs to her husband, then he could actually understand her. Annie needed to be heard and this was much more likely when she was talking and laughing instead of hiding in the sewer.

Annie's intervention was successful because we empowered her to recognize, address, and communicate her own needs. Without this intervention, her marriage was heading for disaster. Her husband couldn't work hard enough to meet her unspoken needs because she was too busy punishing him for neglecting her. It was an impossible dynamic that required accountability and education for Annie to be able to transcend her dysfunctional childhood conditioning;. And in the end, Annie found herself much happier by speaking up and claiming responsibility for her own needs.

Meet Kaylee

Kaylee worked with me for only a few times concerning a disabling depression. It was interesting to explore her distorted perspective from the outside. She was a young, beautiful woman who appeared to have everything going for her — from the outside. But she was deeply discouraged and ashamed of herself because "she had no good reason" for feeling depressed. She had lived an ideal life without any type of tragedy or abuse. She grew up beautiful and healthy, yet had always mysteriously felt deeply depressed. Kaylee was ashamed to admit her depression because she had really lived the ideal life. She was newly married to the man of her dreams and yet had become so disconnected that she was unable to enjoy the blessings right in front of her.

It is more common than you might think for someone to feel ashamed and guilty for being depressed "for no good reason." But, as it usually turns out, there is usually a reason hidden away from the conscious mind that needs to be reworked.

The Dreaded Whitewash Syndrome

I call it the dreaded whitewash syndrome when someone comes into my office dismissing their story before they can even explain it. Imagine someone writing with a dry-erase marker on the whiteboard with one hand about how badly they feel while the other hand erases everything they write. By the time the writing is finished, there's nothing left on the whiteboard. They are so busy falling onto their own sword that there is absolutely no room for acknowledgment or validation of the problem at hand.

Kaylee's guilt and shame about not having any real reason to be depressed was actually making her depression worse. She was punishing herself for not being grateful and thankful for the many obvious blessings in her life. Strangely, she really was thankful for her blessings, but she didn't know how to enjoy them.

It took two visits with Kaylee to discover her hidden conflict. The discovery brought instant tears of relief. As we dug deeper we found buried pain about feeling invisible in her childhood. Again, I want to point out that she was the type of woman whose beauty would capture the attention of everyone in a room, and yet she legitimately felt invisible. With a little bit of digging we learned that Kaylee felt replaced by her younger brother when he was born. Kaylee went from being an only child, who was the princess of the house, to feeling completely invisible when her younger brother entered the world and stole the attention and the spotlight.

Kaylee's younger brother grew older with an outrageous personality full of adventure and flamboyance. He magically captivated the household while Kaylee continued sinking into invisibility. Where did the princess go?

While pursuing the source of Kaylee's depression during hypnosis, we found a significant memory where Kaylee was ignored in a game of Duck Duck Goose. You would think this was just a random occurrence, but for Kaylee it was the final proof that she was invisible. At the age of six she had concluded that she wasn't important, and she closed her heart like Morning Glory closes its petals when the sun goes down. The only problem was she had no intention of opening her heart again. So you see, there were real reasons she was now depressed. Kaylee had many experiences after her younger brother was born proving that she wasn't good enough. Every major success Kaylee's brother scored throughout childhood seemed to overshadow Kaylee's successes and underscore her invisibility.

Her envy and resentment grew without her realizing it.

As you might imagine, Kaylee really believed that she was invisible. She started to pull away from people and close down. She became, in her own words, painfully shy. It was difficult for her to interact with others, so she stopped talking and interacting. Just like I've pointed out with a few of the other stories, when you believe something is true, then it *becomes* true. The more Kaylee withdrew from the other kids, the more awkward she became in her social interactions. She closed the door to everyone and ended up in self-imposed isolation that was reinforced by fear and resentment.

Kaylee's last straw of resentment struck when her younger brother, now a strapping young man, announced to the world that he was getting married *after* Kaylee had announced her engagement. Here he was stealing her thunder again!

She was sinking back into familiar but counterproductive behavior, again isolating herself and withdrawing. As mentioned previously, she was experiencing some secondary gain from this resurfacing problem. She learned as a little girl that if she had a sad face, she would get more love and attention from her family. So her subconscious strategy to protect herself from feeling isolated and lonely was literally leading her into depression where pity would hopefully be offered as evidence of her being loved and being somebody of worth.

This behavior was not rational, but the subconscious mind is not rational! Kaylee's subconscious mind had simply made associations that more love and attention would come when she was feeling sad. She was doing this on auto-pilot. With a little bit of digging we were able to set her free from the perception that she was invisible. She walked away from our second meeting depression and anxiety-free, and was able to be the beautiful woman that she had always been. With the exception that now she could enjoy it, and so could her husband.

Meet Andrea

I only met with Andrea one time, but our meeting had a life-changing impact on her. Through it, she was able to shed some crucial conflicts that had plagued her for a lifetime.

Andrea had struggled with an eating disorder for many years. She spent many years in counseling and was then getting ready to graduate with her bachelor's degree in psychology. But she was completely baffled by her inability to overcome her eating disorder. She was yet another example of someone who had been raised under ideal circumstances. She carried guilt and shame because, by her own admission, her problems should not have been there.

I want to underscore here that **_guilt and shame always lead to a deeper and more despondent hopelessness_**. When people feel like they have no reason to feel depressed you need to understand that they really do have good reasons, but they're trying to "be a good person" by ignoring them through tough love! I will tell you that tough love has nothing to do with guilt and shame. But, it has everything to do with accountability. And when you combine accountability with humility, amazing understanding emerges. You just have to be willing to climb outside of the perspective that has been temporarily blinding. It is easy to be depressed when you can't find a different perspective.

Andrea was incredibly insightful and intelligent, but completely baffled by her self-proclaimed dismal state. I did some visualization with her that absolutely shocked her out of denial. I had her close her eyes and think about the people that she felt she had disappointed. I watched her disassociate and stop breathing as she pulled her visualization forward. Then I instantly disrupted her visualization and asked her who she was seeing. She tried to give me a general answer, "Just some people." I pushed harder and said, "Look again and tell me who is prominent in the forefront of this visualization." She nearly burst into tears once she realized who it actually was. Simply by slowing down her thought process and asking her to be specific, she was able to recognize that the primary person she felt she had disappointed was her father. But how could that be? She absolutely loved her father! In fact, he was the most perfect role model she could have ever asked for. He was everything to her. She was shocked because she was certain that face was supposed to be her mother. She had always argued with her mother and didn't get along with her in her younger years and supposed that their conflict was the reason. But it was dad instead.

The NLP technique I used to deduce this crucial clue is called chunking down. Chunking down basically means I drive Andrea to be specific and don't allow generalizations to slip past my listening filter. This usually requires me to interrupt Andrea often while she is trying to tell me something because I have to qualify every general term she is using so she can be specific with herself. Slowing down her thinking process is really no different than driving her slowly past the park so she can see the colorful flowers.

Andrea discovered it was the face of her father that caused her to feel deep guilt. She broke into tears. Then we simply started digging into her belief system around her father.

We wouldn't have been able to move forward with Andrea without tying this conflict to him. This clue was crucial. She needed to see and acknowledge it was him.

This was a simple case of Andrea feeling guilty and inadequate that, by her own standards, she hadn't lived up to this amazing role model. She was actually subconsciously *punishing* herself as a strategy to become better. The relentless pressure and self-punishment turned into an eating disorder.

Daddy Issues with a Twist

Andrea was the victim of a motivational strategy where she would relentlessly berate herself to drive her to the level of her amazing father. But it was a relentless and unforgiving standard that she was imposing on herself. You will see this standard mentioned again near the end of this book:

As Long As I Am Everything
To Everyone
All Of The Time
Then Of Course I Have Value

Because of this impossible standard fueled by good intentions, Andrea found herself constantly overwhelmed and this drove her to control the only thing that she felt she could — her diet. Except she couldn't control that either! The subconscious lie inside of her mind kept that eating dysfunction alive to perpetuate the illusion of control.

Eating and then purging was an escape from the relentless guilt and shame that was always demanding more. All we needed to do with Andrea was call this to her conscious attention and let her replace that old perfectionist belief system with something that was going to work better in the motivational department.

I'm not perfect today, but I'm good enough!

Andrea left that meeting feeling absolutely free and shocked! She kept saying to me that through all of the counseling she had done throughout her lifetime, she had never been able to figure out that her eating disorder had nothing to do with her mother but was tied to the perfect role model of her father. Who would have thunk?

"And the truth shall set you free." (John 8:31, KJV)

In all of the cases outlined in this chapter, every single person was taking antidepressants to cope with their suffering and pain. By simply digging the truth out they were liberated.

You CAN handle the truth!

When a professional is too quick to give medication to suppress the symptoms, the helpless narrative is only reinforced and the victim accepts this as the new normal.

I don't recall exactly where I heard this next phrase but it really jumped out at me.

Trouble and pain are a portal to understanding.

You Know, That Actually Makes Me Sick!

Psychosomatic Manifestations

I get a lot of questions from people about buried pain and emotional conflicts contributing to physical illness. It is very common in the holistic culture to refer to sickness as disease. I love that the holistic approach includes digging into the core of the problem instead of just treating those pesky symptoms!

DIS-EASE.

Is it really possible that a buried emotional conflict can affect our health and make us sick?

Are You a Low Rider?

Let us consider for a moment the ramifications of driving an all-wheel drive vehicle with a low front tire. The engine light comes on to alert you, but you are just too busy to address it today. You will certainly fix it tomorrow. But you know and I know that tomorrow never comes!

This reminds me of a fun little poem I learned as a teenager and thought it would be as educationally unamusing for you as it was for me:

> *Oh procrastination is a silly thing*
> *it really makes me sorrow!*
> *I think I'm going to quit someday*
> *I think I'll start tomorrow!*
> **— author unknown**

So because of procrastination, the tire gets ignored day after day, and you just keep dealing with the car pulling to the right every time you take your hand off the wheel.

At some point though, when you take the time to address the low tire, you can see that the tire has now worn out. It has not only worn out, but there is a new development.

This low tire started pulling the car out of alignment, and now that the car is out of alignment it is starting to affect the transmission. And with the transmission pulling unevenly, there is undue stress being put on the frame which is now starting to bend.

This all started with a simple problem that required a little bit of air pressure but now requires a trip to the vehicle ER. This doesn't even include the possibility of having a blowout while racing to get there. The car hospital is also really expensive. They are going to have to fix all of the problems that are nothing more than a result of negligence. Negligence can be expensive! This negligence always leads to the agonizing cry that we all know and love so well… "*Why me, Lord?*"

The primary goal of this book is to identify those limitations that have been programmed into our mind and pull them out like the weeds that they are. We have all been brainwashed by different perceived limitations in our lifetime, and I want to declare here that we can overcome these ideas as easily as Julia and Annie did — once we turn on the floodlight of awareness.

The Fisherman and the Executive

In 1963, a German writer by the name of Heinrich Böll wrote the following powerful metaphor about a businessman and a fisherman. This story is set in a small harbor on the west coast of Europe. On vacation, a prominent tourist is taking photographs when he notices a poorly dressed local fisherman napping on a small fishing boat. The tourist is unimpressed with the fisherman's slothful work ethic, so he confronts the fisherman and asks him why he is sleeping instead of working. The fisherman explains that he went fishing earlier, and the small catch would be sufficient for the day's needs.

The businessman insists that if the fisherman increased his workload, he would be able to buy a motor within a year, a second boat in less than two years, and so on. He goes on to explain that one day, the fisherman could even expand and build a small cold storage plant and later, a pickling factory. Then he could fly around in a helicopter, build a seafood restaurant, and export seafood to Paris without a middleman.

The nonchalant fisherman asks, "Then what?"

The vacationing businessman enthusiastically continues, "Then, without a care in the world, you could sit here in the harbor, relax in the sun, and enjoy the glorious sea."

"But I'm already doing that." says the fisherman.

The enlightened tourist reluctantly walks away, his pity replaced with a twinge of jealousy.

Julia already had value that wasn't tied to her performance, she just hadn't seen it yet.

Annie always had a voice but just hadn't learned how to use it.

Kaylee was never invisible and she discovered this once she dug beneath the hidden resentment.

Andrea was already good enough and learned humiliation hurts more than it motivates.

Each of these cases required confronting and redefining limiting beliefs created from childhood conditioning, and forgiving others and themselves.

With some effective NLP and hypnosis, you can go over that wall to figure out what is buried and hidden in the subconscious mind. These tools combined with determination and faith can offer some amazing renovation options that will be life-changing and surprisingly simple.

CHAPTER FIVE

Follow the Path

---o---

Neural pathways are more than ingrained ways of thinking. They are also deeply ingrained ways of feeling.

Consider a fresh blanket of newly fallen snow on your driveway. It is very inconsiderate and frustrating for someone to drive over your driveway before you get the chance to shovel the snow. Why? Because anyone who has ever had to shovel snow understands that the car tires just packed down snow and turned it into ice. And now the effort to remove the frozen blanket of snow has increased significantly.

This packed layer of ice is extremely challenging to remove, and now inspires frustration and procrastination. The procrastinator is only going to get more frustrated each time another car drives over the snowpack and strengthens the ice. This can turn into a vicious cycle. The increasing ice pack is proportionately discouraging, and the procrastinator is eventually unwilling and unable to shovel because the ice is next to impossible to remove. And while the air remains freezing cold, it feels like help from the sun is not an option. So perhaps you stop looking up. You can liken this example to how neural pathways get established and set like hard-packed ice on the driveway of our mind. Once established, these patterns of thought become deeply ingrained and the negative pathways inspire hopelessness and frustration.

This example is a perfect illustration of how our old dysfunctional thought patterns are converted into hard-packed attitudes and beliefs where we actually quit shoveling before we start. We already feel defeated. And by the way, it sure is nice to hide under a blanket with a cup of hot cocoa while the cars keep packing down that ice.

A Rat in the Maze

Scientific studies have been performed with rats in mazes that demonstrate how neural pathways are created and how behaviors become automatic. With brain monitors on the rats, scientists are able to measure significant brain activity in the frontal cortex *while* the rats are initially learning the maze. However, once memorized, navigation occurs automatically without brain activity in the frontal cortex. This essentially means the conscious mind is asleep while the rat goes through the motions. Unconscious competence. Automatic and thoughtless. This automatic pattern can be very helpful when it comes to turning door knobs, brushing your teeth, tying your shoes, folding your arms, driving, walking, etc. We all appreciate the fact that we don't have to relearn these activities at the beginning of every day.

However, this thoughtless navigation is abruptly disrupted once the maze or the location of the reward has been changed. As soon as the change in the maze is detected, the rat's frontal cortex activates and the rat begins the arduous process of rethinking the old story. The learning process has just begun, again.

Now consider unhealthy, automatic patterns of thought that can affect someone who has learned to loathe themselves because of a traumatic childhood. You can see that once any thought pattern of self-loathing or fear becomes established and automatic, the bypass of the frontal cortex guarantees that this person is not consciously participating in the "stinking-thinking" and poor choices that follow. The accompanying self-destructive behaviors associated with these negative beliefs and attitudes are certain to sabotage life and relationships. It can be perplexing, lonely, and frustrating for anyone stuck in this maze. Many people call this phenomenon depression.

This is typically where God intervenes to disrupt our automatic, destructive patterns by *breaking* our maze. We often get angry at God when our patterns and comfort zones get rearranged. It is only natural to believe that the broken maze is more evidence that God hates us. It provides additional fuel for our fire of resentment directed at God. Regardless of our story and justification about the broken maze, our subconscious and destructive patterns get worse and lead to devastating loss such as divorce, disease, and even death. Perhaps my automatic and destructive patterns of thought have caused me to strongly dislike people and avoid them. Maybe my avoidance strategy is to work 16 hours a day so that I am too busy for the "drama" and the extra money masquerades as self-esteem and validation. And perhaps one day, after I lose my job and I suddenly have 16 extra hours in the day to think and feel, I start cursing God because of my new problem of *anxiety* attacks that have mysteriously appeared. You will likely be tempted to cry out: "Why me God?" And if you actually listen to His heartfelt, soft response, you will likely hear something like this: "Breaking your maze of distraction was my only chance of connecting with you again. I've missed you and would like to remove that darkness from your closed heart. Won't you join me so we can rewrite your story and rebuild you into something better?"

It is this paradox pattern that God uses to interrupt our automatic, destructive preoccupation. Hopefully, through some painful opportunities of silence, I can start to listen to the deep yearnings of my heart and acknowledge I really do care about other people loving me. I can be angry at God and blame him for yet another disappointment in life, or I can use my unwanted but *necessary* time-out to engage my frontal cortex, open my heart, and rethink the automatic attitudes and patterns that have left me disconnected and bitter.

The Dot-To-Dot Puzzle

Each connecting dot in a frowny face puzzle represents a painful memory that has associated negative emotions. Now think of each dot as a fencepost for an electric fence. These posts are connected by a high-voltage wire that has electricity running through it, and it is important to understand that this electric fence is hidden from view on the other side of that wall we call the Critical Factor. Remember, like the wall at the junkyard, it can hide painful memories from view, but it cannot block out the associated stench.

Avoid The Void

Consider walking in the dark without any visual cues and with the constant threat of getting jolted each and every time we bump into the dreaded electric fence. *Any* external stimulus that you see, hear, taste, touch, or smell could trigger that electric fence to shock you! And this is just a simple example of a little frowny face with only a handful of negative memories. So what about those people who lived through extensive abuse or trauma for years? What about those kids who were neglected and abandoned for most of their childhood? What about that loner who never had any friends?

The Dragon

What if the number of those dots in the puzzle are in the hundreds or even thousands? Then perhaps your dot-to-dot puzzle creates a large dragon instead of a small frowny face. It is important to understand that these dots are not only connected, but the terrifying picture is also shaded with dark beliefs, attitudes, and irrational fears.

For example, if I've been betrayed over and over in my life by loved ones then perhaps my dot-to-dot Puzzle is shaded in with the belief that:

All people are bad.
People will only hurt me if they get close.
If you knew me, you wouldn't love me.

This common cluster of beliefs is buried in the dragon and forms a subconscious wall of isolation to protect me by locking others out of my life. And when this system is on auto-pilot, there is usually a story of "freedom" or "independence" that tries to glorify and celebrate the isolation. Like it or not, this is usually where God sends in the maze-busters.

Some people want to label isolation as depression. But not me. Remember that the well-oiled maze of depression hides under that black velvet cloak of denial. The deep depression kicks in when we finally completely give up on our dreams. Most people who have given up can usually consciously find the exact time or event where they shut and locked the door of hope. Yes, this is the same door that the Savior knocks upon. It isn't just people that you are locking out. It is also the Divine!

Depression is a natural byproduct of someone lying to themselves that "I don't need anyone anymore, and that no one will ever love me anyway." Accepting the lie creates and reinforces hopelessness and encourages a faster pace while marching in the maze of disillusionment.

An Ambush Predator

Creatures Of Habit

Another interesting way to view neural pathways is to liken them to a deer trail on the mountainside. You don't see any type of vegetation growing where the trail has been cut because the deer use these trails often once they have been established. This makes deer very predictable to mountain lions. Mountain lions are ambush predators and very calculated in their approach when hungry.

So when a mountain lion is hungry, all it needs to do is lie in wait near the trail for the deer to come to him. This is just how Satan works. He knows our patterns of thought deeply. He also knows how to catch us unaware while we are blindly and mindlessly following the established trail systems of our mind. He knows exactly what to whisper to reinforce hopelessness, and understands why we will accept his discouraging suggestions without resistance. In fact, we often confuse the voice of the adversary with our own. If your inner critical voice is addressing you in the second person then you can rest assured that voice is *not* yours! When we believe the lies, we become a willing captive in that cave that likely means we stay angry at God and find some form of satisfaction in refusing to open the door to Him. Satan reinforces the resentment narrative by whispering, "What kind of God would do this to *you*? No God at all!"

It is strange to me that this lie is so effective because the Lord is always at the door knocking and waiting patiently. But He is helpless if we choose to keep Him locked out. The Savior is all powerful but will never violate our agency to choose. This means He *cannot* help us if we will not ask him and open the door.

> *"The significant problems we face today cannot be solved at the same level of thinking we were at when we created them."*
>
> **— Albert Einstein**

Negative neural pathways are a certain way to make and keep you miserable. So these pathways need to be put out of commission like an old bumpy, pothole-infested dirt road. When we stop using these destructive neural pathways they will simply atrophy and die, no differently than a shrinking muscle inside of a cast.

One of the truths that I learned in my NLP training was that when the mind is provided a new decision point of hope, it will choose hope. After a little practice and subconscious negotiation, the positive choice will become automatic! This means that we *want* to build a new pathway that takes us to a different location and simply allow the mind to choose the better of two options. The human mind is incredibly complex and amazing, but at the same time, it is also incredibly simple! So simple in fact that sometimes we look beyond the obvious answers.

Let's Clean it Up!

We've talked about building neural pathways, but what about removing the ones we no longer want? How do we unlearn and let go of things that aren't serving us? Let's explore.

Janitors for the Brain

There are some hard-working janitors in the brain called microglial cells that are responsible for showing up after-hours and deep cleaning the synaptic connections of the brain. These microglial janitors also take the garbage out, but the criteria for what constitutes garbage just may surprise you. We will go into more detail on this below. Meanwhile, these synaptic connections are crucial to the functioning of the brain because they are the highways in which neurotransmitters like dopamine and serotonin travel. These microglial janitors aren't paid to do much thinking. Their job is to come in every night while we sleep and do some deep-cleaning or 'synaptic pruning' for the brain.

Our brain cells will reduce 60% in size while we sleep, essentially creating hallways for these synaptic janitors to move in and do their work. Have you ever noticed how clear your mind feels after waking? Well, it is because these cleanup fairies for the brain came in and did their job. Even a 15-minute nap makes a huge difference.

Use it or Lose It

Typically this statement is used as a motivator for us to improve and grow. But I'm going to put a different spin on this.

Once a neuro-circuit or neural pathway is established in the brain, it becomes stronger. Just like a muscle, the more you use it, the stronger it gets. Consider for a moment the logistics of eating a meal without biting your tongue. Those sharp little chompers we call teeth are slicing and dicing while that wiggly little tongue is hoeing and shoveling. It seems impossible that we aren't constantly biting our tongues, right? Well, this is yet another example of an established neuro-circuit or neural pathways that have been created and are used so often that we don't even have to think about how to eat while we are eating. And funny enough, if you do think about biting your tongue while you are eating, it is likely you will bite your tongue. Sorry about that!

Obsession Sessions

But how do these janitors know what constitutes as garbage to be removed?

These microglial janitors are hired to remove only that which is NOT being used. This means everything you constantly USE or OBSESS about is designated as a top priority to keep around. What if you are constantly complaining about your boss? What if you are obsessing about how sick you always feel? Well, as I say, if these are the most active circuits in your brain, then they receive top priority to stay put! And that means anything new you have been trying to learn between obsession sessions might just get deleted by the janitors to preserve space for your beloved and growing resentment. So remember, if you want to lose it, then don't use it!

What do these little microglial cells do when they aren't working?

Well, they sing in the micro-glee club, of course!

Hypnosis and Free Will

Please understand that a jaded and lonely person cannot be tricked into loving and trusting others simply by undergoing hypnosis. They have to choose to leave the cave and be willing to open their hearts. They must be willing to risk getting hurt again by releasing the dark emotions of resentment in every single dot of that puzzle. I happen to know from experience that the Savior *can* help you do this *if* you open the door and *ask* Him for help. Later in this book, I will explain my own experience with hypnosis where I had this very encounter. But, I want to point out here that the Savior was only willing and able to help me when I was willing and able to ask Him for help *and mean it*.

Part of the process of releasing the dark emotion from each memory in the dot-to-dot puzzle requires forgiveness of those who have hurt us. That means we have to be willing to let go of the resentment *and* the good reasons that hold these conflicts poignantly intact.

NLP has a technique called Core Transformation that allows you to search through your painful memories and replace a negative or horrifying associated emotion with a positive emotion. It is like pouring hot water into cold water to make it warm, so it no longer shocks the system.

There is also a type of hypnosis called "regression-to-cause" that will accomplish the very same thing. We must pinpoint the occurrence when the negative emotion and associated negative beliefs became established. This type of hypnosis provides a direct path to allow the subconscious mind to lead us back to the offending and painful memory that is creating the symptom that causes suffering. This process can be simple in dealing with a client who wrestles with a small frowny face dot-to-dot as I will discuss in the following example. But please understand that this simple approach may not work if there happens to be a large, dragon puzzle filled with thousands of dots. The dragon puzzle requires free will, forgiveness, and divine intervention for the proposed changes to stick long-term.

The Apple Doesn't Fall Far from the Tree

I would like to share with you a simple and true "regression-to-cause" hypnosis example to illustrate how, with a little help, Kevin removed his life-threatening allergy in a single session.

Yes, you read that right. *Removed!*

This allergy was tied to a single memory.

I actually did a television interview with Kevin to discuss his unbelievable and unexpected results. (You can find this interview on my website **MikeSimpson.live**)

I like to refer to this simple example as a case of removing a single thorn from a paw. It is possible that the "medical" symptom someone is suffering from is tied to an irrational thought formed from a single memory that simply needs to be adjusted in the subconscious mind with a little TLC.

And no, I did not say THC!

But as an interesting tangent, like it or not, medical cannabis is taking a significant chunk of pharmaceutical profits by boasting significant success on the pain and anxiety management front. I have encountered many clients who have benefited from the updated laws.

The people have voted and chosen to have legal access to something that grows in the earth that was once outlawed and invalidated by none other than the pharmaceutical industry itself. I've had conversations with individuals who have played key roles in overturning this taboo narrative once established and controlled by big pharma.

I'm hoping we can now make similar legal inroads to giving hypnosis and NLP professionals more legal rights to the freedom of helping victims of depression, anxiety, and PTSD who are currently considered medical-only turf.

Let your voices be heard!

Meanwhile, 'A Thorn in the Paw' Hypnosis Example

In 2016, I was at a dinner party with my wife, Diana, and her sister, Lori, who kept pressuring me to do some hypnosis with her boyfriend, Kevin. This was the first time I had met Kevin, who had a bonafide life-threatening allergy to apples.

No Placebo Here!

Kevin played along and acted like he wanted me to do hypnosis with him, but later admitted that he was just going along with the hypnosis to appease Lori. The truth was he felt extremely annoyed and skeptical. I want to point out here that he didn't think hypnosis would work for him so this amazing result can not be categorized as a placebo. In fact, it was completely the opposite! So, we both reluctantly agreed to do a hypnosis session for his allergy right there at the party on the couch in front of everyone. Fun party trick, eh?

Kevin was one of those subjects that bounced into hypnosis instantly. I slammed him into hypnosis with a rapid induction. In fact, he went into hypnosis so abruptly that I honestly thought he was messing around. He wasn't. Once I established hypnosis with Kevin I simply asked his subconscious mind to take me to the memory that created his deadly allergy to apples. Without hesitation, Kevin started chuckling and said, "I'm here."

I was confused. Normally when I get someone to the memory or root cause that created the problem, I see the client really upset and in tears. In hypnosis, we call this an *abreaction*. But Kevin was instead amused with himself and chuckling. I asked him to explain to me what was happening.

I want to point out that when someone in hypnosis has regressed back to the root cause, they will be reliving the memory, not remembering it. He will speak in the first person as if the memory is happening right now in front of him. Kevin literally traveled back in time! Remember that time does not exist in the subconscious mind. So, reliving a memory typically produces the same emotional reaction and effect as if the event from the past is actually happening right now.

You are the Apple of My Eye

Kevin reported to me that he was in the orchard picking apples with his mom as a 12 year-old boy. Except, that he wasn't picking apples, he was eating them. Kevin was eating apples to punish his mother because his friends got to go fishing while he had to stay behind and work in the orchard. After he ate four or five apples, his mother got frustrated and threatened that he was going to get sick if he kept eating those apples. That's a hypnotic suggestion folks! But Kevin defied her and kept munching away. After several more apples, Kevin got violently ill and threw up. As he did so, some of the apple got caught in his throat. Right there on the couch Kevin started coughing and choking. The party guests didn't really plan on a show before dinner, but they ended up with a real-life drama.

And Voila! A Deadly Allergy Was Born

Kevin's subconscious mind determined right there in the orchard that apples were now an enemy. "Anything apple" entering his body from that moment forward would warrant a class-four alarm that would shut down his heart to protect him from being killed by an apple.

Does this sound rational? Well, remember that rational thought is not a function of the subconscious mind.

This irrational association to apples created a life-threatening allergy that faithfully *protected* Kevin from that sinister fruit for the next 40 years of his life. Kevin is a chef and loves to invent new recipes — some amazing recipes I might add! You should try his jalapeno strawberry jam. And you can imagine how frustrating and scary it was for Kevin to accidentally ingest hidden apple sweetener while experimenting with his recipes. His EpiPen was always nearby. Kevin had many incidents with apples over those 40 years. In fact, he had one encounter where he was pouring apple juice for someone and it splashed into his eye. He said it honest-to-goodness felt like acid burning his eye!

While Kevin was still in hypnosis choking on that apple, we simply cleared his throat and I placed a direct suggestion (command really) into Kevin's subconscious mind that his allergy was gone.

Boom! It was really gone!

And Voila! The Deadly Allergy Was Gone

After the hypnosis session, Kevin was pretty spaced out and shocked that he was able to go into hypnosis, but he was still skeptical. I told him not to eat any apples until he went to an allergist to get tested responsibly. He assured me that he would do this.

But Kevin had other plans brewing in the back of his mind. A few days later, Kevin decided to live-stream himself on Facebook eating an apple fritter and apple pie with an EpiPen lined up in front of him. His mother called him in a panic while watching the show and asked him if he was trying to kill himself!

It looks like Kevin was still enjoying punishing his mother for not letting him go fishing that day.

Kevin had absolutely no reaction to the apples. Nada. None whatsoever. His allergy was completely gone.

And the solution was that simple.

Kevin's allergy has been gone now for 2 ½ years from the time of this writing. The Thanksgiving following our hypnosis session Kevin actually showed up at our home with an apple pie and no

EpiPen. And he ate most of the pie by himself after dinner. It was his gift to us. Well, sort of.

This apple allergy is a classic case of a single memory wreaking havoc in the subconscious mind.

But when we go back to the dragon dot-to-dot example where perhaps thousands of memories are linked together with pain and resentment instead of a single event, then more extensive effort is likely necessary to banish the darkness. It would take far too long to visit each and every memory to replace the darkness with love and light. But, I've discovered a really powerful technique for such a daunting puzzle and will share this a little later.

Stay tuned for the Dragon Slayer!

Meanwhile, Meet Shirley

I would like to share with you another interesting case I worked with over 20 years ago. In this situation, a single hypnosis session with a different hypnotherapist was unable to resolve a case of chronic nail-biting which was so severe that her fingernails were constantly bleeding. But our one and only NLP session was successful because we dug beneath the behavior to unearth and release the real buried trauma. It worked because rather than my addressing the behavior of nail-biting, we regressed and found the root cause — the reason *why* her nail-biting was necessary.

You read that right — necessary!

Shirley had the really frustrating habit of biting her fingernails incessantly until they bled. And she couldn't control it.

Through a one-time, simple guided search with **NLP** we were able to discover that as a young girl, Shirley would often hide under her bed while dad, in a drunken rage, was beating mom. Shirley would bite her nails as a coping mechanism to self-soothe. This domestic violence happened many times during Shirley's childhood. Trying to "suggest away" fingernail biting in hypnosis would be ineffective because Shirley was still living in fear as a middle-aged adult. She was still constantly terrified about everything. And she still felt an uncontrollable need to soothe her fears. Her subconscious mind only knew how to calm her by suggesting that she continually bite her nails as a familiar reaction to the perpetual fear loop.

Shirley had hundreds of painful and terrifying memories buried in her subconscious mind. I would like to point out here that not all of those memories were of dad beating mom. Some of them were just memories of her being terrified that dad *might* beat mom tonight. The threat of violence can be just as traumatic as actual violence because it will still trigger the fight or flight response in one's body. Remember that the subconscious mind cannot distinguish the difference between perceived danger and real danger.

The amygdala in the brain is Command Central for the fight or flight response. It will always take over, anytime it detects a crisis, and trigger cortisol, the stress hormone, to be injected into the bloodstream to help you deal with the crisis at hand. I would like to underscore that the limbic system of the mind can keep you in a fear loop when it is trying to protect you from a perceived crisis, even if that crisis is buried in the past.

For example, I want you to consider someone pointing a rubber band at your forehead for 10 minutes at point-blank range. Even if that person doesn't shoot you in the forehead with the rubberband, you just experienced 10 horrifying minutes filled with anxiousness and terror. Go ahead and try it if you don't believe me. The threat of violence can be just as traumatic as violence. This must be factored in, regarding anyone who was raised in a violent home. Neural pathways become very established as the victims of domestic violence learn to be afraid. Fear becomes a neural reflex that can be efficiently triggered by any external stimulus.

Shirley was raised in continual fear, with fight or flight as her constant companion. This was her "normal," and this was the "ice packed on her driveway." This is how she learned to live and think. Think of the negative neural pathways that were created and reinforced over the years with both the threat and the occurrences of this violence constantly playing out in her home.

Shirley learned how to be afraid because of constant circumstances that were out of her control. And now, nearly 50 years later, she was still living in constant fear because that ice was still, metaphorically, on her driveway.

Her subconscious mind really had no way to cope with this violence except to hide it from her. Please remember that hiding memories from your conscious mind doesn't offer the luxury of hiding the associated emotions.

Feeling terrified in the dark can make one bite her nails! Constantly.

So as an adult, Shirley was still living in constant fear. That little girl from her past needed to be rescued. She needed to be found and brought home to a new, safe place of love and light. And so, we ran a rescue operation for Little Shirley, and went into her past and brought her home for the first time in 50 years.

Most of the difficult cases I take on, where someone is suffering from deep depression, require extensive conversation about the victim forgiving the perpetrator(s). A victim must be willing to let go of legitimate reasons for being upset, and let go of the pain in order to replace it with light and love. But I need to point out here that the principles of agency over self and faith both play a huge role in overcoming the dragon.

For this reason, I reiterate that you cannot trick or sneak depression away from someone. Most people who are shut down and isolated have made the decision to quit caring, quit trying, and they are no longer *willing* to interact with people. They have convinced themselves, through these painful experiences, that all people are bad and will only hurt us anyway.

This faulty premise must be reversed if someone wants to heal. I want you to consider a morning glory flower that has closed its petals to make it through the long dark night. But when the sun comes out in the morning, the flower refuses to open its petals again in protest to the cold night. It would rather just stay closed and hopeless, and stop accepting sunshine.

Holding onto pain does not protect you from pain; this is the great deception. Staying locked away in a dark cave and avoiding the sunshine leaves you with only the cold, damp pain of isolation. It is a deep-in-the-bones kind of cold and is usually more painful than being rejected. This is part of the same great deception. That's why I repeatedly say depression is often nothing more than the effects of loneliness because of self-imposed isolation.

Pain Is Inevitable, Misery Is Optional

You will see this quote throughout the book. Think of it as a "slippery when wet" road sign.

When I take on one of these difficult dragon puzzles, we have to employ a higher power that allows us to drain away the resentment, pain, and fear and replace all of that with love and light. This may seem simplisitc, but in reality it is very simple! And it is the reason why I'm writing this book. The process to overcome the suffering is actually quite straightforward and more accessible to people than they have been led to believe. There is hope. There is **always** hope! And there is a simple approach to escaping from isolation, sadness, and loneliness, but it does require some faith, hope, and willingness to let go of the old story.

Let Go (Of It) And Let God (Take It)!

We have to let go of the pain and the resentment and the suffering if we want God to replace it with something better. And this means we have to choose, with our own free will, that we are willing to let go of that old story or those old excuses, even if those excuses and reasons are good ones. A flower will die if it refuses to open its petals to the sunshine.

The Dragon Slayer

We must turn to the Lord. We can literally ask Him to go into each one of these painful memories and remove the pain and heartache connected to each dot in the dragon puzzle. He can only do this if we open the door and ask him for help using our free will.

I want to reiterate here that some of this pain is impossible for you to remove yourself. We literally have to concede to handing this over to the Savior.

Again, the Lord can only remove the pain if you are willing to release the associated resentment, justification, and entitlement that holds it in place. You have to exercise your faith and free will to be an active participant in the deep cleaning. You have to be willing to concede every good reason that you carry inside of your heart for being angry, closed-down, and/or embittered. You must give it to the Savior and He will take it.

The High Tower

Rapunzel

This particular story is a composite example. I've encountered this "high tower" pattern many times in others and it illustrates a lot of the principles shared before. As you have probably already guessed, Rapunzel remains isolated until she lets her hair down. All the way down.

I want to emphasize that the only thing stopping you from healing is your refusal to let go of your "good reasons." As long as these reasons are within your white-knuckled grasp, the Lord simply cannot remove them from you, because you choose to hold onto them. And so I'm going to ask you:

What is more important, being healed or being right?

Installing the Possibility

The Power of Asking the Right Questions

If I had an hour to solve a problem and my life depended on the solution, I would spend the first 55 minutes determining the proper question to ask... for once I know the proper question, I could solve the problem in less than five minutes.

— Albert Einstein

I have discovered a really amazing insight about the neural pathway creation process. I feel it is an integral part of creating change and healing. Read this next sentence carefully. Really stop and think about it before you read on.

If the possibility does not exist in your mind, then you will never know to consider it.

A few possibilities must exist in your mind in order to understand my example. You must be able to answer "yes" to the following questions before you can do my experiment.

1) Does God really exist?
2) Does He have the ability to speak to you?
3) Do you have the ability to hear Him speak?
4) Do you believe He *will* speak to you?

If you answered yes to all of those questions, go ahead and close your eyes. Ask God if He ACTUALLY has the ability to remove resentment and pain from a single memory of your past. What did He say? I asked him this very question and he answered, "Of course!"

The possibility of the Lord removing pain from a memory has now been established in your mind. But is it believable? Rate it and see. On a scale of 1 to 10 (10 being the highest) what is your current belief level that God is capable of removing pain from a memory? Even if you rate it as a five out of ten, it is significant, considering that this possibility didn't previously exist in your mind. You can now consider this possibility as a seed that was planted, which can be watered and nurtured, and which will most definitely grow! You have now established this possibility. From now on, every time you feel discouraged, this new possibility will "pop up on your radar" when you are considering what to do about your frustrating circumstances.

I heard a quote recently: "Good inspiration derives from good information." To me, this simply means that truth needs to be planted inside of your mind so the Lord can refer you to it when He wants to teach you (or remind you of) something. The Lord is a master at teaching you from the record of your own mind. It will mean more, and be more readily acceptable when the Lord draws from your own experiences to inspire you. This process certainly shows us that He is paying close attention to every single detail of our lives and is watching over us.

So, if you are willing to let go of your pain, the Lord CAN take it. Free will requires you to choose to release it, and to choose to ask for help. If you now believe that the Lord has the ability to take your burden, AND IF you are willing to surrender the whole story, AND IF you are willing to ask Him for help, I WONDER WHAT MIGHT HAPPEN? That is a powerful question. This practical approach is much more productive and powerful than crying out, "Why me Lord?" Or "Please just make me happy!"

You have just begun the process of building a new pathway of hope to possibilities of divine healing.

Simple!

CHAPTER SIX

When a Limiting Belief Is Born

A Strike To The Head

"You are going to love me, Coach!"

These are the words little Johnny announced to me as he introduced himself on our first day of little league baseball practice.

I replied to him with a chuckle, "Oh yeah? And why is that?"

He declared with a big smile, "Because I get hit in the head with the baseball every single time I get up to bat!"

I responded, "You do? Well, I guess we shall see!"

Sure enough, when he got up to bat in our first game of the season, he was struck squarely in the head with the first pitch! I must admit, it was a bit surreal. After a quick chuckle, I ran over to meet Johnny at first base to make sure he was okay. And he was fine because he was wearing a helmet. Right there and then, I decided Johnny needed to learn some important facts based on my observations. Watching him bat from the dugout gave me a perspective that Johnny wasn't able to see while standing in the hot-box.

Since Johnny had been hit in the head so many times at bat, he started creating a story in his mind to explain this crazy mystery. Likely his story went something like:

"Those pitchers really hate me!" or

"I guess I'm just jinxed!" or

"Baseball just isn't my thing!"

But after observing him up at bat a single time, I was able to discern the real answer to his mystery. First of all, Johnny believed he was going to get hit in the head with the ball before he got up to bat. At the plate, he was bracing himself for the impact that was certain to follow. In his mind, he could already see the ball hitting him in the head. He could already hear it hitting him in the head. He could already feel it hitting him in the head. The disaster was certain to come. It was already terrifying!

So right in the middle of the pitcher's windup, before the ball even left the pitcher's hand, Johnny closed his eyes and abruptly ducked away from the dreaded ball of death. And yes, he ducked his head directly over home plate. And while holding his breath with pure terror he stuck his head right into the strike-zone.

The Miracle Bridge

That baseball struck him right in the head. Clack! It was a perfect strike, and yes, pun intended. The crowd gasped. After a bewildered recovery, the hero trotted to first base while shaking his head in disbelief.

"I told you, Coach!" he yelled to me as he stopped on first base. I was musing over the real story I had just witnessed. Johnny was struck in the head by a perfect strike. This is a true story. And it is probably the funniest and most perfect example I have ever personally witnessed of the phenomenon that we call a Self-Fulfilling Prophecy. We create the very thing we fear. And each time that thing happens, our fears and beliefs become more strongly reinforced. We simply create the narrative in our own belief systems that explains and justifies our terrible plight.

We were able to quickly resolve Johnny's head-trip by teaching him to keep his eyes open through the entire pitch. We also practiced with a lot of tennis balls thrown right at his head until he learned how to turn away from the inside pitch.

This new approach was a far superior strategy to sticking his head in front of the perfect strike! So now, little Johnny steps onto the home run path and swings at strikes with his bat instead of his head.

Perception is reality.
Being right does not guarantee that you are accurate.
A lie only works when you believe it is true.
You don't know what you know until you know it.

The Toothpick And The Tire

(When the facts are right but the story is wrong)

This is another true story from my past that sheds some humorous light on how perception can contradict reality. Back when I was 16 years old, my dad got upset with me for driving his truck into our horse pasture where we were working. He abruptly stopped me and told me to remove the truck from the field because there were a bunch of sharp wires on the ground that could puncture the tires. Well, as a know-it-all teenager, I protested as I defiantly pulled the truck out of the field. After I parked the truck in the driveway and got out, I noticed a wire sticking directly into the side of the left rear left tire. Oh no, Dad was right.

I didn't want to admit to him that he was right, so I decided to discreetly drive the truck to the gas station to see if I could get it fixed. As I was driving, the wire kept slapping loudly against the road so I decided to stop and pull the wire out. Bad decision. After pulling the wire from the tire, it immediately started hissing and going flat. I couldn't get the wire back into the hole. Luckily for me, there happened to be a toothpick exactly in the road where I stopped the truck. Thinking quickly, I was able to do a little triage and successfully plug the leak with the toothpick. This stopped the air from leaking out temporarily but as fate had it, there were no tire stores open. So reluctantly, I drove the truck back home with the toothpick hanging on for dear life. Like all teenagers will do, I approached Mom sheepishly and told her about the hole in the tire. She told me she would take care of it. Whew! I left the house quickly to go hang out with my friends.

Meanwhile, Mom took care of the flat tire by NOT taking care of it. She didn't tell Dad. So the next morning when Dad got up to leave for work, the tire was completely flat. As he approached the flat tire for closer inspection, he could not believe his eyes. There in front of him was a toothpick sticking out of the sidewall of the flat tire. He called my mom, "Jerry, you aren't going to believe this! Come have a look!" My mom arrived at the garage and pretended to be shocked at the sight of the flat tire. My dad quipped, "Can you believe these cheap foreign tires? I can't believe a toothpick put a hole in one!" Mom STILL didn't bother telling Dad the REAL story of how the tire was punctured. She let him believe this story about the toothpick for the rest of his life.

In reality, Dad was exactly right about me driving his truck in the field. Unfortunately, and even sometimes comically, indisputable evidence of appearances leads us to form logical conclusions that are completely wrong. Dad lived the rest of his life puzzled, and even entertained, by that toothpick in the tire story. I told Dad the truth about the tire as I spoke at his funeral after he died of cancer at the young age of 63. He was far too young to be taken. The world and my family lost an amazing man. This story brought a good laugh to the congregation and provided a well-needed lift at a difficult time. My public confession *finally* provided Dad with some closure and perspective to solve the toothpick and the tire mystery. We have to be willing to "unlearn" certain conclusions in order to update the story with additional truths. Often the real answers are outside of the box.

Put a Lid on It

Just Look Up!

If you trap a housefly in a glass jar with the lid on it, you can expect it to buzz around and test the boundaries. But once the housefly quits buzzing around, it will usually settle at the bottom of the jar and stop moving around. If you wait for a few minutes and then gently remove the lid, what would you expect the housefly to do? If you guess it stays in the jar, you are correct. It stays in the jar. And guess what happens next? It will die in the jar. You see, the housefly has stopped looking up. It has learned and accepted that there is no escape, and it even has a sore head to prove it. So sadly, once hopelessness is established, the housefly quits looking up and actually starts going through the expected process of dying in the bottom of the jar.

The missing lid on this jar represents perceived limitations. Perceived limitations are limiting beliefs. If I believe it is true, then it is true — at least until it isn't. So, if I believe there is no way out, then there is no way out. I stop looking. I stop trying, and naturally, I've accrued evidence that I am right. And I might be dying in the bottom of the jar with some real resentment directed at everyone who is to blame for my plight. And this resentment is the very thing that reinforces my suffering narrative and actually discourages me from ever looking up again.

We Are Just Fleas in a Pod

This lid-on-the-jar phenomenon is also fascinating with fleas. If you trap a horde of fleas in a jar for three days undisturbed in a dark room and then remove the lid, you will see that the fleas will never again jump high enough to escape the jar. They have been conditioned on how high they can jump. They are literally trapped in the jar without a lid! And thank goodness for that, right? But these fleas are not only trapped in the jar. Even more amazingly, their little baby fleas are born into jar-captivity. These baby fleas literally carry the same inherited but imposed limitations of being trapped in the jar. This is extremely interesting. Especially when you factor in a principle taught in the Bible about the iniquities of the fathers being answered upon the heads of their children:

"I the Lord thy God am a jealous God, visiting the iniquity of the fathers upon the children unto the third and fourth generation of them that hate me;" (Exodus 20:5, KJV)

I find it truly amazing that this negative programming can pass on to us from previous generations. This supports the notion that is becoming more widely accepted — that some of our unresolved issues are actually inherited from previous generations, and are not just limited to our childhood conditioning. Our ancestors have been affected by the same falsehoods, limitations, and dysfunctions that now, perhaps, enslave us on earth.

However, with faith and a new perspective, we can become "the little flea that could."

The Elephant in the Room (That Never Forgets)

Let's belabor the point of limiting beliefs, by addressing the circus elephant. A baby circus elephant is usually tethered to the ground with some type of chain to prevent it from wandering off.

The baby elephant starts to learn through repetition that when the clamp is on the foot, it is not possible to go anywhere. And guess how adult elephants are tied down? Usually with a clamp on the foot and without the chain being connected to anything! That is because the elephant has become conditioned that the clamp prevents it from going anywhere. The elephant has become fully brainwashed to understand that the clamp is in control. So, again, perception is reality. When the elephant believes it can't go anywhere, it doesn't go anywhere. It doesn't even try to leave that spot. There is no fight or will. In reality, the clamp, even when chained, is not strong enough to hold back a full-grown elephant when it exerts its mighty power. The elephant is simply controlled by its *belief* that it is controlled.

I'm Not Going to Take it Anymore! Do You Hear Me?

I often eat lunch at a restaurant near my wellness center. One day while ordering, I decided to be friendly to an employee who was usually not very friendly to me. While waiting for my sandwich, I asked him how he was doing. He rudely and blatantly ignored me. I thought that was incredibly impolite because I had just watched him graciously wave goodbye to another customer who was walking out the door. So after rehashing this blatant demonstration of rudeness, I decided to reflect his attitude straight back at him. I can dish it out, too! So I stopped being friendly. The next few times I ate at the restaurant, I would just ignore him after giving him my order.

Then one day while I was getting ready to pay for my sandwich, this same employee turned his head towards the side entrance to say goodbye to yet ANOTHER customer walking out the door. The audacity! It was at this moment that I noticed a hearing aid in his ear. I instantly understood why he had so blatantly ignored me.

He *couldn't* hear me!

I was so ashamed. He hadn't heard me.

I felt terrible that I had retaliated with *imagined* justification. So, as I say, "perception is reality." But sometimes, when we know we are right and we are fully justified in our own minds, we are very wrong.

This is a perfect example of how misunderstandings happen. It also illustrates how someone can feel so justified in their own story that they are blind to what is *really* happening. I wonder how many people out there are carrying a grudge over something they completely misunderstood. What about those poor unsuspecting victims that have no idea that they were guilty of such a horrible thing? I hope this question can cause all of us a little bit of introspection.

So, what is more important to you? Being right OR knowing the truth?

You Decide

I've worked with many people over the years who have had really sad and compelling stories. It is very common for someone who has gone through difficult times to build a story around why certain things happen to them. For example, someone who was bullied for years starts to believe that he is worthless and isn't good enough. He feels like he's doing everyone a favor by closing down and avoiding all contact with people because he expects that no one will ever love and accept him. And once this pattern is really ingrained and accepted as normal, it transforms from an idea into a belief. The belief will remain concrete until exposed for the lie that it is. That is, if it is *ever* exposed. With this belief intact, the simple thought of interacting with others creates feelings of resentment, depression, fear, etc. Voila, anxiety is born. And anxiety will act like a security alarm system that will go off anytime someone gets close.

The narrative in the victim's subconscious mind reinforces his belief that people are bad and they will cause pain if they get too close. The alarm system is armed and an effective, subconscious strategy is born to keep "intruders" out.

I Don't Need Anybody!

This self-proclaimed loner will prove he doesn't need anyone in his life. And if he keeps up with this narrative, it becomes his truth which is reinforced subconsciously with porcupine precision.

Porcupine precision you say?

Even Porcupines Love To Be Hugged!

If people don't like you, it isn't because of *who you are*. It is because of *how you act*.

It is unfortunate that porcupines don't realize how their hugs feel on the other side of those sharp quills. When a victim has been hurt too many times, he can subconsciously and inadvertently start hurting others who try to get too close. And naturally the subconscious mind can guarantee that this happens automatically and perpetuates a false belief. I will revisit this principle in more detail later, so keep your eye out for the porcupine down the trail.

Meanwhile, there is an interesting process that happens after our self-proclaimed loner has lived in exile long enough. He not only believes he doesn't need people, but becomes impervious to how poorly he is treating others. This hidden energy of resentment and loneliness, combined with his so-called hard-fought independence will create a forcefield strong enough to repulse the dreaded Klingons from beaming aboard.

A Sharp Point to Be Made

The Wasp

I've read different theories about why wasps have an uncanny ability to detect energy fields radiating from people. They are hyper-sensitive to energy.

The energy field coming from someone who is afraid of wasps actually *provokes* the wasp to attack. The energy of fear is irritating and threatening which triggers the wasp's instinct to strike. I've seen wasps ignore people who were calm. The point is, the energy we carry inside of us, whether hidden from our conscious mind or not, affects people around us in immeasurable ways. People will feel and react to what we are carrying. So what do we do to help this self-proclaimed loner change? We have to shake him out of his stupor of denial in which he doesn't care if people don't love and accept him. And it is likely that this person will not come out of denial until becoming extremely lonely and depressed.

When I am emotionally closed down, I am usually the last one to know that someone has an issue with me. I have a perfect story established in my mind to explain away any accountability for creating this mysterious problem of abandonment. I might tell myself that I don't care if people don't like me because I've always been a loner, but deeply buried beneath that facade, my heart still aches to be included. I am in denial that I am lonely because I have stopped *trying* to care. But what I don't realize is that I'm actually driving everyone out of my life because of my deep resentment and fear of being left alone in my world. The lie, that "I don't care," has become my truth. And that truth is going to keep hurting others (and me too) until I revise the story.

Fill Versus Feel

I worked with a man named Bob who was obese. At the beginning of our second meeting, I asked him about his weight. Bob put on the sales pitch that he didn't care what people thought of him. He bragged to me that recently some kids made fun of him for being so fat while he was sitting in the bleachers at his nephew's ballgame.

He bounced and jiggled with a full belly laugh of delight as he explained how hilarious it was that these kids were mocking him.

I paused for a moment and then said, "Yeah, I don't buy it."

Within five minutes, Bob broke down in tears of dejection. He explained his loneliness and compared his life to all of his friends who were married with kids and enjoying their lives. We then dug deeper. He explained that he always felt like the third wheel when he spent time around his friends and their families. And when we dug deeper yet, he said that he started gaining excessive weight after he learned that his ex-fiance had broken his heart by cheating. Bob went through great heartache and rejection in the resulting breakup. He started eating to fill his emptiness. As long as he was "filling" instead of feeling, he didn't seem to hurt as much. Soon, his patterns turned into habits. A day turned into a week. A week turned into a month. A month turned into a year. And after a few years, Bob was *safely* obese and literally insulated from caring about rejection.

Stated simply, Bob's subconscious mind had found an irrational solution to protect himself from getting hurt ever again: OBESITY. Remember, the subconscious mind is unable to reason rationally. And Bob's irrational strategy was so powerfully influential that he belly laughed at rejection instead of crying. Any of us can believe our lies to such an extent that change seems undesirable and impossible because we have closed down emotionally and have given up. Then people will avoid us because our forcefield keeps slapping them in the face.

The Rototiller

Before you plant a garden in the spring, you need to get out the rototiller. The rototiller is designed to tear up the compacted soil, weeds, and rocks after a long, cold winter. I've never seen a beautiful garden that grew from simply throwing a handful of seeds into a rocky, weed-ridden field. The rototiller is necessary. With Bob, the rototiller ripped through his facade of not caring about what others thought. He was still heartbroken from the betrayal of his ex-fiance. He still ached deeply. He was terribly lonely and wondered if anyone could ever love him.

Ironically, Bob's excessive weight added to his misery. It was simply a symptom of a deeper problem — unresolved pain. And an emotional rototiller was needed to convince Bob that nothing in his life was going to change until he made the decision to forgive his ex-fiance and pick himself back up and try to love again. Yes, this decision to try again required facing potential rejection again, and it *might* mean he could get hurt again. But, it also might mean he could find true love this time around. Bob's best chance of attracting love into his life was by choosing to care once more — to care about himself. This included changing the eating habits that had added so much weight to his body. He needed to acknowledge his problem and come out of denial. Bob was as scared as little Johnny was because of being hit in the head by a pitch. But, this time Johnny's eyes were open, and so was Bob's heart.

After working with Bob, he became motivated to try love again. I recently spoke to him and he was excited to report that he had lost 70 pounds! But he also admitted he still has some work to do. He loved the idea of his story being in this book so it could be used to help others come out of hiding.

I have never been able to help a person who was unwilling to undergo the rototiller to tear up their old story. If you aren't willing to be honest with yourself, then you can't be helped. The first step in changing your life is to acknowledge what the problem is and acknowledge when it started. It is often possible for someone to find the moment in their life when they purposefully slammed the door of their heart closed with the intention to never risk being hurt again. I discuss this principle further in the chapter, "The Cave Of Unbelief."

Learning to recognize that loneliness is usually self-imposed is the first step to connecting again.

Are you lonely? Do you feel betrayed and forsaken by everyone? Is there a theme that keeps playing out in your life over and over that you can't explain? This usually means that you are doing something that is affecting others negatively. If you can't acknowledge this, then your story will be just as frustrating to you as it was to little Johnny who kept getting hit in the head with a baseball.

Accountability means that you are willing to take an honest look at your life. Your fear and resentment might be buried for good reasons, but healing remains impossible if you won't admit to yourself there is a problem.

Everyone has an excuse. Everyone has a good reason to be angry. Everyone has a compelling reason to hide.

But happy people aren't using excuses anymore.

Are you?

We See What We Look For

To End on a Personal Note

Diana and I went through a few really painful years watching our son Dylan's confidence and opportunities be destroyed by a basketball coach's hidden agenda. Every parent wants to believe his son or daughter is the best, and that they aren't getting fair treatment. But in this case it was true. Trust me, I've seen it. And I've felt it. I've coached and had my kids participate in enough sports teams over the years to have been on both sides of this equation. There are plenty of politics and inequity in athletics. Someone is always going to get cut from a team. The coach's son is always going to get preferred treatment. Someone is always going to get robbed. Heroes and villains are going to be created out on the field or on the court. Sporting events tend to bring out the ugliness that parents carry in their hearts. So please understand, I reiterate here, that "perception is reality." This means we all believe we are right. And when we feel the injustice of someone else's politics or agenda, we are deeply hurt and betrayed as we watch our kids suffer. And this is exactly what happened with my wife, myself, and our son, Dylan.

Prior to Dylan playing high school basketball, while he was in 4th grade, he went into a deep depression because he was being singled out and bullied by some kids at school. A few of these ringleaders were downright cruel to him. Dylan went from being happy-go-lucky to fully shut down and dejected.

At the lowest point of these tough years, Dylan came home from school feeling really down. He asked why he was even alive in the first place. While in this firestorm of self-doubt and sadness from the cruel campaign, I sat with Dylan one night and did an NLP session with him. I wanted to protect him from these brutal ongoing antics. We decided together that we were going to develop him into the best basketball player he could be. We were going to overcome those painful antics with pure grit, determination, and hard work. We lit a fire under Dylan, and he started practicing day and night. Every time I came home from work, he was out on our little patio in the backyard dribbling and shooting. We made up all kinds of drills and he practiced them over and over. He started wearing out the cement! We were so happy, as parents, that he was channeling his energy towards something constructive. He went from being good to gifted. Since he got cut from the team he had played on, we found other teams that loved having him. And he thrived. He developed incredible speed and agility. He was sometimes flat-out unguardable. He was unorthodox in some of his moves and defenders couldn't quite figure out how to stay in front of him. He became gifted by very hard work.

The Harder I Work, the Luckier I Get

But the point I want to make here is that basketball became the vehicle by which we lifted Dylan out of despair. And so basketball really mattered to us. We ended up transferring Dylan to another school in 8th grade to give him a fresh start. It was the best decision we ever made for him. He was pleasantly surprised in his new school that everyone loved him and wanted to be his friend. He needed this. It was a godsend for us to see him find a new group of friends who cared about him and helped him overcome the negative programming from the previous few years. When 9th grade came around, Dylan was polished as a basketball player. He tried out and made the 9th grade basketball team and had an amazing year. He sank a few last-second, three-point game winning shots and everyone got to see him shine.

I had a dream about Dylan's high school basketball coach the summer before his sophomore year. In the dream, the coach was wearing sunglasses and a hat and was telling me what an amazing basketball player Dylan was. But I could see into his heart and that he was hiding something. I suddenly awoke. I felt that dream was a premonition, and I took it seriously. I tried my best to encourage Dylan to switch schools to play for one of two schools that had really been recruiting him, with the promise to make him their varsity point guard as a sophomore. Unfortunately, Dylan's friends were too important for him to change schools, so we buckled up for what turned out to be a very heartbreaking and difficult ride. The irony of this high school basketball heartache is that Dylan's coach seemed to take a page out of that old bully's book and started that process all over again.

There was one particular basketball game where I watched Dylan get called for traveling three times. That wasn't possible! He was the best ball handler on the team. He was the only one who could handle the full-court press because of his prowess of ball-handling and speed. But he was really traveling! And naturally, after each time he traveled he was immediately pulled from the game. Dylan was starting to *believe* in his coach's doubt. He wasn't playing freely with reckless abandon anymore, but was instead playing scared — second-guessing every single thing that he did so that the coach would not pull him out of the game. And naturally, the coach used Dylan's hesitation and mistakes as justification that he had made the right decisions by giving more playing time to the younger, less experienced kids he was developing for the next season. Interestingly, for this coach, next season never came.

"I feel like a hummingbird in a bag."

— Steve Nash (During an interview regarding team dynamics after being traded to the Los Angeles Lakers)

These younger, inexperienced players on Dylan's team were left in the game as "development opportunities" through their many mistakes, while Dylan sat on the bench wondering why he wasn't playing. The coach created a horrible story, and Dylan started believing it more than he believed in himself.

I am a huge basketball fan. My favorite player of all time is Steve Nash. Dylan and I spent hours studying Steve's tactics. Steve was a joy to watch on the court because he was selfless, smart, competitive, and he made every single teammate better. I cheered for him as a player but more importantly, as a good person. He went through a painful divorce with class and dignity, which was especially impressive. At the twilight of Steve's career, he was traded to the Lakers. It was painful for me to watch Steve try to thrive in that system. I listened to an interview with Steve discussing his new team's dynamics. His response was profoundly sad. I related deeply to Steve's comments as they related to Dylan's high school basketball experience. Steve stated somberly, "I feel like a hummingbird in a bag."

What a tragic mistake it is when a coach uses his power to dim one of his shining stars.

After Dylan's senior year, he went on to play with a competitive AAU basketball team. An amazing coach, Evric Gray, was excited to have Dylan on his team and quickly reignited Dylan's belief in himself. In the very first game, Dylan was back to his greased-lightning self. It is seriously amazing how a coach can make or break a player. Evric believed in Dylan and that's all it took. They played in a tournament in California, and Dylan raised a lot of eyebrows with the college scouts. He was back out on that court terrorizing those large and muscular athletes with his 150 pound body. It was always so funny to see how those big players underestimated Dylan because of his size. But like Mark Twain said, "It isn't the size of the dog in the fight, but the size of the fight in the dog!"

Dylan is now deciding where he would like to play college ball. I have placed one of my favorite video clips from that basketball tournament where in a single play Dylan had a block, a steal, and a coast-to-coast 3-point bucket at **MikeSimpson.live/Dylan**. Thank you Evric! Your influence has forever blessed our lives and also the lives of many others. You are a godsend.

And so, this is the great lesson: if you want to be great you have to believe in your own greatness. Even when others won't. And if there's something preventing you from believing in your own greatness, even if that something comes from someone else that you love and trust, then you had better learn how to disregard that nonsense and rewrite your story.

Sometimes our perception *is* accurate and resentment *is* warranted and injustice *is* real. However, to heal and flourish, we must still have the courage to fight onward and upward and let it go.

And as Fate Would Have It...

Six years after Dylan's bumpy childhood was behind him, I was approached for help by a young man who had bullied Dylan as a boy. I used hypnosis to help him find and release the heartache from his own painful childhood. This young man's resentment, from his childhood circumstances, is what fueled his cruel treatment of Dylan as a boy. As I often say in this book, "Hurt people hurt people." The Lord was not only asking me to forgive this fine young man for devastating our family, but He was also requesting me to *help* him find healing from his own painful past. This was a game-winning assist that even Steve Nash would appreciate.

And we released a hummingbird from the bag.

CHAPTER SEVEN

The Cave of Unbelief

Once in an NLP class, I practiced a technique to elicit subconscious perspectives. I focused on a deep conflict I carried about the effects of my divorce on my young son. He was too little to understand why the divorce was necessary, and his pain and confusion was enough to freeze me in my tracks for several years. I will elaborate more on my conflict in a later chapter, but simply stated, here was my inner struggle that caused me to consider my own happiness as irrelevant.

While I was pondering about this conflict in class, I suddenly went into a vision state where I saw myself standing in the back of a dark, cold cave. I could see the opening of the cave in the far distance, which would allow me to leave the darkness behind. My heart yearned to go out into the beautiful sunshine I could see far ahead.

While standing in the back of the cave, a guide standing next to me, encouraging me to follow my heart and leave the cave. He started ushering me towards the opening, but I revolted and pulled back. "Stop!" I announced. He asked me what was stopping me. I actually didn't know until this experience unfolded further.

I then realized my soon-to-be ex-wife and my son were standing behind me in the corner of the cave. I then explained to my guide, that as soon as I could push them out of the cave, I would gladly follow them. I simply knew that I was trapped in the cave until they could see the light and make the right choice to leave. I could only be happy and free once they were happy and free. My guide then spoke one of the wisest statements I've ever heard:

> *"How long have you thought that being a leader meant pushing someone somewhere you are unwilling to go first? Do you always lead by pushing from behind?"*

This profound statement left a lasting impression on me. I was shown a deeply buried codependency tendency within myself that encouraged me to sit helplessly around waiting for someone else to make my choices for me. This codependency was masquerading as integrity. Somehow, this idea of waiting helplessly, for external conditions to change, made me believe I was a good person. I learned that day how to be a leader and to walk into the beautiful sunshine with the hope that my son would follow me to a new destiny. It was the path leading out of the cave that led me to this path of which I am now writing. But there were some bumps along the way that I will address. In short, it is painful to watch willing captives suffer needlessly in the cave.

The Door

"Behold, I stand at the door, and knock: if any man hear my voice, and open the door, I will come in to him,

and will sup with him, and he with me." (Revelation 3:20, KJV)

Do you believe this? I mean, do you *actually* believe Him? Let's break this scripture down for a closer look. The Savior is declaring that He stands at the door and knocks. Before we begin this discussion, I would like to testify that when I finally opened this door, the Savior was *actually* waiting for me exactly as He promised.

I often hear that people feel frustrated with God because they feel He has abandoned them in their darkest hour. They believe He is there for others, but not for them. The fact that He is not helping them becomes additional proof that they aren't good enough or worthy of His love and help. There is always a dark story as to why they should stay in the cave.

While we are locked in the cave, these dark feelings of worthlessness, isolation, guilt, shame, and resentment add supporting evidence to our story that we might as well just give up and quit trying. The goal becomes to just stop caring, so that nothing can hurt us. If we can hold onto darkness and lower our standards to accept this new definition of happiness, then we *think* we won't get hurt anymore. And we lie to ourselves, "Sunshine is overrated. Perhaps if I just hold onto my pain, it will protect me from more pain. And perhaps one day, after this life of suffering is over, maybe I can go to heaven and finally be happy there. And if I suffer more in this life, then it proves to God that I am committed and good enough. Maybe I'm suffering in God's name, and it makes me more worthy of happiness in the next life."

If any of these rationalizations sound familiar, it is time to acknowledge that you have locked yourself in your own cave and isolated yourself away from everyone. And of course this includes the Lord. Like grandma used to tell me:

Life Can Make You Better Or
Life Can Make You Bitter
I or E, You decide.

Pain Is Inevitable, Misery Is Optional

I have found from my own personal experiences in life, that the Lord does not turn His back on us. Rather, he comes to our locked door and knocks to draw us *out* of our self-imposed prison, the cave. When we feel separation from God, we actually have turned our backs on Him. And some of us have retreated so far back into the depths of the cave of unbelief that we actually stop hearing His call. Sadly, some of us never return. The darkness that lurks with us in the recesses of the cave relentlessly whispers to us that an unjust God has abandoned us in our darkest hour. However, we have literally traveled outside of God's frequency and are hearing a broadcast from the back of the cave in our hopeless ears. Exactly *who* do you think this is lurking in the dark recesses of the cave with us? It is not God. It is the dragon.

Once you discover that Satan is in the back of the cave with you and that the Lord is knocking at the door, you will also understand that you alone, because of your agency, can decide which direction your feet should take you. Neither influence has the ability to force you in their direction. The Lord is absolutely locked away from helping you *until* you open the door and *choose* to ask for His help with faith. It is an act of faith coupled with free will that leads to miraculous healing and escape from the darkness. Through hypnosis, I have found this cave metaphor profoundly effective in helping people rediscover the door and to identify and relinquish the reasons it was closed and locked in the first place. I assure you, the door is real, and so is the Savior. And so are your reasons for keeping Him out. And even though you were once facing away from the door because you were hurt and broken, the Savior was always standing at the door. It is my opinion that depression is nothing more than a hopeless story that has convinced you that the door does not exist.

Sunshine is *not* overrated. Sunshine is essential to living a healthy and happy life. You cannot have access to sunshine while you are locked in the dark cave, regardless of the story that took you there. If you will open the door and ask in faith, the Savior can heal those deeply hidden wounds after you have relinquished the resentment and the story that kept you locked away from Him. He always cares about what you have suffered through and wants to heal you if you will accept Him. He also wants to remind you that He was there with you when you went through those difficult times, even if you don't remember His presence. Countless times, I have helped people discover His divine help during past trauma through hypnosis. It pleases the Lord to remind you how much He has always cared about you. He was always there with you.

A good friend of mine named Bambie shared the following true story with me that shows the Lord's involvement in our lives, even when His love and support comes in hidden ways.

On Top Of The World With Christ - Bambie's Story

My mother, Faye, had been suffering with arthritis and lupus for a long time. Many people around me were dealing with life and physical challenges. It was a difficult time. There was much discussion about whether God wants to know every little thing or just a general overview of how we are.

"Does God really want to hear all the yearnings of my heart, or are we on an auto-pilot mode?"

This concern weighed deeply upon my soul, and I was fasting and praying while studying everything I could get my hands on to read what others thought about this subject. While fasting one Sunday, when I was 20 years old and still going to Business College, I went to a fireside on the East Bench of Salt Lake City, Utah. The view of the whole valley and the surrounding mountains was breathtaking. I emerged after a very inspirational meeting into the morning sun, which was warming my skin. As I considered my whole experience and deep desires to know the answers I sought, Christ appeared right in front of me. A vision unfolded and I asked Him, "Do you care about our every thought and feeling, or are we on auto-pilot to figure it out for ourselves?"

Christ stood beside me and waved his arm out over the valley and said, "Look."

I looked and could feel that He blessed my ability to see clearly. My sight awakened and I could see my mother, 16 miles away in her home in Midvale. She was in bed, due to her debilitating discomfort and attendant care she required at that time.

I could see that her caregiver was there helping her. And I could see there were several other beings there whose spiritual bodies looked much like our physical bodies. I could tell they were there to be of service to my mother on their errand assigned by God.

Knowing that my mother was a good-hearted person who did her best to be a decent human being, I asked Christ, "Well, what about the other people in our neighborhood, especially those who are not so focused on being a good person and those who were actively doing things that were *not* good to other people."

Christ said to me, "Look."

And again, my sight was opened, and I could see that everyone in the whole area was being helped by angels, even when they didn't know it. About this time, I realized that Christ loves each of us unconditionally and is concerned with every little thought of every single person. He is truly there to help us — really help us.

Again, I wanted to know if it were the same for others in the state of Utah…

Whoosh… Yes it was.
Okay, how about the United States?
Whoosh…Yes it was.

At this point I was standing with Christ on top of the world. I could see everyone in the world, everyone as a whole, and each one as an individual. It was a new way of seeing and it was a gift from Christ so I could see for myself.

Everyone in the world is being attended and helped by beings of love, on an errand from God. Everyone! Whether we receive this help or are aware of this help is a personal choice. It requires effort on our part to truly receive the gifts of love, clarity, and life.

At this point, Christ said to me, "Now, since you can see I am taking care of the entire world, is it alright with you that I take care of the world and you take care of your business in your life doing all you can do to be the finest human being you can be?"

I was humbled as I could see now, and deeply touched with this great gift of understanding, love, and light. He truly loves each one of us and is always with us in our darkest hour.

Love and Light to you All,

Bambie

So you see, divine help comes to us in crisis even if we aren't aware of it, or even if we don't remember it. When we open the door, the Lord reminds us that He was always there for us, if we are willing to Let Go and Let God show us.

Labor Pains

One day, after extensive planning and preparation, I led an amazing woman named Nicole in hypnosis to the door of which I have just spoken. She arrived at the door and really opened it. And yes, just as the Lord promises, He was there waiting for her. Through our extensive planning, we discussed at length the buried resentment that Nicole wanted to release to the Lord. In a previous hypnosis session, we had asked her subconscious mind to show us the reason for her deep apathy and depression. We were led to a devastating experience from her past where she had nearly died while giving birth to her first and only natural-born child.

The trauma and aftermath of this experience introduced deep and hidden sorrow and resentment from that traumatic experience. You see, Nicole's ability to have a large family ended with that first and only pregnancy. Both mother and baby survived, but resentment and trauma were born and that conflict ran deep into her heart. It was so devastating to Nicole that she simply retreated into that cave and locked the door with no intentions of ever coming back out. Her heart started to wither like a flower that had been removed from the sunshine. But with some coaxing and extensive work and planning with me, Nicole had decided it was time to turn over a new leaf and release this unearthed resentment and pain.

However, when the opportunity to actually release the darkness was squarely in front of Nicole, she dramatically changed her mind. Her ensuing encounter with the Savior at the door was extremely puzzling and heartbreaking to me. She changed her mind. Nicole was *not* going to give Him her darkness after all. "He's not talking to me. He's not doing anything!" The Lord just stood there and watched her quietly and patiently, but said nothing. I coaxed her to offer Him to remove the resentment that was eating away her life. But she still refused to speak to Him, perhaps in shock that He was really there. She finally reported to me that nothing was happening and now even the Lord's silence proved that she was alone. After this lingering stalemate, she reported to me that the Lord started withdrawing up and away from her.

But as Nicole watched Him lift away, she surprisingly exclaimed, "Oh wait, I guess *I'm the one that is pulling away*." He was patiently waiting for her to offer Him permission to take her darkness from her heart. But she was blatantly rescinding her offer and pulling away from Him! I encouraged her to return to Him and finish what we had so meticulously planned, but instead, she turned away from Him and ended the experience.

What appeared to be a rejection of the Lord's gift, while confounding to me, illustrates the true principle that the Lord's ability to heal us is completely limited by our free will and intent. If we choose to cling to our story and justification, He *will not* and *cannot* take our darkness! On this day, at least, Nicole's reasons to harbor darkness were still stronger than her reasons to release it to the Lord. She was stuck somewhere between unwilling and unable to let it go.

Strangely, I observed that Nicole showed some subtle satisfaction in refusing the Lord's help. Nicole's heartbreaking story had convinced her that He was to blame for the death of her dream of having a large family. That day, Nicole's need to be right was stronger than her need to be healed. We did have one more hypnosis session after this day and made some additional progress of loosening and releasing this resentment, but unfortunately, the last I heard from her was that she was still harboring resentment which led to divorce and hopelessness. But certainly as time continues to pass, this splinter can continue to work its way to the surface for another try. The Lord never stops waiting at the door and patiently understands our reasons better than we do. He is not desperately waiting, but patiently waiting. He is not angry, but concerned. This is not the final chapter for Nicole, but it *is* up to her to approach the door again when she is ready.

On the Lighter Side, He Dances like a White Boy!

She Went Dancing with THE STAR!

I would like to contrast the previous story of Nicole with one of the most joyful experiences I have ever encountered. It will illustrate that the Lord is actually a mirror that reflects to us what we carry inside. I was given a profound quote recently that explains:

"We do not see the world as it is but we see the world as WE are. "

How true! So if we use some artistic license and add a dash of faith, we can liken this quote unto the Lord:

"We do not see the Lord as He is, but we see Him as WE are."

Melinda's story illustrates this mirror phenomenon beautifully. Melinda is a joyful, larger-than-life African-American woman who came into my office to work through some deep-seated heartache and depression. She was a single mother and was dealing with an abusive boyfriend. She also sadly grew up without a father. She hadn't had much success in life with men.

But regardless of these circumstances and Melinda's deep heartache, she had such a joyful undertone about her. We talked at length about the cave and the possibility of releasing her darkness. We found some beautiful common ground that both of us shared, and a deep and abiding love for the Savior. So we talked frankly about the possibility of going to His door and casting her burden upon Him. She was in! And just like that, Melinda proceeded to march with faith to the door through her subconscious mind.

Melinda's reaction to discovering the Lord at the door was priceless. This encounter was as unbelievable and inspirational to me as anything I have ever witnessed. I was spellbound listening to her account unfold. This reunion was as unpredictable to me as the previous story about Nicole turning her back on the Lord. Upon seeing the Lord, Melinda burst into spontaneous laughter and tears of pure adulation! Melinda explained in jubilant rapture that she grabbed the Lord and wrapped him up in a giant bear hug. They were locked in a joyous reunion. And then Melinda declared to me that they both spontaneously broke out into dancing. With Melinda's belly shaking with laughter and her heart filled with pure adoration, she cried out, "I can't believe this! He dances like a white boy!"

1. To every thing there is a season, and a time to every purpose under the heaven:
2. A time to be born, and a time to die; a time to plant, and a time to pluck up that which is planted;
3. A time to kill, and **a time to heal;** a time to break down, and **a time to build up**;
4. **A time to weep, and a time to laugh**; a time to mourn, and **a time to dance;**
5. A time to cast away stones, and a time to gather stones together; **a time to embrace**, and a time to refrain from embracing." (Ecclesiastes 3:1-5, KJV)

After this dancing reunion, Melinda's heavy heart was completely cleaned and renewed. We talked and laughed about her experience afterwards. We were both amazed at what the

Lord had in store for her the day she opened the door with faith and real intent. **She went dancing with THE STAR!**

This experience was as real and profound to Melinda as anything she had ever experienced. A bear hug, a belly laugh, and the jitterbug was apparently all she needed to get her life back on track. I never saw Melinda again, which is usually a sign that our work together was finished. I will always cherish the simple but beautiful miracle of how the Lord was free to jitterbug with a beautiful dancer because that's what she traded for the sadness in her heart. Melinda's releasing of her darkness was like letting a butterfly out of a jar. She was simply restored to her beautiful and perfect self.

28 "Come unto me, all ye that labour and are heavy laden, and I will give you rest.

29 Take my yoke upon you, and learn of me; for I am meek and lowly in heart: and ye shall find rest unto your souls.

30 For my yoke is easy, and my burden is light." (Matthew 11:28-30, KJV)

Back To The Door

Let's first address this door. What does the door represent? The door IS A BARRIER between us and the Lord. And incidentally, the door is a barrier between us and everyone else, too. The door is designed to ensure isolation and always comes with a story as to why it will never be opened again. This door comprises of literally anything in our life that likely had its origin in pain and suffering, but it is still darkness. And when I say anything, I mean worthlessness, guilt, shame, fear, resentment, regret, anger, rage, heartache, pity, injustice, and the list goes on.

Worthlessness is darkness. Shame is darkness. Fear is darkness. Resentment is darkness. Regret is darkness. Anger is darkness. Rage is darkness. Pity is darkness. Injustice is darkness. Darkness is darkness. You get the point.

But bear in mind again, the door IS A BARRIER between us and the Lord. *No matter how good your reasons are for harboring any of this darkness, it is still darkness. And it is still incompatible with the Lord's spirit and it is locked inside of you behind the door. Darkness is darkness. Later we will discuss how we can subconsciously harbor darkness in places we never intended, but please understand that hidden darkness is just as toxic as darkness that is intentionally harbored. When darkness is within, regardless of the good reasons and the story that holds it in place, darkness embitters, poisons, and distorts. It makes us spiritually sick. It makes us physically sick.*

Psychosomatic

Not Always Just Black and White

I would like to share with you a story of a woman named Jane who came to me for help from hopelessness. With a quick subconscious inventory we discovered that Jane had locked herself in the cave of resentment because of her failed marriage and the heartache of her adult children being influenced against her. Jane had lost all hope and was trying to accept the false belief that effort in life would only lead to additional failure and pain. An amazing thing happened to Jane as soon as she decided to surrender her story. After 45 minutes into our first conversation, Jane suddenly looked at me and gasped in shock. I asked her what was happening. Jane responded, "Something just popped inside of my eye." Jane paused and then continued solemnly, "I can see color again from my left eye!" I asked for clarification. I knew nothing about Jane's vision issues. She informed me that recently she had developed a mysterious condition where the vision in her left eye was restricted to seeing only in black and white. This condition left her doctors baffled because there was nothing physically wrong. When Jane relinquished her commitment to hopelessness, her normal vision was instantly restored right in front of us both. Jane's old hopeless story had literally manifested as seeing life in only black and white. In only a few meetings, Jane successfully handed the Lord her burdens and left the cave. It only took Jane a few months before she found a good man that lived up to her new colorful outlook. Wedding bells were ringing.

The longer we harbor darkness, the worse we get. Even our most legitimate reasons for remaining upset can inspire us to cling onto darkness in a similar way we might cling onto a wet blanket while freezing to death in the cold, dark cave. The wet blanket will never make us warm and is actually a deception that hastens our demise. So yes, the effects of unforgiven injustice can become an impassable barrier for the Lord to help you and it serves as the blockade that holds His healing influence out of your life. And naturally, this door also holds the darkness and the excuses in.

Imagine for a moment that you and I wanted to have a private conversation but I decided to sit on the other side of a closed door to speak to you. How effective would this conversation be? The door is a barrier. And because the barrier exists, the Savior actually can't help you UNTIL you open the door. It is a law that is governed by free agency. The Savior can only help you if you do exactly what His invitation states and you open the door. You have to come to the door and open it, regardless of your reasons and the personal suffering you use as justification to keep the door locked and closed. And you need to open the door with the intent to give all of your darkness to the Lord.

By the end of this creation the Lord will have gathered and acquired every single ounce of darkness from every single person and creature. He will present this mountain of darkness and filth to the Father and declare, "It Is Finished."

Yes, this very darkness that you are harboring belongs to the Lord, and He wants it! Eventually, He will add your darkness to his growing collection. And if you think you are doing the Lord a favor by refusing to give your darkness to Him under the guise of some false narrative, rest assured that the price He paid for your darkness in Gethsemane and on the cross has already been paid. Regardless of whether you surrender it now or not!

Clinging onto your darkness for a miserable lifetime does NOT lessen the suffering the Lord ALREADY endured but certainly increases your season of suffering. In fact, your additional suffering adds to the original price He already paid. So an interesting way to look at this is that you are actually lessening your and the Lord's suffering by giving this away as soon as possible! How does that strike you?

When The War Began

4 "And his tail drew the third part of the stars of heaven, and did cast them to the earth: and the dragon stood before the woman which was ready to be delivered, for to devour her child as soon as it was born.

7 And there was war in heaven: Michael and his angels fought against the dragon; and the dragon fought and his angels,

8 And prevailed not; neither was their place found any more in heaven.

9 And the great dragon was cast out, that old serpent, called the Devil, and Satan, which deceiveth the whole world: he was cast out into the earth, and his angels were cast out with him." (Revelation 12:4-9, KJV)

"Before I formed thee in the belly I knew thee; and before thou camest forth out of the womb I sanctified thee, and I ordained thee a prophet unto the nations." (Jeremiah 1:5, KJV)

16 "The Spirit itself beareth witness with our spirit, that we are the children of God:

17 And if children, then heirs; heirs of God, and joint-heirs with Christ; if so be that we suffer with him, that we may be also glorified together." (Romans 8:16-17, KJV)

These scriptures teach us an intriguing insight about our origins before this earth. We lived in God's presence as His offspring — as His spirit children. And at some stage, we fought a great war over different ideologies where a third of the hosts of heaven were lost. We fought to retain our free will, and to continue our development by gaining the opportunity and privilege to have a physical body on a physical earth.

I used to believe that God could do anything. But then one day, while pondering these scriptures I realized limitations are placed on God Himself because He honors our free will. This doctrine of the war in heaven has always captivated me. It was a war of truth versus error, a war of ideologies that divided heaven. And who knows how divided heaven really was as the war began?

How many of our family members were pulled back and forth over the line of truth as they argued and worried about their uncertain and daunting futures of mortality. The unthinkable thing to me about this war is that it was literally fought in God's presence where we actually lost a third of our brothers and sisters. What a tragedy! What a devastating loss for our Father! For us! And then the battlegrounds of this war migrated to this earth where the lies and contention and darkness continue to rage today. But the point I want to underscore here is that a third of our family was actually deceived WHILE in God's presence! How is this possible?

While all of us were in God's presence, we were presented with two plans about our future. We know that Christ endorsed Father's plan and agreed to the great role of Savior and Redeemer. We also know that Satan, the son of the morning, presented a different plan that offered great relief to those who were afraid of the risks presented with an existence on earth. Satan, no doubt, used scare tactics and threats to taunt those who chose to follow the Savior.

We all understood we would pass through the veil where we would forget everything and be subject to the very enemy that would retain memories of us. The very ones who were eventually cast out of Father's presence would become the very ones who would afflict us while on this sojourn to earth. And isn't it interesting that God cast these spirits to THIS earth? The very earth where we were foreordained to dwell? God could have easily cast them into the pit. But why here? In short, their very presence here offers us resistance and opposition for increased growth, perhaps no different than what gravity does for a weightlifter. Eventually, a third of our heavenly family decided to place their faith in a lie which ultimately caused them to lose their place in heaven and turn them into enemies of God. Why would God devise such a plan that would divide heaven with contention, fear, and devastating loss? The question leads us to an interesting teaching of the Savior.

51 "Suppose ye that I am come to give peace on earth? I tell you, Nay; but rather division:

52 For from henceforth there shall be five in one house divided, three against two, and two against three." (Luke 12:51-52, KJV)

Apparently, this scripture applied to not only heaven, but also earth. The truth divides like a sword and it requires faith, courage, and grit to accept and follow the truth. And truth versus darkness always leads to conflict, even war.

And now this pattern is playing out again here in this world but the new casualties are the ones being lost and trapped in the cave of depression, apathy, pity, regret, despair, and shame.

Once trapped in this cave of hopelessness, Satan does a pretty good job of convincing us to stay put. He fuels the justification to avoid the door and tries to use our story as evidence that God does not love us. "What kind of God would send you to a world where you have suffered in so much darkness?" And so the narrative continues to capture souls who succumb to the dark lies that breed resentment and hopelessness. It is my opinion that every suicide takes place in the back of this cave.

Satan's lies were easy on the ears. His plan *guaranteed* no suffering and no chance to fail in life. When Satan's conquests were finally coerced and manipulated into following and believing his attenuated plan, those lost souls placed their faith in a lie. Satan's plan was an ideology that actually opposed free will.

The promised lack of suffering was actually the furthest reality from the truth. Yet, these lost souls followed Satan blindly, locked their doors, and retreated deeply into the back of their cave of unbelief away from God's influence. I would like to point out again that this deception occurred in the presence of Father! How could someone be deceived in Father's presence? Simply stated, placing faith in a lie can create a story and a justification that can reinforce the lie. And that lie can actually begin to fester and swell until it becomes an infection of resentment and hate. This infection can then inspire the soul to retreat deeper into the cave of resentment and more fully justify the deceived to not only denounce light but to oppose it with all the energy available. And this whole process drains the light of Christ from the victim who then accepts the very role of being a direct enemy of light and truth.

As a result, this dark soldier will continue to fight because of his rage that is directed at a God who would have the audacity to promote such a "plan of division and suffering" in the first place. And now, the story of hate is born and fully ripe. And this follower will likely never approach the door upon which the Savior or any of His servants are knocking. The goal now is to deceive the true followers to retreat into their own cave of deception, and use this strategy to bring suffering to the very ones who had the nerve to follow the Savior in the first place.

Leave the cave.

CHAPTER EIGHT

The Victim Can Become The Martyr

We have all been wronged by others, whether maliciously or otherwise. And there are many of us who have been devastated because of the horrible choices of our closest and most trusted loved ones. Yes, "Hurt people hurt people."

What a profound way to explain how a real victim can unknowingly deteriorate into a perpetrator if his or her wounds are not healed. In this chapter, I will elaborate on a heartbreaking case where I counseled John and Abbey, whose marriage was devastated by John's infidelity. Abbey was not just victimized by John's infidelity but had also suffered betrayal by her father's and ex-husband's infidelity. These betrayals ultimately ended in the disintegration of both of Abbey's nuclear family units. Abbey was also sexually abused as a child and had been raped in high school. She had been victimized sexually as a young woman and as an adult.

Buried And Carried

Deal With It By Not Dealing With It

Avoid The Void

To add some subconscious perspective to John's betraying Abbey, I want to acknowledge that as a boy, he, too, had been sexually assaulted multiple times. John was part of a large family and came from a very religious home with a strict moral code and high expectations. His understanding of basic love and acceptance had been confused at an early age by sexual abuse, and further distorted by the continual presence of sarcasm and conditional love in the home. This distorted understanding developed into confusing and destructive sexual behaviors. For John, worth came from connection, connection came from sexuality, and sexuality equaled betrayal of his parents and their core religious beliefs. These devastating sexual patterns created intense feelings of shame, guilt, and worthlessness. Hiding the dark secrets and lies about his sexual abuse and sexual acting out were the beginning of John's subconscious creation of unhealthy protection beliefs and the cultivating, burying, and carrying of his shame and pain. The secrecy and lies surrounding his sexual behavior were the perfect breeding ground for shame, which, unable to emerge from the shadows, developed into a sexual addiction. Secrets created shame and shame created more secrets. Eventually, these feelings of shame and worthlessness became John's "normal," his constant companion and the distorted lens through which he viewed his lack of value in this life. He felt worthless. And frankly, when you really feel worthless, you may act worthless. Not everyone who has been sexually abused will cheat, but I've encountered many cases where this does happen.

Buried Darkness

As outlined earlier, the mind has an uncanny ability to bury painful memories of your past. And when this happens, those memories all too often poison perceptions and belief systems that can sabotage healthy relationships. These irrational beliefs inspire the porcupine quills to come out and scare away anyone close enough to inflict more damage and pain.

This hidden rationale can certainly influence a spouse to cheat. Because the cheater lives in the shadows of lies and secrecy and often betrays his wife's trust, her validation is no longer real. She no longer knows who he really is. How could it be real? In short, "If she really knew the truth, she would leave me and not love me anymore." He doesn't want to hurt any longer and has a driving urge surface to have anyone prove to him that he isn't worthless. He turns outside of his marriage, compartmentalizing his actions. Ironically, he desperately seeks approval from those who truly do not know who he is. He gets intoxicated by any validation and he subconsciously and desperately radiates an SOS emergency beacon to anyone out there who can provide this needed validation. Irrational? Yes. But rational thought only lives in the conscious side of the mind. Remember, irrational and hidden thoughts can serve as that rip-tide of the mind that can pull you out to sea and drown you.

As you can see, this buried darkness from childhood can later surface recklessly and become part of the subconscious self-justification of horrible choices. And it is this very justification that ultimately led John from victim to perpetrator.

I am not justifying John's poor decisions here, but illustrating how his buried darkness can later surface and lead down that dangerous path of hidden self-justification in damaging others whom he loves. And I will show in this chapter how hidden, subconscious, and irrational beliefs will devastate the perpetrator and victim alike. This pattern becomes even more tragic when we see it pass from one generation to the next, where each gets worse like a spreading cancer.

Being wounded by someone else's bad choices is one of the brutal realities of this life. I have met many legitimate victims over the years who have suffered deeply at the hands of others. I have been exposed to many stories of unspeakable abuse and tragedy. It is deeply heartbreaking to learn of the horrible injustices: a child who was sexually or physically abused; the single mother who was betrayed and abandoned; the woman who was raped but locked it away; parents whose child died of a heroin overdose; a loved one who died by suicide, and the list goes on and on. I am acknowledging here that many of us have legitimately suffered tragedy and heartbreak because of the reckless and thoughtless acts of others.

In this book, I recognize and address genuine suffering and miraculous recovery through true understanding and divine intervention. However, it is here I would also like to offer some perspective on how a legitimate victim can unknowingly meander onto the path of martyrdom. This can be a very subtle process that is often difficult to consciously recognize.

The Webster dictionary defines martyrdom as "The suffering of death on account of adherence to a cause and especially to one's religious faith." Many of us have heroes who have died for a brave cause. And we rightfully revere these heroes because of their undying commitment.

But martyrdom is also defined negatively in the dictionary as: "A display of feigned or exaggerated suffering to obtain sympathy or admiration."

It is this definition of martyrdom I would like to address here. And for clarification between these two definitions, I will refer to the latter definition when I speak of martyrdom below. But "energy vampire" is probably just as descriptive.

I would like to add my own definition of martyrdom here as well. A martyr is someone who uses legitimate pain from their past as an excuse and justification to misbehave or mistreat others. Previous suffering does not entitle the martyr to knowingly, or unknowingly, punish others who dare question or challenge the payoffs or benefits of the ongoing suffering narrative.

We've all been in a room where someone is draining everyone else's energy. Everyone in the room dissociates from the exhausting performance while the energy vampire is completely drunk on emotion and oblivious to the negative weight they unpack in the room. And after a well-calculated exchange, the energy vampire then slips away after unloading, venting, and sucking up the sympathies while everyone else feels burdened and depleted.

The Slippery Slope

I have rarely counseled a martyr that consciously recognized he or she had slipped into this pity-party trap. There is a fuzzy area between receiving appropriate love and support from tragedy versus overindulgence and going back for seconds. A martyr becomes extremely proficient in finding unsuspecting but well-intentioned enablers who rush to their aid.

These helpers offer full love and support to the recovering victim who may begin, perhaps subtly at first, to start taking advantage of the helper's kindness. This transition from victim to martyr is initially undetectable by the one going through the subtle transition.

Please read this ten times:

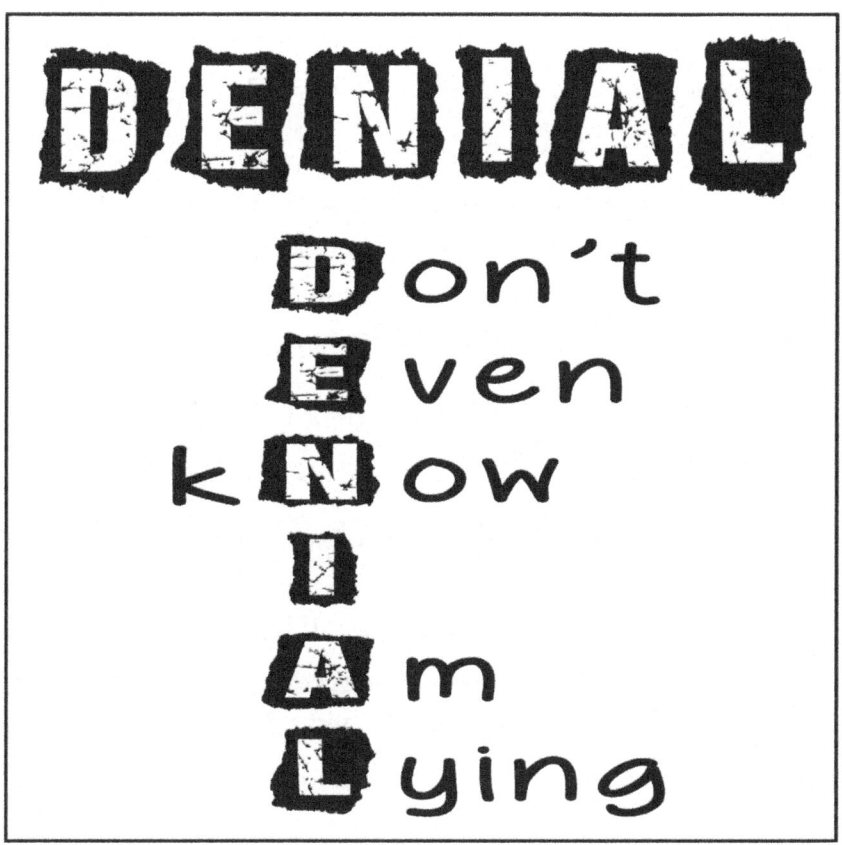

As much as I dislike labels, the following cliche certainly sheds additional light on denial:

You can't read the label while you are trapped inside of the bottle!

If I really don't know that I am lying then exactly *how* do I fix the problem? Accountability.

A Ride On The Martyr Cycle

When The Victim Becomes The Martyr

1 "Take heed that ye do not your alms before men, to be seen of them: otherwise ye have no reward of your Father which is in heaven.

2 Therefore when thou doest thine alms, do not sound a trumpet before thee, as the hypocrites do in the synagogues and in the streets, that they may have glory of men. Verily I say unto you, They have their reward." (Matthew 6:1-2, KJV)

"Yes, but do you realize how much I have suffered?"

"No really! Do you realize how much I have suffered?"

This "trumpeting your alms before men" principle applies just as much to the martyr as it does to a self-righteous performance of fasting and praying in the public square. But I want to point out that an extreme case of martyrdom starts out as a very subtle self-deception coupled with true suffering. If it is left unchecked it continues to grow like weeds in a garden. Eventually, martyrdom can decay into a full case of inexcusable self-justification that will eventually drive everyone out of his or her life.

Martyr She Wrote

Once a martyr and demanding pity and entitlements from others, this person has now transitioned into the perpetrator. One who is guilty of taking advantage of others by running an intensive helplessness campaign: "I've suffered greatly. And because of this I can never take care of myself again. You are only a good person if you protect me and provide for me unconditionally while I remain helpless."

Wait! Where Did Everyone Go?

So yes, pity can turn into a trumpet performance to be seen of men. Bear in mind that a muted trumpet is still a trumpet. And make no mistake, these performances can pay well. Extra entitlements, recognition, special treatment, etc, are not uncommon. But this martyr will eventually find out, the hard way, that once payments have been repeatedly withdrawn from unsuspecting victims, the audience starts to thin and dwindle away. Martyrdom might even lead to financial rewards and deflect accountability by supporting the perception of helplessness. But eventually martyrdom destroys all healthy relationships and leaves the martyr alone to wonder where everyone went. It is here that the martyr feels compelled to create a stronger narrative of suffering to explain the "cruel abandonment" that has mysteriously followed the initial season of suffering.

"After all I have suffered, now everyone has abandoned me, too? Where will this end, God?"

It is here that resentment can now be directed towards any loved one who has the audacity to confront the martyr with accountability. Denial and contention will surely be directed at anyone who tries to address the martyrdom with such "false accusations." If continuing pity and expected gestures of support do not gush forth at an early stage, resentment will escalate in order to reinforce the evolving entitlement. DENIAL has blinded the martyr, and a new villain has been introduced to the thickening plot of the martyr's story.

For this system of manipulation to continue, anyone who has withdrawn from supporting the martyr will likely be demonized with accusations of abandonment or self-righteousness. The martyr, completely blinded by "being right," now inflicts punishments on anyone who challenges his or her narrative and plight. Some victims get addicted to pity when they realize it can be used as a weapon upon empathetic people.

"I suffer alone in God's name. No one could possibly understand the depth of my suffering."

Stop the Martyr-cycle and get off.

This self-deception is now the new narrative of the martyr's reality. This negative feedback loop is actually capable of creating sickness and disease and CAN become true.

I have witnessed profound cases of this self-pity/resentment pattern with extreme cases of addiction. Blame replaces accountability and resentful denial reinforces sickness, whether pretended or real. But eventually the addict finds himself alone and calls it abandonment. And the only friends that remain are other addicts that perpetuate the martyr's narrative.

How Do I Tolerate You?

With addiction, we acknowledge the principle of building tolerance to a substance. The more a substance is used, the less effective it becomes. The addict must increase levels of the substance to get the desired high. And yes, eventually the substance just flat-out stops working. And isn't it ironic that the very same principle of tolerance happens to the pity addict? The story has to get worse and more dramatic to retain the audience's accolades. It can feel like one of those sword fights in one of those popular pirate movies that lasts for 30 exhausting minutes. After one minute, most people get the point. After 30, they are checked out or asleep, or change the channel altogether.

The Addict Will Often Justify...

"When the chips are down, you find out who your real friends are."

So if you are the one who feels abandoned or misjudged by others, choose to be willing to ask yourself and closest loved ones the tough questions:

"What am I doing to drive others out of my life?"

Abandonment is a real reason behind tragedy such as children whose father left the family. So yes, there are plenty of real victims of legitimate abandonment out there. I've met and helped many. But sometimes accusations of abandonment are strategically used as part of the martyr's facade. Martyrdom eventually ends with loneliness and isolation. And in this case, I wouldn't call it depression but rather consequences from bad behavior.

"Wait! After all I've been through, are you saying I'm the bad guy here?"

Perhaps. Let's look more closely.

If you want to heal from legitimate past emotional wounds then you must acknowledge what you are harboring and then *Let Go and Let God Heal.*

If your old attitudes and wounds are blinding you, it is you alone that ultimately decides to take accountability and change your behavior. You can choose to give away the whole story and heal or choose to hold onto it and punish yourself and everyone around you.

Your pain — whether inflicted by yourself or someone else — is still your pain and your responsibility. The darkness of resentment and entitlement can be all-consuming. Getting rid of this darkness has to start with the acknowledgment it is there. And then it requires courage and free will to ASK God to take it from you. It requires faith that He will take it from you. And you have to be willing to let go of it even if it feels like forgiveness condones what wounded you, or somehow invalidates your authentic and legitimate suffering.

What Is More Important To You,
Being Right, Or Being Healed?

Payment From Others — Pity
Payment From God — Healing
You Choose

A recovering martyr often has a difficult time trying to define who they are without the old story.

"But this is the limp I've always walked with! Who would I be without this?"

It requires real effort *and* divine help to build a new identity for the recovering martyr. Once you have raised above the frequency of resentment and entitlement you can hear God much more clearly. At the end of this book I will share with you my metaphor, "Eagles Gathering," that teaches the process of not only letting God remove our character flaws, but just as importantly letting Him rebuild our character. We exchange darkness for God's love. We can only have more of God's divine love and character *if* we make room by letting God do some renovation. Let Go and Let God change you.

Back To John and Abbey

I've elaborated on nuances of some extreme cases of martyrdom, but now it is time to discuss in more detail the real scenario of John and Abbey devastated by infidelity. While counseling with these two individuals, we gained deep, subconscious perspectives and motivations from both the victim and the perpetrator.

Looking at Abbey's backstory, many may be amazed that Abbey even considered working on their marriage. Abbey came from a broken home, a product of her father's infidelity towards her mother. She was also sexually molested as a child by multiple perpetrators. She was raped twice as a teenager. Abbey's first marriage, like her mother's, was destroyed by the betrayal of her husband with another woman. Abbey had been victimized and had her trust betrayed by males throughout her entire life. Professors, psychologists, personal trainers, clergy, doctors, and patients… the list goes on and on of male figures in Abbey's life put in a position of authority and guidance, victimizing her in one way or another. Their actions eroded away her ability to trust, her sense of safety and security, and her sense of control. Here is where I met Abbey, in a space of pure victimization, validated by decades of betrayal and perpetration. Ultimately left with a negative core belief, and most recently reinforced by her pure perpetrator husband John, of "I am powerless." With this as a story, one can see how an individual, with countless experiences of true victimization, can easily pass over into a space of martyrdom. Abbey is now facing the same ironic theme of her life — victimization. She is overwhelmed by sorrow, pain, and fear. She is torn between loyalty to John and not wanting him to suffer further shame from community and societal judgment because of her need to talk to others in a search for support and understanding. Abbey turns to God and receives a difficult but authentic divine message, "Look deeper into this experience, forgiving John will lead to healing you both." This did not mean Abbey needed to stay with John. John had his choices. He could overcome his addiction or lose his family. It did mean there was a chance. However, the message was clear, Abbey's forgiveness would lead to her ultimate healing. This type of mission to forgive can be difficult to say the least. And by her own admission, the infidelity is much less painful if she leaves the cheater. Having to sleep next to the perpetrator who betrayed her is nearly impossible without God's help. We will discuss more on this later.

 I dug deep into John's subconscious to uncover the motivations and irresistible pull of his infidelity. It wasn't long before he was in tears due to his lifelong unhealthy thinking patterns, using the cheating and betrayal to support his belief that he was worthless. He had always felt worthless. Always. The infidelity was just one more piece of evidence as to why he believed the story his subconscious had used to *protect* him for so long. The complexity of subconsciously using worthlessness as a perceived protection is overwhelming to understand. However, this is a perfect example of how the subconscious can create irrational false beliefs as a guise for protection.

The cynical reader might dismiss this as some type of convenient manipulative antics.

"He's only sorry because he got caught!"

The truth is he didn't get caught. John came to Abbey with his confession. Like many perpetrators, John's addiction coupled with his subconscious protection programs overpowered his conscious desire to "do the right thing." Addiction does not establish the addict as a bad or unscrupulous person. Addiction literally changes the chemical and physical makeup of the brain and impedes rational thought processes. Good people are all too often caught in destructive patterns of addiction, depression, anxiety, victimization, and other neurological patterns despite their true and ultimate desire to do the right thing. This is yet another example of a victim (addict) becoming a perpetrator (addictive cycle).

John's background showed he grew up extremely conflicted. Pitted against his learned sexual behaviors as a child and perfectionistic expectations of an intense orthodox religious environment, John developed an extreme sense of worthlessness. John's subconscious created a destructive cycle of intimacy, validation, and shame, which turned John into a sexual addict. The need for validation would create intimacy, which would create shame, which would create worthlessness, which would, in turn, create the need for more validation. Validation would come through John's misunderstood concept of love and connection. This would express itself in the learned sexual behavior from John's sexual abuse as a child. The sexual connection would provide a brief moment of validation and acceptance which John would mistakenly interpret as feelings of worth. This would quickly deteriorate into overwhelming emotions of shame and guilt for betraying his values (parents, religious, personal, marital). This turned his life into a deep, dark cavern of secrets. John lived a life in the shadows. The shadows of secrecy and lies are what breeds shame. Everywhere he went, he carried those shameful secrets like a cold, wet blanket. This was his "normal." Guilt, shame, and worthlessness is a toxic combination to have buried in your heart. And it can turn into something horrible if not removed. In one session, John jokingly told me he understood that everyone has baggage, he was just hoping to eventually trade in his travel trunks for a single carry-on. John's travel trucks were a result of a lifetime of shame and secrets. It was not humanly possible for John to release the shame, the guilt, the self-deprecating belief patterns, and the overwhelming sense of complete worthlessness by himself. The only possible way to accomplish such a task is to surrender to God. This was the place John needed to get to: the seemingly simple belief that he was worth that which was his divine right to claim. That which has already been paid for. That which is given freely and openly. The gift of the atonement and forgiveness.

The Dark Magnet Within

It is extremely difficult to measure the effects of sexual abuse on a child, and I have seen so many heartbreaking cases. Suffice it to say that sexual assault leaves the victim with a residue of seemingly permanent guilt and shame, along with a deeply held conviction that the victim really is worthless. When you legitimately carry these deep scars of abuse in the subconscious realms of your heart and mind, it can turn into a dark magnet that attracts others carrying complementary darkness. Most importantly, validation is forged with anyone carrying this complementary darkness. This is used as a tool by the Great Deceiver. Validation becomes intoxicating for both parties. And then one thing leads to another. Before long, there is this irresistible urge to step over the line. After all, guilt and shame are no strangers here. And neither is worthlessness. And now, with the infidelity, the worthlessness gets reinforced. And that means the emotional black hole is crying out for something else to fill it. And thus you see the increased justification, "I am a good person. I have value. I have worth. She wouldn't engage in sexual behavior with me if I wasn't." This need for justification increases as the depth of the guilt and shame increase. Because Abbey didn't know of John's behavior, John could no longer accept Abbey's validation, therefore the validation would need to come from somewhere else and it would need to be bigger. I am a good person. I have value. I have worth. She knows I am married and would not engage in sexual behavior with me if I wasn't. And yes, this type of self-justification took John over the line. More than once.

Meanwhile, Abbey was filled with legitimate heartache and suffering from this unthinkable injustice, while at the same time, paradoxically, felt asked by God to forgive John. Abbey understood two things. 1) Forgiveness of John would lead to her own healing. 2) By forgiving John she was giving him his very best chances of really changing. She'd been given a commission to help John find that elusive inner peace and healing that will lead to real change. The very thing he never learned as a child.

I would also like to point out that John had genuinely determined to repent, change, and really turn to God once and for all. He had tried many times earlier in life to alter these reckless patterns but with no success. The past seemed to reinforce that future efforts were futile. John already had proof that there was no hope for him. Unfortunately, John was not aware of his destructive cycle. He felt he was a force of nature whose only purpose was to hurt and destroy those who were misfortunate enough to be caught in his wake. By his own admission he certainly did not deserve help from God! He had done too much damage and let God down too many times. God had no use for someone who had promised to stop over and over again and failed to keep his promises. Therefore, he wasn't worthy of God's help or his love. How could God love someone so destructive, who was such a failure, someone so worthless? That narrative was the one we had to destroy in order to give him his best chances of truly changing. To remove that old narrative, John also needed to release the resentment and pain tied to what happened to him so many years before.

John was changing his heart and had found genuine sorrow for betraying Abbey. Accountability was emerging with compassion.

And compassion was something new for John to experience. He had navigated a large portion of his life cold, calculated, and cynical; compassion was something that he had never found on his dinner plate. John was a product of his environment and learned to master his skills of manipulation, compartmentalization, resentment, and interestingly enough, unforgiveness and judgment. John developed some street smarts to be able to survive his childhood and it was these street smarts that now needed to be deconstructed and unlearned.

John was authentically tired of being the perpetrator and being seen as the bad guy. He was tired of hurting everyone. In fact, prior to deciding to repent and truly change, he had been entertaining suicide as a way to protect everyone from himself. He genuinely believed the world would be better off without him. It was a scary place for him to be, and he really was willing to follow through with taking his life. His previous failure had become the final piece of evidence to show him that nothing was ever going to change.

But with his new-found perspective and determination to dig in, coupled with Abbey's genuine love and determination, John decided to look deeply beneath the surface and view honestly what was lurking beneath.

I realize there are cynics out there who want to question the timing of John's repentance, but regardless of what we think, we understand from Christ's teachings that we are required to forgive others seventy times seven or we don't receive forgiveness ourselves. Mercy begets mercy. John could truly repent and change — even if his critics wouldn't believe it or accept it. Even if Abbey refused to forgive him. I helped John understand that it was his responsibility and privilege to forgive himself independently from Abbey attempting to forgive him and heal from his infidelity.

When the Savior asked us to come follow Him, this included the taking up of our cross and our suffering in His name. And yes, even suffering because of other people's poor choices and sins. Isaiah teaches this same principle of redemptive suffering. The idea here is perhaps our own suffering at the hands of others becomes the catalyst of helping the offender transform his life into a true follower of the Savior. Yes, even to go as a lamb to the slaughter.

Paul the apostle is a perfect example of how someone can change their hearts completely. He turned from murderer to apostle. Paul became one of the most prolific missionaries in the history of the world! Perhaps this happened in part because he had such deep sorrow for the lives he negatively impacted during his blind justification. And his new miraculous and abiding love and gratitude for the Savior was so powerful that he just wanted to make it up to the Lord. It would be interesting to measure the net righteousness Paul's life and influence created after he was truly converted to the light. It is certainly interesting to consider whether those whom Paul testified against, including Stephen who was stoned to death at the feet of Saul, could have been some of the very ones waiting to greet him in fellowship after he was martyred in the Lord's name.

I will attest that Abbey's John started believing he could really make a full change, reconcile with Abbey, and repent sincerely because of Paul's example two thousand years after his mortal life ended. Paul's missionary work reached John thousands of years later. So who are we to condemn Paul or John? And now John wants his redemption story to go out into the world to help other perpetrators discover compassion and forgiveness, too. And if John and Paul can do it, then so can you!

Abbey intended to forgive John but still had to overcome a significant portion of heartache and resentment buried beneath her honorable intentions. Her mission was certainly going to require some grace and faith. It was going to require struggle and work. And when I say buried, I mean she was in deep denial that the resentment was present because she was busy genuinely trying to forgive John.

John helped me understand that Abby's resentment would surface often during some of their trivial interactions with subtle payback jabs. But the danger to John during this critical transformation was his own willingness to punish himself because he was sorry for hurting her and felt he deserved the shame and guilt. After all, he already knew and accepted he was worthless. And maybe he did deserve more punishment or consequences from the world's perspective. Abbey had always stood in John's corner and tried her hardest to convince him he was good enough and had value. Perhaps John deserved the punishment, but the Lord required Abbey to open her heart so He could remove the resentment and sting. She had as much right and responsibility to heal as John did.

But, still, Abbey's subconscious jabs at John were reinforcing the negative programming that directed his life in the first place. And from a practical standpoint, Abbey's passive aggressive payback was the very dynamic that would push John easily back into hopelessness, shame, and guilt. Ironically this "deserved" shame and guilt could fuel the dysfunction that would inspire John to quit trying and return to familiar patterns of again seeking validation elsewhere, like a desperate swimmer starting to drown.

In Summary

Trying to help Abbey recover from being betrayed and trying to help John let go of the addiction and accompanying guilt and shame turned out to be a delicate balancing act. Each one of them had to constantly remind themselves that neither one of them were entitled to be resentful or hurtful towards the other person. The Lord requires Abbey to forgive John if she wants to heal. But the Lord also requires John to be compassionate about Abbey's pain and suffering and quit cheating.

John was not entitled to Abbey forgiving him. He made that very clear to John in an inspired dream. In the dream, the Lord showed John that he had no claim to Abbey's forgiveness. He simply needed to be compassionate and patient about Abbey's plight and grateful for the atonement of the Savior. Abbey's deep heartache of being victimized and betrayed many times in her life required her to open her heart and invite the Lord to remove all of the pain she had suffered. She was choosing to open her heart to the Lord and begging Him to take away her resentment, pain, and good reasons for the suffering. Abbey's entire story needed to be surrendered so she could heal.

If she would have been seeking out pity from people who would certainly have given her the accolades of the victim then perhaps John could have never found his way to the point of true repentance and forgiveness. And what would his life have become?

Perhaps another tragedy. Her mission to forgive came from God to save a floundering soul who had injured her.

The bigger picture here is that Abbey was given a mission by the Lord to set John free. Free from the suffering that not only was imposed upon him, but that he was imposing on her because of his reckless reaction to the buried heartache and pain that lurked within.

True love and humility were required by two humble and willing children of God to overcome this horrible tragedy and heal. As of right now this looks like a success story to inspire the perpetrators and victims alike to turn to the Lord for legitimate healing.

The final outcome of John and Abby's journey is not yet determined. Regardless of whether their marriage can survive, I am hopeful that both of them will open their hearts and heal independently and move forward with faith. And hopefully, this can be together. But each party has the responsibility to receive the necessary grace and healing independently of the other spouse's choices.

Loved People Love People

CHAPTER NINE

Are You The Enabler?

When I was studying NLP and realizing I was an enabler, I decided to write a little metaphor that could be used to teach people like me how to come out of denial and actually change. Enablers are usually well-intentioned people who do anything they can to stop others from suffering. And remember that a martyr or an addict loves these enabling do-gooders because they give away so much for free, no strings attached! I'll feature myself as the enabler in the story because I wrote this metaphor for me.

Little Birdie

One day Little Mikey was taking a walk all by himself in the park when he came upon a very sad scene. He walked right past a small tree and heard Little Birdie crying out in sorrow from her nest.

"Everyone abandoned me and flew away. I'm all alone and starving to death! If only some kind person could bring me something to eat, then I would no longer be dying, all alone!"

Little Mikey announced excitedly, "Wait! I am a good person! What a coincidence!" Little Mikey also happened to know that birds *loved* worms. And, of course, Little Mikey was the biggest expert in the whole neighborhood at catching them. He had done it zillions of times! So Little Mikey rushed over to the nearest dirt mound and started digging. Within moments Little Mikey captured a large juicy worm. He ran over to Little Birdie and felt so happy to give her the juicy treat.

The moment was beautiful! Little Birdie danced with glee while eating the big juicy worm. Little Mikey bounced with excitement because he had been the hero by saving Little Birdie. The day couldn't have been better. Little Mikey continued along and skipped his way home.

The next day, Little Mikey again decided he would take a walk in the park. He was such a big boy. While in the park, he decided to take a peek in the nest. And much to Little Mikey's delight, he saw Little Birdie again crying out from the nest with a *sad* tale to tell. Little Birdie cried out, "An amazing blessing that you would show up just as I was ready to die a horrible death! Here I am starving, and you show up and answer my prayers again! You are such a good person. If you would only bring me another juicy worm, then I will be safe for another day!"

Well, of course, Little Mikey was happy to be a good person. So he ran to the dirt mound and easily captured another juicy worm. He raced back to Little Birdie and handed over the slimy delight. And after the feast, Little Mikey happily skipped home again.

The following day Little Mikey had a big birthday party at his house. All of his favorite cousins and best friends came over to have an amazing party with presents and cupcakes and pizza. It was an amazing day. Little Mikey was too busy to take a walk in the park on his birthday.

But the following day, Little Mikey decided to take another walk through the park. As he was approaching the little nest he suddenly heard Little Birdie screaming angrily.

"I thought you were a good person! Yesterday I nearly died of starvation because you didn't come and feed me! I can't believe you could be so selfish to let me sit here and suffer all day long with nothing to eat at all!"

Little Mikey replied to Little Birdie, "I'm sorry I missed feeding you… But I had my big boy birthday party."

And Little Birdie angrily exclaimed, "Well, isn't that just fine that *you* could have a birthday party while *I* am suffering and dying in the nest? How *dare* you leave me suffering while you have a party!"

Little Mikey was confused. He asked Little Birdie where the rest of her family went. Little Birdie sharply replied, "They abandoned me and flew away!"

Little Mikey asked Little Birdie, "Why didn't you just fly with them?"

Little Birdie snapped, "Because it is terrifying to jump out of this nest, and I would most certainly die if I tried!"

Little Mikey asked, "Did any of your family die when they jumped out of the nest?"

Little Birdie screamed, "That is not the point! How dare you be so judgmental against me! I am sickly, and they were all strong. And they had the *nerve* to abandon *me* while I was too sad and scared. And now you have abandoned me, too! I can see that you have abandoned me. Just go away and I will die in this nest because you have chosen to be selfish!"

Little Mikey felt really sad in his heart, but suddenly he had an idea: "Wait! Why don't you just jump and fly and go find your family?"

And Little Birdie screamed again, "Can't you see that I am far too sick to be able to fly like the other birds? So if you do not hurry and feed me, then I will die and it is your fault!"

But this time Little Mikey stood tall and announced with his outside voice, "If I had wings, then I would jump out and fly and go find my family!"

Little Mikey started crying and raced home as fast as his little legs would take him.

When Little Mikey got home, he cried to Mother through giant tears, "Little Birdie is angry and dying and it's all my fault! I'm a bad person, Mommy!"

And of course Mother had a very important lesson to teach Little Mikey.

Mother taught Little Mikey that kindness always matters but sometimes we get confused about what kindness really means. She then explained that fear is not the same thing as a broken wing and that hunger was the very thing that would drive Little Birdie to jump from the nest. Little Birdie was never truly going to be happy until she was fulfilling her destiny by using her God-given wings. Mother also taught Little Mikey that *if* Little Birdie happened to die in the nest that it wasn't him that killed Little Birdie, but it was instead her own fear. Mother explained that

God had given Little Birdie hunger and wings as a gift to help her fly.

Flying or dying was up to Little Birdie.

Then Mother declared wisely and solemnly, "Say a little prayer that Little Birdie won't find someone else to feed her. She needs to fly and learn to feed herself."

Meet Sofia

Sofia is a client of mine that came from a tragic and difficult childhood. Her past had now caught up with her and created some reckless and dangerous behavior that was destroying her life and dividing her family. This is what brought her to me for answers. Sofia was astounded when I read her this story of Little Birdie. She instantly understood the dysfunctional dynamic that had been destroying her life. She recognized instantly that she was Little Birdie in the story and that her birth parents had jumped from the nest and abandoned her. It was after I read her this story that she decided it was time to jump from her dysfunctional nest and fly. Sofia wanted to include her story in this book in the hopes could help others out there who are struggling with similar issues.

Sofia and her brother were abandoned by alcoholic parents in Russia when she was only three years old. These children were placed into an orphanage and lived there for the next four years of their lives. It is difficult to measure the impact of the foundational years of her life that were filled with uncertainty, violence, and abandonment. The orphanage was sterile and the children were not given love and affection. During this time, she endured physical abuse from some of the other unsupervised children. Sofia learned how to close her heart and stop feeling. Remember that survival strategies such as this can get someone through a legitimate crisis, but often leaves them emotionally closed-down long after the crisis is over.

Sofia and her brother were eventually adopted by some wonderful parents from the United States when she was seven years old. It was an ideal situation except for the fact that Sofia's heart was still closed. As she grew from childhood into adolescence, she found that she had a difficult time interacting and fitting in with others her age. She felt like an outcast by her peers, but found she was able to interact and relate with adults better. She carried these fears that her peers would never accept her and, unfortunately, this reinforced her belief and social skills that she was unloved and unwanted. The perception of being unlovable was deeply ingrained in her subconscious mind, even though she now actually had a supportive family that deeply loved her and contradicted her negative beliefs. But her family's love and concern alone was not enough to heal this gaping wound.

In Sofia's desperation to find love and value, she became addicted to meeting up with strangers from her dating apps. These relationships almost always ended with sexual encounters followed by abandonment. She became defiant against her parent's attempts to control this reckless behavior, and found her so-called "freedom" so intoxicating that she just couldn't, and wouldn't, give it up. The men she met told Sofia anything she wanted to hear in order to get sex from her. It felt dangerous, yet exciting and intoxicating to meet up with these men. Remember that she grew up with danger and abandonment as her constant companions, so this dynamic was part of Sofia's "normal." Her sexual encounters with strangers were Sofia's desperate attempt to fill her emotional void. As "fulfilling" as these relationships seemed while she was with these men, she found herself constantly abandoned by them afterwards. Ironically and sadly, these encounters reinforced her worthless narrative because these men always disappeared after they used her for their own gratification. Sofia also learned that she was actually not capable of feeling compassion. She had never learned how to care about others in her foundational years. As a young woman, she finally found a boyfriend who really loved her and was committed to her, but she sabotaged this relationship by cheating on him with strangers because she was ironically terrified that he, too, would abandon her if she committed to him. Strangely, his commitment to Sofia actually triggered her to act more irrationally. Love did not feel safe to her.

Before working with me, Sofia and her parents constantly fought over her reckless addiction. This contention drove her away from them. Sofia needed real healing. For her to find this healing, she needed to be willing to take a good hard look into her subconscious mind to see that her heart had closed.

Before Sofia had a true change of heart, she needed to be willing to acknowledge in herself the void and forgive her birth parents for abandoning her. She must acknowledge and release the fear and resentment she felt about her awful circumstances that obviously destroyed the foundation of her childhood. She needed to Let Go and Let God. Sofia chose to release the story and the heartbreak into the Lord's hands in hypnosis. The resentment and fear were literally taken away and replaced with a divine endowment of compassion. That compassion instantly replaced the darkness that once occupied precious real estate in her heart. Sofia was transformed by this process that she now considers divine healing which literally transformed her life and allows her to feel safe with love.

"A new heart also will I give you, and a new spirit will I put within you: and I will take away the stony heart out of your flesh, and I will give you an heart of flesh." (Ezekiel 36:26, KJV)

"And Jesus said unto the centurion, Go thy way; and as thou hast believed, so be it done unto thee. And his servant was healed in the selfsame hour." (Matthew 8:13, KJV)

You Complete Me!

Little Mikey's enabling is the yin to the martyr's yang. Likewise, Little Birdie's martyrdom is the yang to Little Mikey's yin. They both play a crucial role in keeping codependency alive and well.

Little Mikey learns that encouraging helplessness in others will keep them helpless. A kind gesture can be misguided and actually prolong Little Birdie's suffering. Little Mikey discovers a strength of character when confronting Little Birdie with accountability and challenging her to use her wings. He will require this newfound strength to thwart Little Birdie's ongoing attempts to discredit him if she refuses to change.

Little Birdie needs to be accountable to her own fears that prevent graceful flight. Both Little Birdie and Little Mikey have something they need to change and they need to do this independently from each other's choices. The nature of their relationship will improve dramatically when they are both living in integrity.

Passive Aggressive

Without breaking the Martyr Cycle, Little Mikey would remain under its spell until a crisis of faith occurs. The new narrative would likely be, "I'm sick and tired of being a good person! All I ever do is help others at my own expense. But I am so tired and miserable! What kind of God would do this to me after I have done so much to serve others?" It is not much of a stretch to see how Little Mikey could then also fall into the martyr's trap.

Boundaries And Consequences

The first step in repentance (or change) is to acknowledge the problem. Little Birdie would need to acknowledge that taking advantage of Little Mikey's good intentions is wrong and she shouldn't do it. Deep down she knows this but continues lying to herself to embellish the suffering narrative.

I assure you that Little Birdie will only be happy when she becomes independent and strong.

The most empowering belief that will help Little Mikey is to teach him that conflict is often necessary to disrupt codependency.

Both of the offenders need to change their perspectives, but their individual outcome needs to be independent from what the other one is willing to do.

Little Mikey needs to set some boundaries with some consequences for Little Birdie's best chance of changing. Even if Little Mikey has never done this before, it is now time to do it.

So Little Mikey will need to inform Little Birdie that he will no longer be feeding her, but he will continue encouraging her to jump and fly. They can remain friends only if Little Birdie stops the manipulation. And if Little Birdie does not comply, the consequence of Little Mikey withdrawing will be Little Birdie's doing. Not the other way around.

When you are setting boundaries, you have to also establish and communicate unwavering consequences. This is tough love. It is tough for both the martyr and the enabler but it is necessary to create lasting happiness.

Boundaries without consequences are nothing more than a head fake or an empty threat. And you can rest assured that the perpetrator will not honor the boundaries if the consequences aren't real. Once consequences are communicated and agreed upon, then the perpetrator needs to understand that he will be responsible for the outcome. Not the enabler.

In the case of a husband battering his wife, it is the wife who needs to lay down the boundaries and the consequences of her leaving permanently if he lays a finger on her. And when she leaves because he breaks this agreement, then he has only himself to blame. It is not her that has left him, but it is his choices and behavior that drove her from his life. His behavior is completely unacceptable regardless of his excuses or reasons. And this does not make the battered woman the villain. It makes her the hero. And hopefully, her boundaries with consequences will teach the abuser to get some help and really change.

To rise above dysfunction requires belief and courage to overcome peer pressure and self-doubt. This journey can feel scary, unfamiliar, and lonely at times, but the rewards exceed all expectations. The pull of destiny can be felt deeply in your heart once your mind has become quiet and surrenders to the great divine.

Just look up.

CHAPTER TEN

What If I Don't Deserve To Be Happy?

I want to share with you a little metaphor I wrote that demonstrates the principle of forgiving yourself even if the very ones you have injured refuse to forgive you.

The Lunker Of Kalamazoo

Jimmy was really excited to go on the big family fishing trip in pursuit of the Lunker of Kalamazoo. This fish had been spotted multiple times, and it had been rumored that it rivaled the size of a whale. And in the spirit of fairness, we have to acknowledge that some fish stories get a little exaggerated. Nonetheless, Jimmy's family had been meticulously planning this trip for an entire year and the time had finally arrived. Jimmy could hardly contain his excitement.

After arriving at Lake Kalamazoo, everyone quickly got their fishing lines into the water with hopes of catching the legendary Lunker. Jimmy was the last one to get his fishing line tied. After the final touches were made to his hook, Jimmy cast his fishing line out into the water. Unfortunately, in his exuberance and excitement, Jimmy accidentally cast his line directly over the top of all of his family's fishing lines that were already strategically placed out in the water.

"Oh no!" Jimmy cried out.

He had broken the golden rule of fishing. So he hurried and reeled in his line as fast as he could, but it was too late. Everyone else's fishing lines were already tangled up with Jimmy's line. He unwittingly reeled everyone's fishing lines onto shore in a giant, tangled mess.

Everyone was angry at Jimmy, and for good reason. They all stood around arguing and complaining about Jimmy's carelessness. Jimmy was so sad that he had ruined the entire day. He sat there dejectedly, looking at his feet while everyone complained and berated him. Of course, Jimmy accepted the punishment because he was a good person.

While Jimmy's family all stood around complaining, the Park Ranger happened upon the scene. He asked everyone what this ruckus was about. Jimmy simply replied, "I ruined their fishing day by tangling up their lines. It's all my fault!"

The Miracle Bridge

The Ranger asked Jimmy if he meant to do it. And Jimmy responded, "No, it was an accident, but it's still my fault because I'm a bad-casting fish face!"

And the Ranger said, "I have my knife here. All I need to do is cut your line, and we can get you back out on the water fishing again in no time at all."

However, Jimmy was reluctant to do this because everyone was so mad. The Ranger went on to explain to Jimmy that he had the right to cut his line free from the tangled mess he had created, and that each family member had the same opportunity to forgive Jimmy and cut their line free. Or they could stand around and complain about it all day. Everyone had a choice, but unfortunately, Jimmy's family chose to continue moaning and complaining.

With some coaxing, Jimmy finally decided to accept the Ranger's help. Jimmy couldn't quite put his finger on it, but there sure was something special about that Ranger. They quickly cut Jimmy's line while everyone else protested. The Ranger then quietly escorted Jimmy away from the angry anglers, and over to a hidden cove he called "the secret fishing hole." The ranger fixed up Jimmy's line with something he called secret bait and then showed Jimmy where to cast it into the water. With a little help and guidance from the Ranger, Jimmy's cast was perfect.

The Ranger winked at Jimmy and said in a hushed voice, "I think you'll like this fishing hole." Jimmy's attention was suddenly drawn to his fishing pole as it was nearly ripped out of his hands. Jimmy went on to catch the Lunker of Kalamazoo at the very moment his family stood in the background, arguing about their plight. It was a new record! Jimmy was featured on the evening news, and even had his picture and story put on the front page of the Kalamazoo Gazette. Jimmy was crowned as the new, undisputed Fishing King of Kalamazoo.

That Lunker of Kalamazoo was so large that it required Jimmy's entire family to hold it for the picture. Jimmy was the only one smiling in the photo.

"And he said unto them, Cast the net on the right side of the ship, and ye shall find. They cast therefore, and now they were not able to draw it for the multitude of fishes." (John 21:6, KJV)

The Savior's teachings require us to forgive others if we want forgiveness.

The Unmerciful Servant

21 "Then came Peter to him, and said, Lord, how oft shall my brother sin against me, and I forgive him? till seven times?

22 Jesus saith unto him, I say not unto thee, Until seven times: but, Until seventy times seven.

23 Therefore is the kingdom of heaven likened unto a certain king, which would take account of his servants.

24 And when he had begun to reckon, one was brought unto him, which owed him ten thousand talents.

25 But forasmuch as he had not to pay, his lord commanded him to be sold, and his wife, and children, and all that he had, and payment to be made.

26 The servant therefore fell down, and worshipped him, saying, Lord, have patience with me, and I will pay thee all.

27 Then the lord of that servant was moved with compassion, and loosed him, and forgave him the debt.

28 But the same servant went out, and found one of his fellowservants, which owed him an hundred pence: and he laid hands on him, and took him by the throat, saying, Pay me that thou owest.

29 And his fellowservant fell down at his feet, and besought him, saying, Have patience with me, and I will pay thee all.

30 And he would not: but went and cast him into prison, till he should pay the debt.

31 So when his fellowservants saw what was done, they were very sorry, and came and told unto their lord all that was done.

32 Then his lord, after that he had called him, said unto him, O thou wicked servant, I forgave thee all that debt, because thou desiredst me:

33 Shouldest not thou also have had compassion on thy fellowservant, even as I had pity on thee?"

34 And his lord was wroth, and delivered him to the tormentors, till he should pay all that was due unto him.

35 So likewise shall my heavenly Father do also unto you, if ye from your hearts forgive not every one his brother their trespasses." (Matthew 18:21-35, KJV)

You must give mercy to receive mercy.

I Am Not Worthy Of Being Forgiven

I encounter the belief of unworthiness *often* with genuine people who have good intentions. This narrative is surprisingly common with sincere people, but yet this belief of unworthiness is often the very obstacle that *prevents* a suffering soul from divine healing. Often we feel so guilty about something from our past that we actually reject forgiveness to prove we are sorry. This stalemate with God is our evidence and strategy that demonstrates accountability and integrity. From time to time, I will encounter a narcissist, who dwells on the opposite end of the spectrum. He is filled with blame instead of sorrow, and where accountability is nowhere to be found. But this chapter is directed to those souls who are truly sorry for their mistakes but have been unwilling or unable to forgive themselves.

Good people are willing to punish themselves endlessly if they believe this is the price demanded of them by God. Refusing to let go of this limiting belief will certainly prevent the suffering captive from hearing what the Lord is *actually* saying through the door.

Please don't interrupt me Lord, I am too busy punishing myself for you!

Guilt is a God-given gift to act as a compass to keep us on the path of integrity, but it is designed to be a temporary means to an end that is intended to lead us to higher ground. Shame is a tool used exclusively by Satan to trap us in perpetual unworthiness. There is a proper protocol of repentance endorsed by the Lord: we acknowledge our wrongdoing with admission and sorrow, make restitution if we can, and really change our hearts and behaviors with the Lord's divine help.

Am I Worthy Of Being Forgiven?

I use the term "false humility" to explain the oxymoron of someone refusing to forgive themselves because they deem themselves unworthy of being forgiven. You can compare this idea to a sick person feeling unworthy to go to a doctor.

"I'll go to the doctor *after* I make myself better."

The doctor is for sick people. The Savior clearly taught this principle:

"When Jesus heard it, he saith unto them, They that are whole have no need of the physician, but they that are sick: I came not to call the righteous, but sinners to repentance." (Mark 2:17, KJV)

I shared this scripture with my Client Brennan who then related to me a quote that simply must be stated here:

Me + More = God (No, No, No. You've got the cart before the horse!)
Me + God = More (Yes, Yes, Yes! The horse can now pull the cart!)

But What About Those Innocent Souls Who Punish Themselves for Something Out of Their Control?

Forgiveness is not just for sinners. In this chapter I am going to discuss a few tragic cases where good people refused to forgive themselves for horrible circumstances that were completely out of their control. These individuals were haunted by shame and regret, and refused to forgive themselves because they are good people. Remember, this standard, although honorable, is the very obstacle that guarantees ongoing suffering.

Meet Chris Smyres

Chris is a close friend of mine featured in the Foreword of this book. He approached me in 2017, desperately seeking help from a tragic case of PTSD and addiction. Chris had suffered deeply for 18 dreadful years. Over that time, he had tried many different therapists and programs to overcome the overwhelming effects of PTSD with absolutely zero success. Chris approached me after a failed attempt at suicide. Death seemed the only escape from nearly half a lifetime of living in a nightmare. He is a man of integrity who questioned his worthiness to be alive after an unthinkable tragedy when he was forced at gunpoint to take another innocent man's life.

Chris' story was a tragic case of being in the wrong place at the wrong time. As a 20 year-old man, Chris was driving to a night catering job and ended up taking a wrong turn that led to a dead-end. Chris pulled his car under a streetlight to check the map for directions to the catering event. After putting his car in park, the engine started shaking and cut out. Chris got out to look under the hood to get the car restarted. While looking over the engine, Chris was approached by two men who acted like they were going to give him a hand. After gaining his trust, they knocked him unconscious from behind and started beating him. After they had beaten Chris down, they dragged him into a nearby ravine along with another man they had also kidnapped. At gunpoint, Chris and this other abductee were forced to play a cruel game of Russian Roulette. These evil men were going to force an innocent man to kill another innocent man. Chris was the survivor of this horrible game.

There is really no adequate language to explain what went through Chris's mind throughout this entire nightmare. He explained how this twisted game went on for what felt like hours. He went through every thought and fear about dying each time the trigger was pulled. He just knew he was going to die. Finally, the gun went off in Chris' hand, and tragically killed the unfortunate stranger. Chris made a break from the men after the gun went off, narrowly escaping their gunfire. He ran from their sight and slipped deeper into the ravine. Chris laid hidden in the brush for hours before their taunts and jeers finally stopped during the darkness of night. Finally, after hours of hiding in the cold dark, he made a break for his car. Miraculously, he still had his car keys in his pocket and the car actually started on the first attempt. He managed to escape in his vehicle but was certain the gang was going to ambush him from behind again. Chris had to pull the car over multiple times to vomit while frantically finding his way back home. After a terrifying drive, he was able to somehow find his way home despite the horror and disorientation from the nightmare he had just endured.

That tragic night of terror destroyed many people's lives. The body of the victim was never recovered. Chris descended into the abyss of extreme PTSD and became recklessly addicted to alcohol as he tried to manage and dull the non-stop symptoms of terror and mistrust. Nothing could take his frantic mind off his feelings of worthlessness that constantly haunted him. He had an ever-present desire to die. Chris found us 18 years after that horrible night.

Chris and his dad made a call to my office after hearing about me from a hopeful relative. This is the call that was to transform all of our lives. Though skeptical and mostly hopeless, and after a recent failed attempt of suicide, Chris agreed to do a full program at our wellness center. A truly amazing thing happened the first day I sat down with Chris and his parents. I felt like Chris's mother should have a session with our audio-visual entrainment that takes people into deep meditation and hypnosis. She agreed. While she was in this session, she had a vision where she saw Chris standing at a podium speaking to a large group of people. When she finished her session, she had tears running down her face and explained what she had just witnessed. I knew instantly that this was a sign from God that Chris was going to get better. I felt a pure conduit of light pour through me. It bolstered my faith, and I simply knew God was part of this.

After Chris's many failed attempts with previous programs and therapists, he finally found complete relief from the PTSD that had dominated his life. In order for Chris to overcome the PTSD, we needed to replace his shame and unworthiness with gratitude and a meaningful purpose. He had to be willing to forgive himself. Chris reluctantly accepted a new spiritual quest to let go of the unchangeable past and embrace a new future that included a mission to move forward and help others. With some deep hypnosis, we not only re-encoded Chris's moments of trauma, but created within his heart permission to forgive himself so he could dedicate his life to helping others who had suffered as he had. It was the perfect way to honor the other fallen victim and make that terrible loss meaningful.

It was during the very last hypnosis session of Chris's program that I finally took him back to that horrific event to rescue him from the past. He was shocked and delighted to discover that he was not alone at the scene of that tragedy. Instead, Chris was greeted by multiple aspects of his soul that were waiting to embrace him. In that electric moment of Chris meeting his literal dream team, he exclaimed with tears of gratitude, "I'm not alone! I was NEVER alone!" He was overwhelmed with peace as he grasped to take in the scene before him. Right in front of his eyes stood a better "version of Chris" waiting to merge with him. This was his mighty, "future-self." Also waiting to join Chris was a mysterious but inspirational character that he named "The Universe Man." Chris named him this because he has the shape of a man but also somehow reflected the depth of the universe. Universe Man was there to join the cause! When our hypnosis session concluded, we spoke of Universe Man and simply felt that he was the very man who had died on that tragic evening many years ago. We understood that he was coming to Chris as a partner in a combined mission of hope. Together, Universe Man and Chris would move forward and help many others in this world who had been through similar trauma. It made complete and perfect sense that this union was necessary to allow Chris permission to forgive himself and rise to the occasion. Chris was fully committed to the cause of using this tragedy as a stepping stone to help himself and others rise above hopeless despair. This was a miracle! And it was happening to Chris right in front of our eyes.

There, in that sacred hypnosis session, Chris partnered up with *Universe Man* on a mission to go out and change the world, one person at a time! Chris found permission within himself to climb from the depths of reckless disregard and unforgiveness onto the platform of public speaking to educate the world about hope after tragedy. Chris now educates others on the real dangers of PTSD, including his own success story of escaping the daily nightmares and constant dysfunction that kept him a prisoner for over 18 years until his triumphant ascent out of the abyss.

Chris remained completely symptom-free from PTSD for 15 straight months and during that time spoke to multiple groups of mental health professionals and law enforcement, educating them on the unpredictable nature of people who are suffering under the oppression of PTSD. After 15 months of independence, however, Chris had a few drinking setbacks that sent his mind spiraling back to that old poisoned perspective of shame and unworthiness. His PTSD returned with a vengeance to accompany his newly fueled "worthless" narrative. The reality is, healing is as permanent as you are willing to make it. Before this season of setback, Chris' nightmares were gone, the shaking was gone, and the effects of alcoholism were gone. He had completely taken himself out of the unspeakable nightmare and managed to stay in that powerful place of purpose that fueled his new mission of hope.

After a few months of setbacks, Chris's poor decisions led him back into some of those old negative thought patterns that are easy to recreate when you are locked back inside of the bottle. His PTSD was back in full force. His permanent recovery is completely dependent upon his staying passionate about his mission of hope. Chris's decision to start drinking again illustrates the reality of ongoing commitment and lifestyle choices to maintain healing. Perhaps this is no different than reckless driving after repairing your car in the body shop. Although shiny and new again, the driver can not evade the consequences of reckless driving if he chooses to continue old destructive patterns. Chris found complete healing through the protocols that we used with him and it absolutely transformed not only his life, but the life of everyone who knows and loves him, including me. But moving forward, it is Chris *alone* who will decide his fate as he carries a significant torch in this great war of good versus evil. He has combined his voice with mine, to bring hope back on top where it belongs!

A few months after Chris's return to chaos, I was able to work with him again for a few hypnosis sessions to remove that recurring story of worthlessness. And it worked, again! It really is amazing to see someone unwilling to receive forgiveness because of their sorrow for what has happened in the past. But this outdated version of integrity was going to destroy his life if he wasn't willing to Let Go and Let God take it. I would also like to point out that Universe Man showed up in our hypnosis sessions to remind Chris to let go of the past baggage once and for all so they could move forward in their new mission.

One of the triggers that sent Chris back into the abyss was his attempt to write a book. Thinking about finding the family of Universe Man who lost their son, brother, and friend. Chris's father informed him after he had recovered from PTSD that he had preserved the bloody shirt from that horrible night. Chris was recently approached by a judge who is willing to raise the money to do DNA tests so that they might locate the family. I am looking forward to personally accompanying Chris while meeting with this family once they are found. Chris will be able to bring this poor family closure to the questions they have been asking for 20 years.

I fully expect Chris to be involved with me at future speaking events where we will be joining our voices together to create some visibility of miraculous possibilities. I would like to share the words of Chris's mother after she got him back.

Here are her words:

My son Chris suffered from severe PTSD and alcohol abuse because of a terrible incident that happened to him. He suffered 18 years of hell. He went on non-stop drinking binges for a week at a time, would get himself extremely sick, sober up, and do it again. He couldn't stay sober for more than a month unless he was in rehab or jail. He also went to many different therapists. We thought we found someone who could help him, a Vietnam vet that had suffered from PTSD. On his website, he claimed he really knew what PTSD sufferers went through and he really "got it." I believe he did, but he didn't have a way to cure Chris's suffering and self-abuse. Nothing worked.

One night, we got a call from our son telling us he couldn't take it anymore and he was going to kill himself, and he hung up the phone. You can imagine my panic at that thought. I didn't know what to do or where to turn. Out of the blue, I got a phone call from a relative telling us about Mike's Wellness Center. My husband called and talked to Mike. He was skeptical that this would work for Chris because up to this point, nothing else had worked. We knew that he had to change his way of thinking about himself or the result would be a failure, just like the many attempts to recover in the past.

The result of Mike Simpson working with Chris is nothing short of a miracle. It seems almost impossible, but Chris is truly better. He does not have any guilt about what happened to him and looks at the past 18 years as a nightmare he woke up from. The PTSD and alcohol abuse is gone and I have my son back. Mike is so gifted and skilled at what he did that it is beyond words to explain. He truly is a miracle worker.

What Mike Simpson does actually works! If you know someone who is suffering from severe PTSD or addiction you are probably desperate for help like we were. You need to send them to Mike's wellness center. It will be the best money you ever spent.

Just Look Up

I would like to add my own words to Chris's mother's words. What I do works if *you* work. Life requires commitment! And it is difficult to stay on course if you are paddling without a destination in mind. Just floating is a dangerous place to find yourself. Please use this story of tragedy to rekindle your own commitment to align yourself with the true principles of healing, and engage yourself in a meaningful and important cause.

Don't be surprised to see me speaking at public events in the future with Chris by my side. This message is far bigger than any one of us. My mission will continue, and I will value and cherish my time and experience with Chris and use his inspirational story to inspire as many people as we can to "Just Look Up!" I pray daily for Universe Man and his family. And I dedicate his tragic loss and Chris's amazing transformation to my mission to change the world one person at a time! Won't you join me? Go to **MikeSimpson.live** to learn more about the community we are building.

"The only thing necessary for the triumph of evil is for good men to do nothing."

— Edmund Burke

Meet Phil

Back when I was in the 6th grade my family moved to a new town. It was hard to move away from all of my friends. When I got to this new area, I quickly became friends with Phil. He was a natural-born daredevil that could pull off any stunt without a hitch. It was nice to find a good friend in him because he was as tough as nails, and it was nice to have someone by my side to help me transition into a new school.

Just before I moved into Phil's neighborhood the unthinkable happened — while helping his older brother Ronnie on his paper route, Phil witnessed his idol, big brother, and best friend, struck and killed by a car. A little more insight into the relationship between Phil and his older brother Ronnie — Phil was always the little 'Dennis the Menace" type. He was mischievous and curious about everything. This curiosity led him into doing things that would get him into trouble and, many times, into physical danger. Ronnie was always the responsible and reliable brother, pretty much the polar opposite of his little brother, Phil. Ronnie had his hands full looking out for Phil and trying his best to keep his little brother out of trouble. But, he did a very good job. The two brothers were pretty much inseparable. They did everything together, even sharing the same bedroom and sleeping in the same bed together as they were growing up.

My moving into Phil's neighborhood soon after this terrible accident, with both of us needing friendship, led us to become like brothers. We were always together. Phil and I went through many tough times supporting each other. He was even there for me when I went through my divorce.

Here we are many years later and still brothers. After I had been doing hypnosis for a few years, I welcomed Phil into my office to do a session with me. It turned out to be profoundly beautiful... and fitting. In a way, this miraculous transformation of Phil's life, with my help, seemed like divine providence — bookends of a sort. On one end, I was dropped into his life by God right after Ronnie's tragic death, and I benefited so richly from Phil's friendship. On the other end, it would be me who got the prompting to step in and help Phil release the trauma that had haunted him for the better part of 40 years. Phil had always felt deeply guilty ever since that frigid February evening when he had crossed the highway like frogger without hesitation or thought. Once on the other side of the highway, Phil looked back to see Ronnie taking too long, cautious as always, looking for a safe opportunity to cross the highway during rush hour. Phil, freezing and impatient, yelled back to Ronnie, "Hurry up!" Since Ronnie's death, Phil has always carried a profound guilt about yelling at his brother to hurry up. Phil would go into a deep depression in the early part of every February during the very month he witnessed that tragic event as an 11 year-old boy. Remember, time does not exist in the subconscious mind. The traumatic association to the month of February was burned deeply into Phil's subconscious and he always sank deeply into depression during that time of year.

But with Phil in my office, we were going to change his life and transform February. We were going to go in and set the record straight.

When I took Phil into hypnosis, we went back to that horrible scene of the accident. There at that tragic site, in the middle of the road, we found Phil as an 11 year-old boy, standing terrified and *unwilling to leave his brother!* There he was, a horrified and suffering 11 year-old boy trying to wrap his head around the scene of losing his older brother, his hero, his best friend. Phil absolutely refused to leave Ronnie behind. We had the adult Phil go embrace little Phil standing on that road. Big Phil sobbed and held little Phil. We told little Phil we had come to bring him home to the present. And then Ronnie arrived to join in our conversation. Yes, Ronnie, as an adult spirit was deeply concerned about his little brother holding onto all the guilt and shame he had been valiantly harboring for the better part of his life. Phil was subconsciously unwilling to let go of that guilt because it seemed to be the only thing he had left of Ronnie to cling onto. But Ronnie wasn't going to have any of this. Phil reunited with Ronnie right there in that experience, and Ronnie begged him to move forward and let go of guilt and shame. Ronnie did not want to be remembered in that way. And in that magical reunion, Phil honored his brother's request and finally let go. From that moment forward, any thought of Ronnie was filled with peace and love and gratitude. Ronnie had now been re-encoded into Phil's mind exactly the way he wanted to be remembered. This gave Phil permission to rise above the old patterns and embrace a new and higher place of consciousness. Phil and Ronnie were now connected the way it was always meant to be. We just needed to go back and rescue little Phil from the past. Now little Phil travels with big Phil and he is like a kid again, back to those crazy stunts and amazing accomplishments.

I really appreciate Phil's willingness to share this story because it is deeply inspiring and demonstrates the very reason I wanted to write this book in the first place. Here are Phil's own words explaining what he noticed when he was finally able to let go of that old trauma which was buried deep in his soul...

In Phil's Own Words:

The guilt I felt for so many years after my brother was struck and killed by a car on a cold February night was always a heavy burden, and weighed on my heart and soul. I can remember very vividly the events, feelings, situations, and the people of that night... It's almost haunting. I always felt like it was my fault he was killed. I had never talked to anyone about what I yelled at my brother that night after I had so haphazardly crossed the highway first. My guilt and shame were always too daunting to share with anyone. I kept it to myself and merely pushed it down inside of me. I always thought it would fade away with time. It never did.

When I went to Mike for help, it was a time when I felt desperate and broken after a divorce. All through my life it seems Mike was the person I went to for help and insight. He seemed to have a special gift of perspective and reason. As I reflect back on my life, Mike was my replacement "Ronnie," that rock that only a brother/best friend can be. The thing I remember most and will never forget is when Mike carefully took me into a place of tranquility and peace. I do not remember how we arrived at the scene of the night my brother was killed, but I was there as my 11-year-old self again. I found myself running out in the middle of the street where my brother lay unconscious and broken. He had an enormous laceration on the underside of his face that I couldn't see at the time. However, a pool of blood started flowing from it and I remember it growing rapidly and pooling up on the pavement. I was terrified and scared. I was yelling, "I'm sorry… please wake up! Please don't die!" A man rushed to us and started what seemed to be examining my brother. I was yelling, "He's my brother" over and over. The man in a very calm, concerning, stern voice told me to calm down and said, "Everything will be alright." I don't remember how long I was in panic at my brother's side. It seems like a few people gathered around to see if they could help, and I remember someone pulling me away up off my knees and talking to me. I don't know who the person was or if the person was a man or a woman. However, as I was under hypnosis, this time I turned around and looked at the person… It was Ronnie. He had warmth in his eyes and a concerned smile on his face, a kind of a tight-lipped smile. At this moment, I was instantly enveloped in what seemed to be his loving warmth and care, and I was no longer worried. It seemed as if everything that was happening so tragically at that moment on the road… faded away. I remember him putting his hands gently on my shoulders, and softly, as a loving parent would do, looking into my eyes. He was communicating with me but his mouth wasn't moving. I could hear him telling me to, "Let it go… I am always with you." He eased my heart and mind by helping me to understand that I did not lose him and he did not lose me. Furthermore, it was very important to him that I know that his death wasn't my fault. As soon as he realized I knew that… he was gone. As I woke up out of hypnosis I was sobbing, not from sadness, but from the overwhelming love I had just experienced being in the presence of my brother again, and having received his reassurance of not being at fault for his mortal death.

February is no longer a month of regret and shame. It is now the month of deep reflection of Ronnie. It is now his month. I make a greater effort to ponder the good and great memories I have of the short 11 years I was blessed to have with my best friend, my role model, my protector, my idol, but most importantly, my brother.

My friendship with Mike throughout my life has been much, much more than that. He is my brother. He always has love for me and those around him. Mike and I have countless experiences and memories together, both good and bad. Thank goodness mostly good. All through our adolescent years we were inseparable. Now, as I reflect on our past together, Mike has always had a special kind of insight and discernment. He was never shallow. He has always been a deep thinker and a man of reason. He never ceases to amaze me. I have watched and admired him as he has worked diligently over time to become an incredible instrument in God's hand. In retrospect, it is clear to me the step-by-step growth he has been blessed with is because of his spiritual diligence to God's plan and his relationship with Him. He has always taken great advantage of the opportunities and gifts offered him. Whether it was teaching himself to play the piano and guitar by ear, or writing beautifully heartfelt and meaningful music. It is easy for me to see that every little thing he has learned, every gift he has received over time has accumulated for the blessing, betterment, and healing of those in need of his gift. Mike is worthy of such. There are many times when he had taught me something in the scriptures or merely something about life in general, and I wouldn't realize it until years later when the deeper meaning of what he was teaching me came to light. I would have one of those enlightening "Aha" moments when I would say to myself... Daaaang, that's what he meant! I could go on and on about Mike. For me, it all just boils down to... I am greatly blessed to be his friend/brother and I love him with all my heart. Anyone who has any kind of contact with Mike will be better somehow... some way. I don't doubt it in the least.

— **Phil Cook**

Phil's Request

Phil convinced me that this book would not be complete without including the following story I wrote over 30 years ago. This story is dedicated to Chris, Phil, and everyone else out there who has the desire to make the transformation to heal and rise above tragedy.

Paddy The Mud-wallowing Slug

Once upon a time, there was a slug named Paddy who lived in the bottom of a muddy old pond. He was happy enough, at least at first. He had a lot of friends, a nice cool, muddy pond bottom, and all of the little critters he could ever possibly eat. But as time went on, Paddy started feeling deep stirrings he couldn't quite understand. He was confused because occasionally one of the other slugs would make its way to the reeds in the bottom of the pond and climb up and away, never again to return. These outcasts were always ridiculed as they climbed. "Why would they leave such a beautiful muddy bottom?" he often thought.

Finally, Paddy gathered his friends together and asked them what they thought of those slugs that had left. All of Paddy's friends started mocking and teasing him in unison. "Obviously, only the rejects want to leave this paradise!" one friend taunted. But when Paddy didn't laugh, they all became concerned. Mugsy, the ring leader, then spoke for the group. "Look, we've been trying to mind our own business but we've all noticed you acting a little strange. Everyone is talking and we want to keep you from making a huge mistake. Everyone will disown you if you keep talking this nonsense."

That night Paddy went on a private wallow to ponder and further explore the uncommon yearnings of his heart. After a long night of soul-searching, Paddy joined together with his friends and announced that he had made up his mind and he was going to make the climb. He needed to know why no one ever came back. The mud-crawler gang reacted exactly as he had expected, but Paddy was determined. Paddy promised them, "I will return to tell you what is up there."

Paddy went to the reeds and started climbing. He could hear some of his fellows jeering and teasing as he climbed slowly out of their sight. "Paddy is grimy, Paddy is slimy!" He ignored them and hastened his climb.

Paddy climbed and climbed. As he moved higher, the water was strangely becoming clear and blue. It was so peaceful. He could also see far into the distance with such clarity! It was mesmerizing. He stopped to muse over the beautiful scene when suddenly he saw a dark shadow from the corner of his eye. And just in the nick of time, he was able to narrowly escape the mouth of a giant catfish! It was a close call! Too close! He started climbing back down the reed in pure terror thinking perhaps no one ever returned because that catfish ate all of them. But, after he calmed down, Paddy stopped descending and decided to climb higher in spite of the danger of the clear water and the hungry fish. Paddy determined to climb more slowly, and very carefully.

Paddy started feeling extremely nervous and tired. He rested a while, clinging to the reed. He didn't know how long he had rested, but thought he should continue upward. His skin started to burn a little as instinct pushed him yet higher and he pulled himself from the water. "What was that bright light above?" he thought. "Am I dying?" All of a sudden he felt like his skin was being torn from his body. Paddy pulled himself higher and felt a surge of warm light burst over him as he instinctively lifted above the pond with his new... what were these? Wings! Paddy looked at his reflection in the water and was amazed at what he saw looking back at him. "Who is that? *What* is that? *Is that me?*" Paddy was looking into the eyes of a newborn dragonfly. He had just made the transition from Paddy the mud-wallowing slug into Paddy the sun-loving dragonfly! He lifted up into graceful flight in the golden sunlight. There are no words in the slug language that could explain his joy. Those deep stirrings had driven him to this beautiful destiny.

After Paddy had completed his first flight, he gracefully landed back on the very reed of his transformation. Paddy then remembered the promise he had made to return to tell his friends what was up above. So with determination and reluctance, he dived into the water with the intent to descend back to the murky bottom. But something was very wrong. He couldn't get past the surface. He tried over and over but simply floated on the warm water until he had to quickly leap into the air to escape the shadow of that same sinister catfish! "That was close!"

Paddy would never return to the bottom again. Even if he could, the slugs would not recognize or accept him. This was his new home. The pond that once *retained* him, now *refrained* him.

Paddy learned the great lesson that day why no slug had ever returned from climbing the reeds. And now before Paddy's eyes there appeared a greeting party of dragonflies in all their glory. Here were the leaders who had led the way.

To know what was above the murky bottom, the slugs would have to listen to their own deep yearnings, overcome their own fear and complacency, and make the climb for themselves. But as for Paddy, he had discovered heaven on Earth.

"He is not here for He is risen." (Matthew 28:6, KJV)

CHAPTER ELEVEN

The Blended Family

I would like to share some insights and a true story about divorce and blended families with the hope that it will help others struggling with similar issues. The experience from my divorce and blending my new family have increased my understanding of the deeper nuances of human dynamics. My trials have provided me a dark foundational canvas upon which the Lord would paint a radiant and colorful masterpiece of understanding and healing.

"For in much wisdom [is] much grief: and he that increaseth knowledge increaseth sorrow." (Ecclesiastes 1:18, KJV)

"Happy is the man who finds wisdom, and the man who gains understanding." (Proverbs 3:13, KJV)

I have worked hard to learn and apply healing principles outlined in this book to allow the Lord to lift me above some of my own weaknesses and struggles.

"Cast thy burden upon the Lord, and he shall sustain thee: He shall never suffer the righteous to be moved." (Psalm 55:22, KJV)

Back When I Was Yellow

In my freshman year of college, I enjoyed a psychology class where I learned some interesting concepts about the Color Code. I was fascinated. I learned back then that my personality was fun and easy-going. My color was mostly yellow.

A few years later, however, when I found myself in a failing marriage, the yellow exterior seemed to fade into a dingy gray. We can learn a lot about ourselves when confronted with difficult circumstances, whether in or out of our control.

Pain Is Inevitable, Misery Is Optional

Basically, when the press is being applied, we get the exciting opportunity to discover character flaws that are buried beneath the surface.

Can We Enjoy A Little Heavy Mettle?

met·tle

noun

A person's ability to cope well with difficulties or to face a demanding situation in a spirited and resilient way.

It's Time To Test Your Mettle

Trials and difficult circumstances offer the honest truth-seeker the opportunity to recognize holes in our own character. Each of us have character flaws buried beneath the shiny surface we present to the world. But trials and great suffering do not guarantee we will become better. Grandma's wisdom comes through again:

Life Can Make You Better Or
Life Can Make You Bitter
I or E, You decide

In the final chapter of this book, I share a metaphor I wrote called "Eagles Gathering" that demonstrates what can happen when we face the stormy seas of life with God's help. I hope you will take the time to really study through the metaphor, and savor some of the hard-fought wisdom I was able to glean from some tough years.

When The Going Gets Tough, The Tough Get Going!

Yeah, I know. This saying used to irritate me, too, when my dad would say it to me as a kid. I always knew this meant he was going to ask me to do something hard. But dang it if he wasn't right. He was always right! Tough circumstances offer each of us an opportunity to take a deeper look at our own character. Hindsight provides a clearer perspective and wisdom we often lack when we are in the furnace of affliction. But remember, you cannot have solid gold without this furnace melting it into a liquid, allowing the dross to float to the top and be removed by the Savior. God sent us here to leave better than we came. This can only happen with His divine, and sometimes painful, help.

We all get hurt by others. But ultimately, each of us must decide for ourselves if we want to get back up and dust ourselves off or lie down and quit.

If You Have Quit, Then It Is Time to Un-quit

Wow, this is getting heavy. Let's take a little fishing break.

Two Lunkers

The summer after my senior year in high school, I went on a trip to Lake Powell with my best friend's family. On that trip, I was standing by the shore with my friend's little brother, Mark. I was teaching Mark some of the finer points of fishing after we found a little piece of twine connected to a swivel. I told Mark that if we put a slice of a pickle on a swivel and dropped it into the water we would surely catch a fish. Mark looked at me in disbelief and asked me if I was serious. I said, "Of course I'm serious!" And of course I wasn't. I was just pulling his leg. So we went ahead and loaded up the pickle and dropped it in about four inches of water. And honest to goodness, as soon as the pickle hit the water, a giant catfish shot out and grabbed it! And we literally pulled the fish out of the water. I couldn't believe it! Mark's reaction was priceless.

He looked at me as if I was some type of fishing god. In reality, I wasn't much of a fisherman at all but more of a jokester.

In any case, the point I would like to firmly establish here is this: catching that catfish was about as likely as me catching my wife, Diana.

I have been questioned by every friend and person I know, trying to figure out how she ended up with me. I'm just going to say here that I loaded up a pickle on a swivel and caught a lunker! Twice!

Consider the Children

I have not only been through a divorce myself, but I have also counseled with countless people who were victims of divorce. Most of these victims were children facing extreme turbulence and uncertainty.

"Whosoever therefore shall humble himself as this little child, the same is greatest in the kingdom of heaven. And whoso shall receive one such little child in my name receiveth me." (Matthew 18:4-5, KJV)

But whoso shall offend one of these little ones which believe in me, it were better for him that a millstone were hanged about his neck, and that he were drowned in the depth of the sea." (Matthew 18:6, KJV)

Divorce can be devastating for children, especially when guilty parents use them as pawns in their games of revenge. Children suffer and pay the price for their parents' blind justifications and dysfunctions. I've seen far too many cases where good and decent parents turned into perpetrators as soon as their children began to be raised by someone other than themselves.

As already stated, our character flaws will not be visible to ourselves without some serious upheaval. Perhaps the dynamite that blows open the mine is necessary to penetrate deeper towards the gold. But the price for gold requires struggle and honest effort. We must sometimes hammer, chisel, and remove the heavy stones of our deeply buried flaws. Most of these stones are far too heavy for a human to carry without the Lord's strength.

Meet Jacob

I worked with a teenage boy named Jacob, who was deeply angry and suicidal. We dug deeply into his conflict about watching his parents divorce after his mother's infidelity devastated the family. Jacob's father eventually remarried another woman who had children from her previous marriage. Jacob was angry at his mother and living with his father at the time of his remarriage. Conflict and contention with Jacob's new blended family ensued immediately after the marriage. I would like to acknowledge that Jacob was already wounded and displaced from the divorce. This is also true for his new step-siblings that now lived with him.

There was something deeply sinister happening in Jacob's new family that caught Jacob unfairly in the crosshairs of a brutal revenge campaign from his step-mother's ex-husband. To add insult to injury, Jacob was being blamed by his stepmother for all of the contention. At the height of this family blending turmoil, Jacob was devastated when his new older step-brother severely beat him. Jacob's stepmother naturally blamed him for the fight.

Broken and hopeless, Jacob reluctantly moved back in with his mother. How was any of this fair? It wasn't. What had Jacob done to deserve such treatment and instability? Nothing. It was pure injustice.

Jacob was now estranged from his loving father and felt replaced and demonized by his step-family. Jacob started seriously entertaining suicide. It was a real and constant threat to his life. And his father was so busy officiating the contention that he was oblivious to Jacob's plight.

Jacob's own parents were divorced because of his mother's infidelity, and now his dad was in a different family that mistreated and rejected him. And Jacob hadn't yet learned about that diabolical campaign being run by his step-mother's ex-husband. It was after this season of upheaval that Jacob found me. There was much work to do to get him off of the slippery slope of suicidal ideation.

One day after a powerful and healing hypnosis session with Jacob, I asked him to bring his father in for a meeting to convey our progress. This conversation yielded devastating new information. Jacob's father admitted to Jacob and me that he had recently learned his wife's ex-husband had actually encouraged and rewarded his children to maliciously cause contention with Jacob. It was an evil campaign of revenge. You read this right. That man was rewarding his children to create contention and chaos in his ex-wife's new family.

These step-kids were constantly cruel to Jacob and received their father's approval in return. And this evil campaign was bringing satisfaction to the ex-husband, who wanted revenge.

It is absolutely heartbreaking to see how an adult is capable of such vindictive behavior. Jacob had a divine healing encounter in hypnosis once he was willing to release his *legitimate* resentment. His decision to forgive everyone who had injured him was hard work. Jacob's miraculous breakthrough required divine help from the Lord because this boulder in his mine of discovery was far too big for him to manage.

Jacob's step-mother's ex-husband eventually did confess and apologize to his ex-wife. But the damage he inflicted nearly ended Jacob's life in suicide. It is unthinkable that a jaded parent can be so blinded and justified by rage that someone else's life is nearly extinguished. Unthinkable. Horrible. Preventable.

"Hey, sorry about that."

Friend, if you or anyone you know is going through an ugly divorce then please have the parents read this story!

With any campaign of revenge, whether justified or not, there will always be innocent children devastated. Please use these true stories as incentive to rise above the dark influences that have injured you.

Jacob, I'm so proud of you for having the courage to forgive and heal to share your story with others. Your courage will change someone's life out there. It certainly changed mine! Thank you.

Full Disclosure

Was I a perfect father and stepfather to my children? Is my relationship perfect with my children? Definitely not. But these principles of awareness and forgiveness play a huge role in putting the mistakes of our past behind us and in building the bridge to peace and harmony. Although this bridge is real and tangible, it cannot help us if we don't cross it with our own free will, accountability, faith, and humility.

The Past is Behind Behind Me, It's Gone

The Blender

Can someone please tell me who came up with the term "blended family?" I love smoothies as much as the next guy, but this friendly term seems to omit the part where the blender is decimating everything you just dumped into it.

When that power button gets pushed, there is an immediate ear-piercing, terrifying shriek as everything gets chopped into oblivion and sprayed all over the kitchen ceiling. "Why me Lord? Where did you hide my lid?" Obviously, this is not the right question to ask. Instead, you should be asking Him, "Where did I put my lid?" If you direct this question to God, He will be happy to remind you where you left it, and might even help you clean up the mess.

What If I Won't Forgive Others Because They Aren't Sorry?

What if the person who hurt me is not sorry or won't be accountable? I have found this reality to be far too prevalent. However, why would we carry the poison of someone else's choices inside of our own heart? The Lord can only remove this poison if we let go.

What If They Won't Forgive Me?

What if someone I have injured rejects my apology and attempt at restitution? Would it then be my responsibility to *unforgive* myself to appease their grievance? Well, the answer to this question falls back to the Lunker of Kalamazoo story from Chapter 10. If I want the prize, I must accept the Ranger's help and get that fishing line back into the water, even if the others protest. At the end of the day, forgiveness of others and of self remains squarely my own responsibility. It takes courage to change and move forward, especially if those from our past refuse to forgive us. When we leave this world, it is the Lord's opinion that matters most. So let us focus on what we can control today, and go forward with faith and accountability. It is never too late to change. This path that we have chosen to walk together has no room for resentment. There is too much good to do!

For those of you who have chosen to change and forgive yourselves, but still suffer persecution from the ones you have injured, I share this poem:

The I Of The Storm

O They Think They Do Serve Him
As They Rail Like Fierce Wind
Yet Their Outcast, You See
Are God's Chosen, Within

— Mike Simpson

You must release your own mistakes and also the mistakes of those who have injured you before you will be able to cross The Miracle Bridge. It is impossible to be in the present if *"the fear of what if"* leaves you obsessing about the past or the future. Jacob had to let go. I had to let go. You have to let go.

The Fear of What If Will Ruin What Is
God's Gift is The Present

CHAPTER TWELVE

My Own Buried Pain

One day, after 12 hours of advanced hypnosis regression training, I asked Diana to guide me in hypnosis so I could practice a newly learned technique. This was the deepest hypnosis session I have ever experienced. While in hypnosis, I went into a visionary state where I was able to acknowledge some extensive emotional wounds from my past that were deeply hidden from my conscious mind.

I saw thousands of large hooks buried into my ribs. These sharp hooks were attached to high-tension cables which were attached to the hands of the people who had injured me throughout my life. And yes, each of these hooks represented the pain I had suffered at their hands. Each hook was a separate incident. These hooks were a reflection from deep within and highlighted very real resentment and pain I was unknowingly harboring. This particular darkness was tied to the cruel choices made by others who deeply injured me throughout my lifetime. I was honestly stunned to witness the mountain of injustice that had accumulated. I also noticed I had a pitchfork stabbed into my back and a big crowbar buried into my collarbone. These large weapons represented two significant incidents of betrayal from loved ones.

In awe, I explained to Diana what I was witnessing. She asked if I could see who had injured me. In the background, a sea of blurry faces faded into view. Then in answer to Diana's question, each face systematically floated forward in a single file as an associated hook illuminated to match it. Each face alternated to my left and right. It was surreal and absolutely unintentional and unrehearsed. I was now officially out of denial about harboring resentment.

Diana suggested I go ahead and remove the hooks. I gasped — if she could only see what I was experiencing! I half-heartedly tugged at a single hook and had my suspicion confirmed. It didn't budge. It was cemented into my rib. These hooks had large barbs on them to prevent them from coming out. I didn't realize the Devil was a hook designer! But maybe there was a smaller hook somewhere?

I searched until I found what appeared to be a small, innocuous hook that perhaps I could remove. Nope. I knew exactly who this "small" hook belonged to when I touched it. I went ahead and tried to pull it out, and it lacerated my hand. "Ouch!" Then I pulled at it with my other hand, and it sliced me again. It really hurt! The tension on this "small" hook was so tight that it was impossible for me to detach it. This hook caused the deepest pain I confronted in the experience. In fact, this "tiny little hook" turned out to be prophetic. It was connected to a person who had used and manipulated me through a major portion of my life. As I stated earlier in the book, it is difficult to forgive those who aren't sorry.

These hooks weren't going anywhere by the strength of my own hands. I told Diana that the only way these hooks would come out was if the Lord took them. I instantly recognized that the Lord was standing in the background, observing patiently. I knew He could and would remove these hooks *only* if I asked Him, *but* I had to ask sincerely. So then, Diana suggested (as any good wife would), "Oh good. Then go ahead and have Him pull them out."

At this juncture, I encountered my own stubborn, tremendous resistance. It was like feeling the brakes on a car screech me to a halt. There was *no way* I was going to let Him take those hooks out!

I could see now from the inside of my subconscious mind that I was unwilling to relinquish these hooks because they were proof and validation of the unfair suffering that I endured throughout my life. The evidence was squarely in front of me, and it was significant. But I started wrestling with the possibility of letting them go. Like any good hypnotist would do, I asked myself, "Do I want to hold on to pain to protect me from pain?"

Yes, I was manipulating myself, but certainly for the better.

I started to feel like a bit of a hypocrite. You see, I had been counseling people for years to let go of that injustice, and now here I was facing my own personal collection and I was completely unwilling to let go. Somehow, choosing to let go of those hooks felt like I was condoning what others had maliciously done to hurt me. Furthermore, it felt like I was setting myself up to be seriously hurt again and again.

The perceived benefit of my buried hooks was to make me a little tougher, a little more resilient, and less inclined to let people control, manipulate, and intimidate me. Reluctantly, I came to the enlightened understanding that this treasure was still darkness.

Ugh. At that moment, I Let Go and Let God take the hooks. I simply exhaled and declared, "Take it!"

Instant Noodles Gone with a Slurp

Instantly before me, I saw those hooks turn into soggy spaghetti noodles. Faster than I could blink, they were sucked out of me in the most hilarious and unpredictable manner. It felt like being on a roller coaster where you lose your breath.

I laughed out loud.

Are you kidding me?

No joke, the Lord was totally messing with me. Don't get me wrong, He was cleansing me, but He thought it would be clever to do this hook removal in an unpredictable way that would tickle my funny bone. It worked, and I love that about Him! I love that He is joyful and has a sense of humor! Those hooks leaving my body literally looked like wet noodles getting slurped from a bowl. Afterwards, there was nothing but gaping holes throughout my rib cage. I apologize in advance for the pun: *Had I become holy?* I couldn't resist. At the end of this experience, I watched swirling light filling in and healing all of my old hook wounds. The Lord was exchanging my darkness with His charity. And remember what Paul taught, "If I have not charity, I am nothing."

Another amazing effect from my spiritual liposuction was the instant relief I felt as these hooks were removed. After gaining my composure, I told Diana that it felt like my blood pressure had just dropped significantly. Again, I not only witnessed these hooks being removed in real-time, but I also *felt* them leave. I tangibly felt the darkness withdraw and it was immediate. Instant healing through the atonement is possible. I have witnessed it with many others and also now, personally. It is important that you understand that this was my own personal and sacred experience, and not just a fun story.

Before the Lord pulled those hooks out of me, I was wrestling with the internal dialogue of who I would be without these hooks. And I felt the Lord ask me if I required to know the answer before I would allow Him to take the hooks. It is extremely important to note that my terms of surrender *could* have prevented the Lord from removing these hooks. Finally, after deep consideration, I just took the jump and said, "Go ahead and take them." I was willing to risk who I would be without them. And I am sure glad that I did, because that transformation started a new chapter in my life.

What I learned about myself after that darkness had been removed was a rather unexpected side benefit. I had been like a clogged drain that had just been flushed clean. I felt like truth and life were flowing through me in a profound new way. I started having more vivid dreams that I could remember when I woke up. I started to feel instant information pouring into me when I was helping other people with NLP and hypnosis. My discernment and intuition increased. Thinking this over, it made a lot of sense. When we get rid of the darkness, revelation flows easily through our open heart.

I want to reiterate that I was not the one who made me a clear vessel. Becoming a clear vessel was the Lord's doing when I asked Him to help. You can read more about this principle in the final chapter where I share the story of Eagles Gathering. The Lord was simply waiting for me to realize that I was polluted and helpless and that I really wanted His help to change — to really change. And so, He took all of that resentment and pain from me.

And perhaps as a side benefit, made me more effective at doing His work.

If I Can Do It, You Can Do It

Drop Your Baggage If You Want To Come Higher!

Once in a counseling session, a woman shared a vision where she saw herself standing at the bottom of an escalator with a large suitcase in her hand. The Lord called down from the second floor that she would have to drop the baggage if she wanted to go higher.

What a beautifully simple metaphor for healing. You can only climb higher if you release everything that is incompatible with the Lord's spirit. You have to give it up!

What If The Only Thing I Am Harboring Is Self-Loathing?

Self-loathing is still darkness. It is inconsistent with God's plan for you. And it doesn't matter if you hate yourself for good reasons. Self-loathing is always darkness.

Meet Heather

The first day I met Heather, she was attending one of my free information classes. Heather came in without any makeup and wore a baseball cap. She spent most of the class looking at her feet. She was absolutely dejected and helpless. I proceeded to teach Heather about some of the more intricate points of hypnosis. I was extremely impressed with her understanding of the human psyche.

She informed me that she had been to counseling for many years and had been to many programs to address her depression and self-loathing. She could almost finish my sentences for me during the presentation but yet she was still struggling and suffering from the very things she claimed to understand.

But why should I believe you?

Heather had a disposition of distrust towards me because she had tried so many things without success. In fact, she had also done hypnosis with other therapists without any lasting results. So let's just say that she was skeptical for a good reason.

Heather had struggled with suicidal thoughts and depression for many years, and really didn't know what else to do. Her mother seemed optimistic at the class, but Heather wasn't convinced. We went ahead and set up an appointment for her to come in and meet with me. The first time we met, I only used NLP. At the end of that meeting she was shocked. She felt like we had assessed as much or more in one meeting than she had learned in a lifetime of counseling. This was simply because I was drawing from her subconscious information that was normally hidden on the other side of the wall.

I would like to reiterate that intellectually understanding something does not release you from the suffering. She needed more than to simply understand.

Heather decided to set up a second appointment with me to give me one more test to see if she could trust me. We had another deep NLP session, and she was again amazed at what we were able to pull out of her subconscious mind. Even more surprising to Heather, was how it was done through what seemed to be a regular conversation. Let me assure you that it was *not* just a regular conversation. When I'm working with NLP, every single question has a specific intent to elicit subconscious beliefs.

After our second meeting, Heather felt that she was in the right place. We went ahead and set her up to do a 28-day program at our wellness center. When someone does a program of this length, they usually work with me twice a week for a month. We have many modalities at the wellness center that are designed to re-pattern the brain. The reason for the length of the 28-day program is so that we can actually establish and build new neural pathways.

Some More Thoughts on Neural Pathways

I would like to deviate from the story for a moment to elaborate more on neural pathways. Neural pathways get created when we learn something new and it gets reinforced through repetition. Some of these neural pathways can be neutral. For example, we have all established neural pathways to learn how to brush our teeth. We have established neural pathways to learn how to navigate our phones. For everyday tasks that we do often, we have already established neural pathways.

I want you to try a little experiment. I want you to set this book down for a moment and fold your arms. Then I want you to wait for a few seconds and then reverse the way you are folding your arms. When you do this you will see that folding your arms the first time required no thought. This is called "unconscious competence." But when you reverse the way you fold your arms, you will notice that it is more difficult. On the second attempt most people really struggle to figure out where your arms need to go. The reason is because you have probably never folded your arms that way. And so you have not established a neural pathway for folding your arms in that prescribed manner.

And not all neural pathways are created equally!

We have some very helpful neural pathways to help us navigate our lives. And we enjoy being able to use a door knob without trying to figure out how to do it every time we see one. But not all neural pathways are good.

If we have learned as a child how to despise ourselves, you can rest assured that neural pathways are at play. Deeply ingrained patterns — whether negative, positive, or neutral — are still deeply ingrained. And this explains why we have to be able to create new neural pathways if we want to start thinking and acting in a different way.

I've taken a lot of care to explain how some of our hidden belief systems sabotage our lives and prevent us from feeling like we are worthy of being happy. And in order to move forward, these limiting beliefs must be dug up and replaced with something positive.

Remember that a belief is nothing more than an idea in your mind that you have accepted as true, and therefore you will follow and obey religiously. So if you have an irrational conviction on the subconscious side of your mind that you are not worthy to be happy, then you can rest assured that you are not going to feel happy.

False Humility is when someone punishes themselves in order to prove to God that they are sorry for not being enough. I have met with many strongly religious people who have developed the propensity to punish themselves constantly to prove to God that they were sorry that they were less than perfect. And because they think this pleases God, they "faithfully" reject happiness.

It is sadly ironic that someone will punish themselves in God's name to seek out His approval when He wants nothing to do with this destructive behavior. How many times as children did we start building a version of God in our minds that reflects how we were raised by our own parents? I will assure you that this usually is not a good thing. When we project false and negative character traits onto God's true and delightful character, then, of course, we will be repulsed by the untrue version of God we create in our own perception. These punishers have a definite plan to stay in the back of the cave as far from God as possible with no intention of ever approaching the door upon which He so persistently continues knocking. We discussed this in a previous chapter, but sometimes these false ideas of God inspire us to stay locked away from Him in the cave.

Back to Heather's Story

In Heather's case, because worthlessness had already been firmly established in her mind and heart, she would be ambushed constantly by that old trusted friend, self-loathing. A simple whisper from the adversary could send her into a negative loop for weeks.

Heather had established deeply ingrained, negative neural pathways of self-loathing. And previously, all conversations with loved ones and therapists only increased her resistance to change because of the Critical Factor. Do you remember that wall we talked about? The wall that has the attitude of a lazy two year-old that doesn't like to learn new things? The barrier that rejects good and bad from getting in to the subconscious mind? Yes *that* wall!

Heather's wall was constantly rejecting all positive feedback as foreign ideas because they so deeply contradicted her entrenched negative identity.

So one day, we decided to place her into hypnosis and find the true origins of her self-loathing.

I placed Heather into a deep state of hypnosis and asked her subconscious mind to take us to the source of her self-loathing. Heather became very uncomfortable in the chair and squirmed around. She was instantly scared and agitated. I asked her, "Where are you? What is happening?" After a few moments of being disoriented, Heather replied with a shock: "It is dark! I don't know where I am... Wait. I'm in the womb! I am three months old inside my mother's womb!"

As I mentioned in an earlier chapter, hypnosis is a state of consciousness where you can be 20 times more aware than normal. And time does not exist in the subconscious mind. The subconscious mind does not know how to differentiate between a memory or something that is actually happening in real-time. Heather was certainly in one of these pure states of hypnosis. She was actually back in the womb!

A Womb With A View

Heather was back at the moment in time when her unwed teenage mother discovered she was pregnant. This young unwed mother was horrified at this discovery. This acknowledgement filled her with guilt and shame. Heather actually imprinted on her mother's dread with this irrational acknowledgement and cried: "*I'm a mistake!*"

And with this acknowledgment came the tears and anguish hiding within Heather. We had just hit the mother load. The negative emotion that was established when Heather's mother discovered she was pregnant was stamped into Heather's soul and was now poignantly coming out into the light of day for the very first time.

Again, because time does not exist in the subconscious mind, memories are just sitting in there like fruit on a tree and are still attached to the emotions associated with those memories. Heather wasn't only remembering that memory in the womb — she was reliving it! And like I mentioned with minivan mama, this can be a good thing or this can be a bad thing. In Heather's case, this was a very painful thing. This was one of the core splinters that was buried deeply in her soul that was manifesting in such powerful ways that Heather had never been able to honestly love herself. Because rational thought is only a function of the conscious mind, this fear of being a mistake was far out of sight from Heather's rational mind and therefore could not be reasoned with intellectually. It was a weed that needed to be ripped out of the garden by its roots.

Certainly Heather's birth mother had no intention of injuring another life through her own guilt, shame, and regret from her reckless choices. But don't you find it amazing that Heather imprinted on her birth mother's guilt and shame and it became the very source of her own inability to love herself for 30 years?

That shame and guilt was so deeply ingrained inside of Heather that no amount of conscious effort was able to budge that deep-seated, irrational belief.

Something magical happens when someone learns the source of a problem like this. Once Heather's rational mind was able to understand this, it went to work. When Heather was able to consciously understand what the source of her self-loathing truly was, she started to cast the light of conscious perspective on this idea. You can think of this conscious process as wiggling around a loose tooth that you have decided needs to come out. Naturally she did not want this self-loathing inside of her anymore.

After Heather learned the source of her self-loathing, she agreed to go through the session using Audio Visual Entrainment, or AVE. You can read more about AVE on **MikeSimpson.live/Technology**. While she was using this technology, Heather went into a vision state and suddenly saw herself holding hands with her birth mother and birth father. She looked at both of them and announced that she was not a mistake but that she was a blessing! And without acknowledgement she let go of both of their hands and turned into a butterfly and flew away. I will tell you what else else then flew away: her self-loathing. Heather had found a spiritual release from the self-loathing. I want to point out here that I was not the one that created this experience for her. It was her own subconscious mind and spirit that created this healing experience. And for many years prior to this experience, no amount of rational conversation was enough to rid her of this plague of self-loathing. You see, there was a higher spiritual power at play here. Heather was a spiritual person and spent a lot of time pondering and praying about what we had experienced in hypnosis. By looking up she was able to find an actual solution to a deeply buried problem.

After Heather excitedly reported to me her experience while using the AVE, I decided to record one of my new hypnosis soundtracks and include some of Heather's experience in the soundtrack. There are two particular statements I make on those hypnosis tracks that can be traced back to Heather.

*"I am a BLESSING,
A butterfly on a summer breeze"*

Heather's own healing experience had just miraculously removed the core of her own self-loathing once and for all! Now, this doesn't mean that the temptation to punish herself or be hard on herself simply vanished. She still had neural pathways established that made her extremely efficient at punishing and hating herself. We had simply removed the core negative emotion that was attached to the hidden memory that guaranteed sabotage and helplessness in her life. What Heather reported to me after this healing experience was that she still had bouts of feeling tempted to punish herself. but she would recognize it consciously and found that she could fight off that inclination much more effectively. And the more Heather consciously rejected that old pattern, the more automatic it was to dismiss. Heather was now building a new trail system in her mind and placing a fork in the road for self-loathing. The trail sign read something like this:

Warning! Choose The Right!
Self-Loathing 2000 Miles to the Left
Self Esteem One Step to the Right

This new fork in the road was offering Heather a conscious decision point to negate self-loathing before it started. And because she could now recognize when these destructive thoughts were trying to ambush her, she would just take the new trail to the right instead. And that mountain lion sure despised Heather's new unpredictable travel strategies. She was now learning to walk in terrain that exposed and thwarted ambush tactics.

Heather made the transition from unconscious incompetence into conscious territory. Heather was now vacillating back and forth between conscious incompetence and conscious competence. Sometimes she could take the fork to the right. And sometimes she would still take the fork to the left. But even if she chose left, she knew she could backtrack and take the other option. And now, she did this consciously! This conscious decision frustrated Heather, but at least it was now a choice.

Heather could now see the enemy coming because she had new ninja skills. With practice, she became much more efficient at taking a right at the fork. And after some continued reinforcement, she began to arrive at unconscious competence. Automatic pilot. And the trail to the left grew in with beautiful vegetation. There would be no more decision point or fork in the road. The old path vanished, and only a single track remains that leads to self-esteem. And there are no ambush predators on this trail.

Heather still had bad days once in a while but it would be just that, a bad day. In her old patterns, a bad day usually turned into weeks, months, and even years. Now Heather was learning to rebound quickly from disappointment and frustrations by choosing the path to the right. And I spent more time and effort teaching her how to adopt a more productive belief system than punishing herself as proof to God that she should be a better person. The better approach is to include God and ask Him to lift you higher, rather than keeping Him out of your life until you can lift yourself higher. The second scenario never plays out well.

Heather: In My Own Words

Sometimes, it's hard to remember the person I was before I worked with Mike Simpson and went through his wellness center. But I have years and years of journals if I ever need reminders. I have family and friends who remember the hard times and can't believe the change in me. I have my own dark memories — though I don't let myself dwell on them too much, except to acknowledge how far I've come. It's been over two years since I finished my program, and I have had no major depressive episodes or suicidal ideation or crippling anxiety since then. I still have had ups and downs and disappointments. I even went through a very painful break-up, where someone I loved did not love me back. But those things that would most definitely have sent me into a huge depressive downslide before — with no ability to stop myself or pull myself out — now those events are only disappointments. Road bumps. Things to be sad about. But, not lethal accidents. I can be upset and grieve like other people without my entire life getting sidetracked. I can have setbacks and heartbreak without it sending me into the dark abyss that I am unable to escape from. And it's because Mike helped me get rid of all that faulty automatic programming that had been running my life for so long. Before, every day was a struggle. I was constantly battling my self-loathing. Pretending that I was okay and living my life took every ounce of energy and strength, and then I would crash frequently. Eventually, I couldn't fight it anymore, and I'd completely break down. I was always tired and weary. Another program that we found in me built around the belief that I was a mistake was that "I shouldn't be alive" and my body would literally find ways to attack itself and try to kill me, and it would almost succeed every two to three years. My subconscious was just doing what it was programmed to do, but it made life so hard.

Now, I don't spend each day just surviving. I have the energy and strength to do as I like. I have peace and happiness as my auto-pilot instead of self-loathing. I can see the things that used to trigger me, and choose not to acknowledge them. I can handle disappointment and life's ups and downs without being thrown off course.

And there were some things that even after my program ended, I still needed to work on. The majority of my program was spent understanding the source of my self-loathing, suicidal ideation, severe depression, and crippling anxiety. Once we found the reason I hated myself at the core, we made huge steps. But there was more. Because that happened when I was so young, other events in my life built upon and reinforced that belief system. It was one of those "self-fulfilling prophecies" types of things. My subconscious was looking for and finding all sorts of evidence to back up the reasons that I was a mistake and shouldn't have even been born. And there were some traumas, too. I had been abused as a young child by a trusted neighbor, and that was devastating as well. However, letting go of that became much easier once the self-loathing was gone. I could recognize that I didn't deserve what happened (where before a part of my subconscious believed that I had deserved it), and I was able to forgive and release that darkness so I didn't have to be affected by it anymore. It no longer had power over me, to wreck my hopes and dreams. But without Mike, I hadn't even been able to access the memory that my subconscious was hiding, because it was so painful and my subconscious was trying to protect me. I couldn't remember it. I only had nightmares and feelings and bad patterns in relationships to hint at the abuse that my subconscious kept hidden. After several sessions in my program with Mike, my subconscious was finally ready to acknowledge what happened, and the memories returned. Mike helped me navigate through that, too, and the technology helped me process and release the emotions. It went so quickly, working with Mike and the amazing technology.

People will ask me sometimes, "How long will it take to get where I'm healed with Mike? How many sessions?" The answer is: I don't know. I had a lot of bad programming in my subconscious to deal with. I definitely needed the 28-day program. I met with Mike before my program, and I did a few visits after. Not because it didn't work — but because IT DID. Whatever I worked on with Mike, we resolved. And we resolved it much faster than traditional therapy. Even now, I look at Mike as a resource that I will always use, if I ever find there is an area of my subconscious that seems stuck or faulty.

One example is that when I did my program, I wasn't dating. That wasn't an issue when I was just trying to survive and not kill myself. Several months after finishing the program, I started dating. Very quickly it became apparent that there were some subconscious programs that were not serving me in that area of my life. But here's the thing — the fact that I could even recognize them and see that I did not want them — that was huge. And going to work with Mike, I could tell him what the problem was, and we could quickly focus on it and work on it — all because of all the work we'd done before. We didn't have to talk around the problem for months. We discussed it, found it, and resolved it. Also, a lot of what he taught me as I worked with him in my sessions, I was able to take and do many of the same processes myself at home with the AVE equipment. Mike has been working on ways to teach and help others more. This book is one of those efforts.

I should mention that at this time, I do work for the wellness center. I started volunteering there after my program because I wanted to be a part of this amazing process. Eventually I was hired as a technician, and then promoted to Office Manager as well. I love being a part of the amazing healing process in other people's lives. I get to help them as they go on the same journey I went on myself. It is very rewarding. I may not always be at the wellness center, but the wellness center and Mike Simpson have forever changed my life. And I will always be grateful for that.

Meet Laura

Laura was a troubled teenager with a challenging past. She was born to a single, drug-addicted mother who ended up giving her away for adoption. Adoption is a difficult and painful subject for anyone who might feel "thrown away," but certainly a topic that needs to be discussed and explored. A common irrational identity statement I often hear from an adoptee is: "If my own mother didn't want or love me, then nobody will."

Laura had also been sexually abused multiple times while living with her addicted mother. Strangers were flowing in and out of the house constantly. Laura paid a heavy price for her mother's negligence. And sadly, these circumstances tripped Laura up right out of the starting gate of life. It was completely unfair.

As also discussed with Sofia and John in previous chapters, sexual abuse as a child often unlocks those appetites prematurely where sex can masquerade as love and acceptance. When resentment, fear, and self-loathing factor in, then the risk of unplanned pregnancies with struggling teenagers dramatically increases. Many families have been blessed with children from these circumstances through adoption, but I have also counseled many suffering women who chose abortion and then spiraled into deeper worthlessness, regret and shame.

Laura started experimenting with sex as an escape from her feelings of worthlessness. Truly, a valid reason to be concerned. One devastating part of Laura's past was her birth mother's choosing to keep custody of her younger brother while sending Laura away: "What does that mean about me if my own mother gave me away but kept my brother?" This is a painful question, and can easily reinforce the story of worthlessness. Remember that these ideas and fears that get buried into the subconscious mind will often wreak havoc with a teenager struggling to find an identity.

Who Would Ever Accept Me If My Own Mother Didn't?

This narrative can happen even when adopted children have been placed into a healthy and loving home. It is absolutely shocking for a child to discover that their origins are different than what they were raised to believe. What a betrayal. "You lied to me?" Then, "Who am I?" This new narrative of having once been devalued by the birth parent(s) now threatens to invalidate the adoptee's entire identity. "I am different than everyone else."

This topic is often considered taboo by the adopted child because they genuinely don't want to hurt their adoptive parents. So it becomes a conflict that cannot be discussed or examined openly but only buried deeper.

Laura's parents brought her to me hoping to resolve the ongoing contention and chaos. They were absolutely debilitated because nothing they tried had helped. It did not take long after sitting down with Laura to uncover the deep conflict that was fueled by her resentment. Of course, she did not understand these dynamics from a conscious perspective, "I'm just like any typical teenager who is angry at her parents because they just don't understand." she rationalized. She didn't understand or account for why she had been so reckless and angry. When you feel worthless, you can act worthless and this usually leads to reckless disregard.

I Don't Need Anyone

I had the opportunity to work with Laura's mother privately before working with them together. This first conversation with mother was absolutely electric. I was able to sufficiently disrupt her denial to demonstrate her own painful past being triggered by Laura's recklessness and chaos. Unknowingly, the mother became the martyr that actually fueled the contention with Laura. When you get two people living together who both share similar wounds, then they become mirrors for each other to reflect and project pain.

Pain is a Door to Understanding

This dynamic is akin to two people, both containing dark magnets in their hearts, that forcefully collide together with pure, irrational attraction.

Darkness clings to darkness, and pain instigates pain. Both parties are blaming each other. Both parties could pass a lie detector test claiming that they are each right.

When I was able to help Laura's mother realize her hidden contributions to Laura's problems, she was shocked out of denial — at least temporarily. Mother's martyr campaign demanded external validation from her sea of sympathizing supporters who had painted Laura as the villain. Tragically many of these people were Laura's own family. This campaign reinforced Laura's feelings of worthlessness and alienation. Sadly, this is not the first family from which she had been alienated.

Laura felt completely misunderstood and rejected by her parents and fought against the perceived injustices every time she could because she was angry and scared. When Laura's adoptive mother temporarily realized that she was guilty of martyrdom, they both broke into tears.

Wait! I'm the bad guy here? Mother answered her own question and broke down into tears and begged Laura's forgiveness. It was validating and healing for both of them.

All along, Laura's biggest complaint was that her mother never listened to her. Finally, in this meeting, mother was listening.

"Well, you are the one who made me do this!
It isn't my fault!
Hey everybody, can't you see I am right?"

Mother's pain was provoking Laura into contention. Likewise, it was Laura's pain that was baiting mother into contention. Magnets.

Meanwhile, the Lord is an opportunist. He often uses sharp corners to knock off sharp corners. But this process works only if we will be accountable. Unfortunately, Laura's mother changed her mind about her contributions to the dysfunction following another argument with Laura. Validation was now withdrawn. Mother snapped back into denial. Laura was again on the outside, looking in.

With Laura, I had to address the legitimate reality that her mother would likely not change or acknowledge Laura's improvements. That's why I needed to place accountability with Laura to remain committed to the change even if invalidated by her mother's renewed denial.

Was this young woman willing to change if her mother wouldn't? Would Laura hold onto her hard-fought changes in the face of her mother's justification and denial? Could she? Laura needed to let go of the worthless story that was forged and reinforced by both of her mothers. We were able to do this in a hypnosis session once Laura agreed to release the justified resentment and injustice. I took Laura into a sacred place where she had a divine encounter with the Lord. There, He literally showed up and embraced Laura. We asked the Lord to remove the darkness from all of her painful memories and the resentment to both mothers so she could free herself from the past and the present struggles. The Lord did exactly as we faithfully asked. This experience softened Laura's heart dramatically and changed her from the inside out.

Laura was the only one who could control the outcome of her life. I reminded her she needed to include the Lord in her daily battle. Right after I suggested this, Laura suddenly looked at me with a puzzled look. She had just seen a quick vision and asked me if I had a piece of paper so she could draw what she had just seen.

After drawing the image, Laura explained she saw a vision of herself as a young girl. She was covered with black tar, but she could still see her blue eyes and her golden heart shining through the costume of circumstance. She also saw herself with a golden crown on her head. This beautiful revelation came because Laura's mind and heart were open to her true identity, despite her painful past *and* present. Laura committed to change regardless of her mother's skepticism. Laura allowed the Lord to remove her negative charge. She became as a neutron where there was no positive or negative charge. Her mother could retain her negative charge, but Laura's transformation could neutralize her mother's emotional reactions if she remained committed to these principles of forgiveness. Yes, unfortunately, you can always bring back the darkness if you choose.

"A soft answer turneth away wrath: but grievous words stir up anger." (Proverbs 15:1, KJV)

Even Jesus was doubted and rejected by his own people. Laura is in good company.

"3 Is not this the carpenter, the son of Mary, the brother of James, and Joses, and of Juda, and Simon? and are not his sisters here with us? And they were offended at him.

4 But Jesus said unto them, A prophet is not without honour, but in his own country, and among his own kin, and in his own house." (Mark 6:4, KJV)

Our authentic improvements may not always be recognized by others, but that doesn't matter to the Lord. He wants us to accept His acceptance and reject the world's rejection.

If you knew me, you'd love me.

CHAPTER THIRTEEN

Be Careful What You Wish For

As mentioned earlier in the book, we have to be prepared for our lives to change when we find healing. Sometimes we get so accustomed to our problems that we actually get disoriented without them. This idea reminds me of a tree on our property. Over the years, this tree actually grew around a steel fence post that was buried near the tree's base. Isn't it interesting that the tree eventually embraced the post as part of itself and fused to it?

We can do the same thing with the buried steel posts from our childhood. Sometimes experiencing a desired change can introduce new and unanticipated problems. And later in this chapter, I will share a few poignant examples of this.

Meanwhile, there are times where we are reluctant to let go of old problems because there we expect some type of payoff or secondary gain.

Secondary gains? Problems with benefits?

While working with a new client, I always ask some basic questions designed to discover any secondary gains that come from the person's existing problem(s).

A true-life example of this principle occurred while working with a teenage girl named Sherry. She and her mother approached me to address a frustrating case of migraine headaches that put Sherry out of commission often for three or four days at a time. About 30 minutes into our first and only session, Sherry started to legitimately see she could lose her headaches. With this sudden realization and disorienting shift in perspective, I observed Sherry recoil in panic at the thought of losing the headaches. That's right, I saw her visibly recoil.

The Suffering Narrative

My NLP protocol involves keen observance of unconscious nuances instead of naively trusting what story the mouth and conscious mind are pushing. The client's words will usually parrot the rehearsed suffering narrative, while the unconscious gestures contradict the story. This is called incongruence. In Sherry's case, it was clear that these headaches were serving a purpose.

To understand Sherry's secondary gain from her headaches, I asked her a few simple questions:

"What would you risk if you lost your headaches?"

And

"What do you gain by keeping your headaches?"

The expected initial response to these questions is typically spoken quickly in pure denial. "Nothing."

This expected answer is usually the outermost layer of the onion we are peeling away. After a little needling, the secondary gain starts surfacing into conscious awareness. When this happens, I can typically expect a disoriented reaction from the person who is emerging from denial. This state of confusion is called an impasse.

An impasse is a similar reaction you might expect when you walk out of the dark theater into the sunshine. The first few moments of this intense sunshine are painful on the eyes. This bright new perspective will show you much more than you could see in the dark theater. When I see this impasse, I know we are close to hidden information.

After Sherry's impasse, she suddenly understood the secondary gain of her headaches. Her headaches were *rescuing* her from stress in a similar way a fuse might blow after too much electricity surges through a power cable. Sherry coyly admitted that she welcomed those "dreaded headaches" like an old friend dropping in unannounced. Suddenly Sherry wasn't too sure she wanted to lose the headaches because she didn't know how to manage her stressful and demanding life without them! She didn't know how to say No and didn't want to disappoint her parents, coaches and teachers who had big expectations. Who would've guessed?

The Relief of Pain

Sherry was involved with cheerleading, a demanding school schedule, piano lessons, dance, and a starring role in the school play at the young age of 14. She had become accustomed to becoming Wonder Girl by observing her older siblings overachieve for validation, approval, and *value*. Sherry was following the same pattern that previously brought her older "successful" sister to me for help with depression. Both of these girls struggled with the same conflict. Their mother's structured and demanding expectations relentlessly drove them to excellence. Most of us can agree that idle hands are the devil's workshop. This may be true, but overdoing it can *also* be considered the devil's workshop. Eventually, this unrealistic pursuit of perfection will wear the tread from any over-achiever's emotional tires. Excessive pressure can easily result in despondency and depression if not managed mindfully.

At the young age of 14, Sherry had already fallen into the trap of basing her value on her performance, and it was giving her migraines. The remainder of our session was no longer about headaches but on how to set boundaries to enforce balance.

A Voice and A Choice

We identified and eliminated Sherry's subconscious belief that her value was based on her performance. When she realized that she could have a voice and a choice in her own life, then the headaches were no longer necessary. But she did have to risk disappointing some people by saying No. Is saying No, always selfish? No.

Sherry's migraines disappeared after our first and only NLP session. I will elaborate more on the faulty principle that was driving Sherry's life, but I will first share another interesting example of secondary gain.

Big Puppy Dog Eyes

Here is a true account of working with a man we will call JD, to overcome his dysfunctional addiction patterns. We made great inroads with JD for these issues. In fact, in the final session of his program I felt we were finished with the addiction work, so I asked him if he had anything else he would like to address. He sheepishly admitted, there was something.

"There is one thing my wife asked me to bring up. I have allergies to dogs, and my wife asked if we could get rid of them."

I agreed we could work on these allergies in hypnosis, but first, I needed to discuss the benefits of the allergies and the obvious incongruence to his request. His nonverbals were screaming to keep the allergies. He chuckled and said, "I don't have any benefits from dog allergies." But after five minutes of needling and reviewing some of his addiction patterns, tied to rebelling against life's overwhelming demands, he actually recanted his offer to lose the allergies. By his own admission, being allergic to dogs was the *only* way he *was NOT* going to get pressured into owning a dog because he is such a pushover when it comes to disappointing his wife and kids. He just KNEW he would *have* to get a puppy if those allergies were gone, and that would mean more responsibilities at home that he didn't want to assume.

I must admit, this is the first time I've ever had someone request an allergy boost to protect the kids from disappointment! Secondary gain won the allergy debate and left puppies to be enjoyed from a distance through a pet-store window. JD chose *not* to disclose this decision with his wife so as to avoid being in the dog house.

Human Being Vs Human Doing

My NLP instructor, Suzanne, taught me about this conflict in my first NLP course. She experienced this painful conflict in her own life because she was exceptionally gifted as a child. You read that right. Conflict doesn't *always* come from tragedy.

Suzanne was reading full books at the age of 2. Her amazing intellect and ability generated a lot of notable and understandable fanfare. She was the amazing little human being who could do amazing things.

Suzanne graduated high school with a 4.0 GPA and made an easy transition into college, where she graduated as Valedictorian. But then something happened. The engine of the car mysteriously seized up. Around this time, she had a full breakdown. Simply stated, from a young age Suzanne had learned that she was special *because* she was gifted and smarter than others her age. But being special came with pressure and expectations. Throughout her years of development, Suzanne was driven by the notoriety and relentless pressure to remain special. She felt a constant need to stay ahead of everyone all of the time in order to maintain her own value. This relentless pressure to be better than everyone else to maintain her gifted status was constantly nipping at her heels. This faulty value system eventually wore her down emotionally, and made her physically ill. She was mysteriously broken. It was a tragic relief.

It was at this stage that Suzanne needed to rework her map of reality with something that was going to be more conducive to a healthy life. It is wonderful to be gifted as long as she doesn't rely upon her abilities to prove her value.

We saw this earlier in the book::

*"As Long As I Am Everything
To Everyone
All Of The Time
Then, Of Course, I Have Value"*

Both Suzanne and Sherry had adopted a belief system that stated unequivocally that their value was tied to their performance. This belief system is extremely common, especially in religious cultures where people are striving to be productive, and even unrealistically perfect, so they feel they will have value to God. The problem inherently built into this belief system is that your health will start failing when you can no longer keep up with the unrealistic demands driving you to be a super-achiever.

With this performance-defined-value belief system intact, you can only retain your value based on your next performance. This is cleverly designed by the Enemy to destroy us from the inside.

In reality, we have value because we have value, because we have value, because we have value. Hopefully this is not too redundant for you.

We are unique; each of us is irreplaceable; we cannot be exactly reproduced. Most significantly, we are legitimately the children of God. Our value is inherent in our existence and has nothing to do with our performance or abilities. Once we realize that God loves us independently from our achievements, we will still feel inspired to achieve amazing things. But now, we will do them for the right reasons.

16 "The Spirit itself beareth witness with our spirit, that we are the children of God:

17 And if children, then heirs; heirs of God, and joint-heirs with Christ; if so be that we suffer with him, that we may be also glorified together.

18 For I reckon that the sufferings of this present time are not worthy to be compared with the glory which shall be revealed in us." (Romans 8:16-18, KJV)

Less is more...
More or less...
Give or take a little...

Sherry's migraines went away after our first meeting. She was absolutely relieved to learn a better version of reality that didn't constantly demand emotional devastation.

Am I advocating here that we should strive to achieve less? Absolutely not. I believe in striving for greatness. But I equally believe in pursuing our passionate interests realistically and for our own reasons — reasons that are not contaminated with the fear of what someone else will think of us if we disappoint them.

One of the reasons I was able to excel at NLP and hypnosis was because of my desire and passion to help others. My gifts were not forged in fear. They came by faith, not by the fear of being worthless if I couldn't do it.

Doing the right thing for the wrong reason is still the wrong thing! But doing the right thing for the right reasons is the right thing!

Sherry decided to discuss the insights about her migraines with her mother. When she did, her mother was absolutely shocked that her own motivational and productivity strategies played such a crucial role in her daughter's value system AND suffering. Mother had been blinded by the trail systems of her own mind. Rather than Sherry being terrified of being worthless because she couldn't meet all of her mother's unrealistic demands, Sherry learned that she could speak up and play a lead role in her own life. But this also meant Sherry had to risk disappointing her mother. And so you see, once you claim your freedom and apply balance, then you can excel for your own reasons. You can be free, fulfilled AND have balance.

Meet Carson

Carson is a young man that I worked with a few years ago. Carson had some deeply buried beliefs and fears that were driving him into a constant state of anxiety. In his first session we had a life-changing conversation that included NLP and hypnosis. This was one of the most miraculous cases I have seen happen in a single visit. After our session, his mom reported to me that he had changed dramatically for the positive. She was shocked that he was finding himself more loving and patient and she just could not get her head wrapped around it. He had been suffering for so long that he was on several different medications with many negative side effects, including jittery distraction.

After our meeting, his family made the decision to take Carson off of his medication. To do this they enlisted the help of their psychiatrist. He was dumbfounded by the change in Carson. By his own admission, he called Carson's transformation a true medical miracle. Many of the techniques to create these amazing results with Carson are principles you have seen outlined in this book. And even though it is miraculous, the point I'm exploring here is not how Carson created the miracle, but rather to examine the problem that was introduced by losing his old problems. I know that may sound confusing, so I will say it again: I would like to outline for you the new problems that were created by Carson losing his old problems.

Because of Carson's constant state of panic he had been placed in Special Education classes at school. He spent several years associated with the other kids that were considered special needs. I do not need to point out here the cruel stigmas that are sometimes aimed at these kids. But now, with Carson's miracle, his family decided it was time to move him into the regular classes. He wanted so badly to fit in there.

Becoming a Small Fish in a Big Pond

All of Carson's comfortable friends were still attending the special education classes. And for him to be transplanted into a different school, a bigger pond, he found himself suddenly overwhelmed with the pressure from his more demanding classes. He found himself terrorized and even resentful from the bullying that accompanied his transition. The students were very cruel to Carson, and they refused to acknowledge that he had changed.

I stayed in contact with Carson and his family and met with him occasionally to talk about these demanding circumstances that were requiring him to go through some difficult growing pains.

About a year after Carson's amazing transformation I met with him to catch up. He began to present a story that his mind was starting to go crazy again and that he was reverting to his old self. I sat and looked at him closely. A spirit of discernment came over me and told me that he was lying. I confronted him on this.

"You're lying to me, aren't you?"

He gave me a quizzical look and acted like he didn't know what I was talking about. I pushed again.

"You are lying to me, aren't you?"

Suddenly Carson's face cracked with a smile and irritation, and through an exasperated sigh, he admitted my hunch was right. You see, Carson was trying to make a case *through me* that his change had only been temporary and that he was mysteriously broken again.

The Stamp Of Disapproval

This would be similar to suicide by cop where you provoke the officer to shoot by pretending to pull a gun. If Carson could just get me to announce to his family that all hope was lost, then he would happily get transplanted back into the easy pond. He was hoping to get my stamp of disapproval that he had reverted to his old, broken self so he could go back to his old "easier" life that had less pain and pressure. Less pain was certainly debatable. He had an interesting case of denial and amnesia where he had *forgotten* how painful his old existence was.

So our conversation turned from him being "broken again" to discussing the deep resentment he held towards these kids for how they had been treating him since the pond-swap. As I dug a little deeper, I was able to learn that because of Carson's deep-seated resentment towards these kids, he actually found great satisfaction in annoying them every chance he got!

I'm Here, People, And You Are NOT Going To Ignore Me Any Longer!

Carson insisted to me that he could not control the fact that he was so annoying to these bullies. But through some painful accountability talk, we were able to eventually resolve that Carson needed to take accountability for acting annoying if he wanted to survive in this new pond. That old pond was no solution at all. And he needed a reminder. If Carson decided to keep irritating those people who had previously not accepted him and let resentment fuel his disruptive behavior, then surely the lack of acceptance, ridicule, bullying, and rejection would continue.

Let's just admit it folks: sometimes it is downright satisfying to irritate those people who have ignored or hurt you. But that can backfire, too.

Wait! After All I've Been Through, You're Saying I'm The Bad Guy Here?

"A soft answer turneth away wrath: but grievous words stir up anger." (Proverbs 15:1, KJV)

As unfair as Carson's treatment was from these bullies, he was the only one who could change his part of the problem with some good old-fashioned accountability and forgiveness. He needed to decide if he was going to slip down the martyr's slope with some considerable justification or choose to Let Go and Let God take it.

It was tempting for me to fall into Carson's pity trap during our conversation. But feeling sorry for him and arranging his pond-swap was not going to help him become the person that I could see inside of him.

The only thing that was going to change those circumstances was for Carson to stay off of the martyr cycle and embrace his new existence. He was almost there! Carson needed to let go of the resentment that was there for some extremely painful and good reasons. And he needed to be willing to look in the mirror and recognize that his resentment-fueled irritating behavior was only going to get him picked on more. So he was at another crossroads.

The Point Of Atae

The point in a flight at which an aircraft will lack sufficient fuel to return to its starting point.

The Point of No Return

The stage at which it is no longer possible to stop what you are doing and when its effects cannot be avoided or prevented.

I Am Somebody...

Carson was at the point of atae. He had miraculously healed and changed but was now filled with fear because of the daunting demands of the transition he was now confronting. And yes, Carson is a bit of a prankster who was having fun poking the big scary bear with a stick. A sharp stick! Let's just say that he was enjoying making people acknowledge him.

Carson decided to take accountability and drop the resentment and martyr act. And once he changed, something happened with those bullies. They left him alone!

I AM SOMEBODY!!!

VIP!

I was invited to give a speech while Carson was in the audience and couldn't resist featuring him as my VIP. I arranged that he would come up to the stand with me for a few minutes. He was surprisingly honored to do it, so we put things into motion.

What an amazingly beautiful experience it was to call Carson up onto the stand in front of a large crowd of people! With him standing proudly next to me and my arm around him, I proceeded to tell everyone Carson's story of triumph. He stood speechless and proud and tall. I asked the members of the audience to raise their hands if they had ever been bullied. I was shocked to see that more than 75 percent of the audience raised their hands in the air.

I honestly felt Carson gasp as everyone fixed their eyes directly on him. It was incredibly powerful. We could feel everyone's love and concern and faith directed squarely at Carson. This was Carson's day in the sun — this was Carson's rite of passage!

While planning this speech I had the most powerful idea flow into my mind about how to feature Carson. So right there during the speech, I explained to the audience my very strange but powerful impression. I simply asked the audience to all roar like a lion as loud as they could if they disagreed with how those bullies had treated Carson.

RRRRROOOOOOOOAAAAAAAAAARRRRRRRRR!!!!!!!

Prior to this I'd never been on the receiving end of 600 roaring lions, but I will tell you it was one of the most beautiful experiences of my life — of Carson's life — of the audience's life. **THIS WAS CARSON'S MOMENT!**

He was standing in front of these people as a new man of courage and power — beloved and validated.

"The wicked flee when no man pursueth: but the righteous are bold as a LION." (Proverbs 28:1, KJV)

Mike Simpson

The Big Fish In The Big Pond

When Carson walked down from the stage, he got a high five from every person in the aisle as he made his way back to his family. Something beautiful had just happened. The human spirit is powerful and amazing and is capable of overcoming adversity, fear, and resentment. Carson had made the transition from cub to lion. I don't know who was impacted more that day, Carson or the audience. But I'll tell you one thing for certain, he left the speech a different person than when he arrived. He left knowing he was believed in. He was the hero of his story.

It changed the way he walked. It changed the way he held his head. The bullies stopped bugging him and strangely stopped ignoring him. Do you think that bullying went away by accident?

When you stop acting like a slave, there are no masters.

I also worked with Carson's brother, Austin and he also found transformation. Their mother was gracious enough to write a few of her own words to explain the miracle of her two children's lives being transformed by Letting Go and Letting God Heal.

Please enjoy Mother's perspective:

Carson's Miracle

All Carson wanted was to be "normal." As his parents, we tried our best and went to extreme measures to help him accomplish this. To understand why this was his dream, it's important to understand a little about him. He was always a very hyper child who was diagnosed with ADHD at age 5. As he entered Kindergarten, we learned quickly that his little body and mind simply could not do what the other children could do. He was unable to sit still, concentrate, listen, and comply with simple instructions, and he struggled with being very impulsive both physically and verbally. This affected him greatly in school, and especially socially. We sought help from many doctors and counselors, and tried many different medications to help him simply function daily. This went on for many years. He was put in a special class at school designed for children with behavioral special needs. He was in this setting all through grade school. As he got older his desire to "be normal" grew, and we did everything we knew how to help him achieve this, but seemed to fall short.

Everyone who knew Carson struggled to love him. He was most often very hard to be around, and was commonly referred to as the "annoying kid." This, as you can imagine, created a very emotional rollercoaster ride of a life for him. Some medications made things better for a time, but some made things a lot worse. There were times his own family members feared for their lives. This, however, did not distract us from wanting to help him.

When Carson was 12, we learned about a hypnotherapist who could possibly help. We were apprehensive to meet him, but figured why not? It couldn't possibly hurt to give it a try. The day we met with Mike he had a very busy schedule, which didn't give us any time to fill him in on all of Carson's history. This made us a little nervous. All Mike knew was Carson struggled with ADHD, was on medication, and that he wanted to "be normal and fit in."

After one session with Mike, Carson was a different kid! He was happy and calm, and had a different countenance. These changes were so obvious that everyone who knew him noticed. He went off all his meds and went to regular classes at school. It truly was a miracle! He is healthy and happy and now has friends that he hangs out with. His psychiatrist was shocked and even stated it was a miracle!

With so many changes in himself, he had to learn how to be this new person. This didn't come without challenges, but the desire in himself to be this new kid outweighed the old him. Mike met with him a few more times and taught him how to repattern his way of thinking. He has struggled with being bullied since the change, but that has recently stopped and he continues to progress daily. It's been over a year, and the miracle continues to amaze us. He is doing so well! Carson's future is so bright and filled with such promises he never knew were possible!

Austin's Battle with Depression, From Mother

Austin was not a typical teenager. He suffered from depression which controlled many years of his life. It started in his early teens as he became more and more withdrawn. He slowly stopped caring about anything and everything in his life. He stopped turning in assignments which led to near failure in some classes at school. Austin used to love gaining knowledge but his desire to learn completely stopped. None of his old hobbies interested him anymore. Even planned vacations such as a trip to Disneyland failed to excite him. He was so smart he could have easily gotten over a 4.0 GPA and attended any college he wanted, but he just didn't see the point. He distanced himself from friends and family alike because he saw himself as a negative influence. Every day was just a repeat of the same cycle. Wake up, go to school, go home, maybe eat, and then go to sleep.

Austin saw no future for himself. He was sick of hurting all the time, and didn't want to continue living a life so miserable. He felt ashamed that he had been raised in a great situation compared to many other people, but he still couldn't bring himself to be happy. He even experimented with cutting and burning himself to try to externalize the pain and sometimes just to feel anything at all. As his parents, we asked him on several occasions if something had happened. He would say nothing was wrong, this is just who he was. Knowing he was capable of so much more, we took him to doctors and counseling sessions to try and help him.

During each session, the doctor would ask some questions and then either prescribe a new medication or alter the current dosage. Sometimes Austin would feel better, but it never lasted long. During one psychiatrist appointment, the doctor asked him if he had thought about taking his own life. This was one of the hardest days of my life, listening to him say "yes" and then describing in detail how he would do it. Those thoughts, he described, would come and go depending how he was feeling. This put him on suicide watch and the doctor visits became more frequent. Unknown to anyone until years later, Austin once attempted to overdose using stolen Opioid painkillers.

Something had to change, but what? In his senior year of high school, the opportunity came to see Mike Simpson and try hypnosis therapy. He talked it over with us, and we strongly encouraged him to give it a try. He did some of his own research on hypnosis and concluded there was scientific proof it can be helpful, so he figured he had nothing to lose. This one hypnosis session proved to be the miraculous change his loved ones had been praying for. Austin walked out a new person. Instead of asking some questions and then prescribing some pills, Mike listened to him, talked with him, and made him feel understood like no one else had before.

Austin was only hypnotized for several minutes, but during that time was able to root out many subconscious fallacies and imbalances that were causing the depression. On the three hour drive home, he wouldn't stop talking. He was happy! We were in awe at the complete change. Austin continued to visit with the psychiatrist and even went off his meds without telling him. After the third visit off his meds, he told the doctor what he had done. The doctor was completely surprised he was off his meds and doing so well, but happy he had found something that worked.

Austin graduated high school and is currently attending college and doing fantastic. He even started dating and doing things socially. What took place in that one hypnosis session with Mike was life-changing for Austin. He talks so much now it shocks everyone he knows. Every single person that knows Austin has recognized the change in him and is thrilled to see him doing so well. He has returned to reading a lot and is even enjoying learning a lot of new things in his college classes. He is finally starting to enjoy life and all it has to offer. While he still struggles sometimes, he can now recognize the depression and take steps to stop it before it begins to control him. There is no telling what his future has in store, but it is brighter than ever thanks to this miracle!

Some Closing Thoughts from Mike

I am so grateful for the opportunity to work with these people. It is not always easy, but is so rewarding when I have the privilege of witnessing people like Sherry, JD, Carson, and Austin transform. We learned about the secondary gain from problems, and how faulty beliefs can create sickness and depression. Each one of these people had a story that trapped the darkness within. Each one of these people had the courage to rewrite their story. Well, perhaps there is one small exception when it comes to JD's fear of puppies. That is nothing to sneeze at!

CHAPTER FOURTEEN

Spiritual Opposition
PG-13

In this chapter, I address some topics that children may find disturbing and scary. Please read through this chapter first if you intend to have your children read it.

- Entities
- Spooks
- Demons
- Evil Spirits
- Ghouls
- Ghosts
- Hitchhikers
- Satan
- The Devil

Call them what you will, but call them something. If you believe in God, then it is impossible to dismiss the reality of their existence. They are the opposite of God and thrive here in this world, mainly because we generally don't understand or believe in them. These evil influences are real and they do cause real trouble. They don't go away by ignoring them. They can get inside of you when you are vulnerable, and most hide once they are inside. And they certainly influence our thoughts and emotions.

Evil spirits are extremely prevalent in this world and addressed at length in the New Testament. I have had extensive experience with these entities throughout my lifetime. As a teenager, I was attacked by them often in my sleep. I would get rattled awake when they attacked, as they held me down to prevent me from speaking. They bothered me until about the age of 18, when I had finally gained enough strength and faith to keep them at bay. I'd had enough. These experiences really prepared me for The Enemy. If you practice fighting with a plastic sword long enough, you will feel comfortable fighting with a real one. I told a few people about these experiences while growing up, but was rarely taken seriously. I mostly kept it to myself.

I encounter and confront these dark entities often in hypnosis. As mentioned in the Cave Of Unbelief chapter, the adversary plays a *huge* role in the campaign of depression and hopelessness. A careful study of Christ's healings in the New Testament shows that roughly 75-80 percent of his *recorded* miraculous healings included casting out evil spirits. After I started doing hypnosis full-time, I encountered these entities just as frequently.

A big reason I encounter so many entities is because they have a difficult time hiding from us while in hypnosis. Remember that a true hypnosis is heightened awareness that allows us to be 20 times more perceptive than normal. It is worthwhile to note that these entities do their best to hide once they slip in through the cracked window of resentment, anger, pity or fear. These entities are opportunists, really no different than a leech attaching to an unsuspecting swimmer in a murky pond.

Most of these entities avoid theatrics and fanfare. Instead, they go deep inside and remain silent while they fester in a black nest of depression, resentment, hopelessness, and darkness. We often leave them undisturbed because generally we don't believe they exist. I would like to also note that while entities are lurking within, their thoughts are often confused with our thoughts. And of course, their thoughts reinforce hopelessness and depression. Their hidden presence can legitimately extinguish all hope and obscure the sun like dark storm clouds. While hiding within, entities will often speak to you from the second-person perspective. We often falsely refer to them as *our* critical voice. But it is likely not our voice at all. It is theirs! For example, who is really speaking when we hear phrases such as: "Who are *you* kidding? No one is ever going to love *you*!" or "Look how ugly *you* are." These phrases are usually being directed at you from someone or something else.

6 "But when he saw Jesus afar off, he ran and worshipped him,

7 And cried with a loud voice, and said, What have I to do with thee, Jesus, thou Son of the most high God? I adjure thee by God, that thou torment me not.

8 For he said unto him, Come out of the man, thou unclean spirit.

9 And he asked him, What is thy name? And he answered, saying, My name is Legion: for we are many.

10 And he besought him much that he would not send them away out of the country.

11 Now there was there nigh unto the mountains a great herd of swine feeding.

12 And all the devils besought him, saying, Send us into the swine, that we may enter into them.

13 And forthwith Jesus gave them leave. And the unclean spirits went out, and entered into the swine: and the herd ran violently down a steep place into the sea, (they were about two thousand;) and were choked in the sea." (Mark 5:6-9, KJV)

This desperate legion of spirits begged Christ not to condemn them before their time. Well, this legion certainly took the swine over the edge. And if these evil spirits worried about being cast into the pit then, just imagine their desperation now. They are worried and scared about their time of reckoning. By pleading permission from the Savior to enter into the swine, these spirits demonstrated determination to occupy *any* type of body.

Exactly how does the medical narrative of the day categorize entities? I've been laughed out of a room by breaching the topic. Entities rarely appear in the medical conversation unless being disregarded as outrageous imagination, or rebranded as mental illness.

Two Types Of Spirits

There are two categories of spirits. One category is disembodied spirits who are the departed spirits that haven't moved on. These are they who have previously lived on Earth, but have chosen to stay behind after death to seek out their old haunts. They find second-hand pleasure from someone else's body if they can gain access. Sometimes they won't move on because they are uncertain or afraid. Not all of them are malicious or dangerous, but they are breaking the rules by staying behind.

The other category of spirits are unembodied spirits. These are the fallen angels from heaven who were never granted a body in this world. They have a more sinister goal of making everyone miserable who chose the plan to follow the Savior on earth instead of Lucifer, The Son of the Morning. I have found this class of spirit typically malevolent and vengeful with motives to hurt and destroy. They are on assignment from Satan to create suffering and answer to him for any of their failed attempts of debauchery.

I encounter both types of spirits hiding inside of people during hypnosis. Typically I encounter more unembodied spirits than disembodied.

When I was younger, I found the amazing book titled "Return From Tomorrow" written by George G. Ritchie, M.D. This is a must read. At age twenty, Ritchie temporarily died in an army hospital. He returned to life ten minutes later, after witnessing the vast spiritual realm.

Ritchie recounts his inspirational out-of-body experiences. While out of his body, he witnessed disembodied spirits hanging around bars diving into unconscious, intoxicated people. These departed spirits were so desperate to experience drinking again that they would dive into anyone who had passed out from too much alcohol. Ritchie also had a sacred visit with the Savior at the pinnacle of his journey and was shown by the Savior how love is the greatest commandment. What a profound and important witness for us about the spiritual realm that surrounds us in this world.

I find it unthinkable that most Christians who believe in the Bible have a hard time accepting this reality of evil spirits, but readily accept Western medicine's labels. Why were evil spirits so prevalent in New Testament times and yet now irrelevant? They are still here.

Meanwhile, this so-called infallible enlightenment of science still leaves the experts scratching their heads. Mental illness is still as mysterious as the common cold.

One of the principles that we are taught in hypnosis training is to allow someone's experience to be what it is without interference or projecting our own ideas into the client's experience. Often someone's hypnosis experience does not conform to the hypnotist's world-view. Unexpected things often happen that we can't explain, but we are trained to roll with it. I'm not afraid of these entities, and that's why I can effectively deal with them when I encounter them. I can do this because 1) I know they are real, 2) I know how to find them, and 3) I know how to send them away.

Why isn't any of this crucial information about entities or hypnosis taught to traditional medical professionals? I've spoken with many licensed professionals in the mental health industry who expressed frustration at being highly restricted on this topic. Healthcare professionals are forced to approach entities the way they have been selectively educated.

I acknowledge again that my "normal" and your "normal" are likely different because I've been dealing with these entities for a long time. I suppose entities in hypnosis are no different than an electrician encountering rats and cockroaches on the job, or the fisherman fighting mosquitoes while on the lake. It is just part of the territory and something for which to be prepared.

As I've stated often, just because we don't understand or even believe a principle doesn't mean it isn't profoundly real. And if we deal with these dark influences by ignoring them, then this darkness will certainly claim a certain type of power or influence over us so as to mitigate our positive influence in this war against evil.

I have taken up the practice to evict these entities upon discovery instead of ignoring them. If I were a car mechanic, I would suggest to the car owner to also replace the worn timing belt while the car is torn down to fix the broken transmission. There is no sense paying for the expensive procedure of tearing down the car twice.

Here are a few unbelievable stories that demonstrate how these menacing entities are affecting people in adverse ways, and how dismissing them is playing a significant role in emotional healing.

I See Dead People

A few years ago, I brought a man and his wife into my office for a hypnosis session. She had been audibly hearing scary voices that were constantly threatening her. These spirits were wreaking havoc in their lives. This couple was hopeful that hypnosis could help. This case was uncommon because the husband, who chooses to remain anonymous, has the uncanny ability to easily see into the spiritual realm. He has spent the better part of his life living in what he calls, "The Twilight Zone" — being privy to the hidden forces of both good and evil. We began his wife's session, but I was unable to get her into hypnosis. Finally, after an exhausting 90 minutes, I ended the session completely drained. I then had a private meeting with the husband where he informed me that he had literally just observed three evil spirits threatening her while I was attempting to get her into hypnosis. He watched these spirits *fighting* against me desperately as if holding the lid to her subconscious mind shut. Wow. This explained why I felt so exhausted after this failed hypnosis session.

As I have stated before, it is very common for me to encounter spirits while someone is in hypnosis. And this typically happens without trying to find them. I've had cases where the spirits attacked my client while in hypnosis to try to stop us from disrupting their black nest. When discovered, they do their best to frighten the client away with some pretty impressive scare-tactics. I have learned that spirits are much easier to expel from a person *while* in hypnosis because they are extremely susceptible to the laws of suggestion. In other words, you can bind these spirits with restrictive suggestions, and then they can be removed with little resistance. They are much harder to expel through the conscious mind.

Meanwhile, in this meeting with the husband, it occurred to me that we should cast these entities out of his wife *without* hypnosis and use his spiritual eyes for feedback and verification. After all, they couldn't hide from him. So, we brought his wife back into the room and proceeded to remove these spirits. I taught him my preferred technique to expel, and he picked right up on it. As we cast away these spiritual hitchhikers, he watched them angrily but reluctantly leave. That day this man added to his spiritual arsenal the ability to not only see and hear spirits, but to powerfully and efficiently remove them. He proceeded to keep an eye on his wife after this session and continues to clear her, but it is a full-time job because she actually *chooses* to let them in! So this just goes to show you that casting entities out is temporary unless the person rejects them and releases the negative story that invites them back inside.

Since I've been involved with the wellness center and doing hypnosis and NLP full-time, I have encountered many spiritually gifted people. I must admit, this man's ability to see these spirits is at the top of the list of spiritual gifts I have encountered. After learning these techniques, he became efficient and powerful in removing spirits by himself, and continues to aid me with my clients today. Here is a man who can see and hear what most of us have to accept by faith. The realm of light is as real as darkness, but light is certainly more powerful. Once we lose our fear of these dark forces, we can effectively keep them at bay while we build our lives around true and sound principles of light and freedom.

Past-Life Regression Revisited

I would like to share my theory for you to consider about past-life regression. Yes, this is quite common to encounter in the hypnosis field, and we are trained to let these experiences play out without interference. There are some impressive documented past-life regressions in hypnosis where people recall memories and even speak in languages they have never learned in this lifetime. It is difficult to explain and ignore this phenomenon, but since I have made it a point to clear spirits out of people before doing emotional work, I have only encountered a single past-life regression over the past three years of doing hypnosis full-time. Is it possible that these past-life memories are actually being recalled by the spirits hiding inside of people? It is a question worth pondering, isn't it?

Meet Kreedon

Kreedon came into my center looking for help with deep depression and schizophrenia. Constant chaos from many voices was his normal. Imagine trying to function in this world with countless voices constantly spinning around in your head.

Kreedon's parents made the decision to have him come in and do an extensive program with me. The first day I did hypnosis with Kreedon, not surprisingly, we immediately encountered and confronted enough entities to fill an entire auditorium in his mind. Right as Kreedon went into hypnosis, he instantly sat back dismayed and said, "Wow" with his mouth hanging open. I asked him what he was experiencing. He said, "There are so many people here." He was silent for a moment and then we proceeded to usher all of them out of his body into a large auditorium I created in his mind. We ushered them all into the chairs in front of us. We informed the spirits they would not be staying and gave them a choice of two doors to exit through.

After the legion was given their options, they all systematically bowed their heads. Kreedon watched all of them remove hideous demon-looking masks. Yes, masks. The scary faces were gone and there in front of Kreedon was a large group of normal-looking spirits locked in their chairs watching quietly. They all agreed to leave peacefully through the first door we showed them. The second door was not going to be as pleasant. But they knew it would be one door or the other, and they were no longer welcome to stay inside of Kreedon.

After this mind-blowing hypnosis session, Kreedon was absolutely stunned and literally speechless for a few minutes after emerging from hypnosis. With a huge smile and after a long pause, he asked, "Can you hear that?"

I asked him, "What?"

He responded, "It's so quiet!" And he sat back, unable to wrap his mind around what he had just witnessed. This was the first time Kreedon had heard silence in his mind for over ten years! He could not stop smiling in awe. For me, this was pretty much standard protocol, but for Kreedon, his life had just taken an unexpected u-turn.

Kreedon was *not* schizophrenic after all. He was gifted. He is still gifted. And his gift is very similar to the anonymous man I introduced in this chapter. The spirits that had been inside of Kreedon exploited his gift to see and hear and had been simply jamming his lines of communication with constant chaos. This chaos had been blocking the voice of God from getting through. But now we were doing some long-overdue spring cleaning. Kreedon left our meeting on top of the world.

The night before Kreedon met with me a second time, he was attacked by more entities from within. They started threatening and warning him to stay away from me. They desperately tried to convince him that I was evil and could not be trusted. They knew another confrontation was coming. They also knew I was not afraid of them. Kreedon had a chaotic night and ended up getting injured by trying to evade these voices with alcohol and recklessness. But he did limp into our next session the following morning.

It was really interesting for him to note that the moment he walked through the door of my office, the voices went silent. Dead silent. They were hiding again.

When we started our session, he told me that our previous session may have not worked because he was still hearing voices after he left. I put him back into hypnosis, and we quickly identified another group of entities that were large enough to fill a second auditorium. We learned that these remaining entities were hiding from us during the first session, and we received confirmation from those entities that the first group had not returned. So, I offered these entities the same exit options as the first. And again, surprisingly, all of them did exactly what the first group had done, and walked single file through the door. Gone.

Now the voices were gone for good. And believe it or not, Kreedon's new problems were just beginning. Imagine how difficult it would be for you to go from being "broken for life" to now having to live in a world where you have miraculously changed! Suddenly Kreedon had pure silence in his soul, but he had never really thought about living a functional life. So now, Kreedon's mental silence was loud and glaring. Perhaps some of the lepers that Christ healed experienced a similar identity crisis? How am I supposed to live now without my old problems?

Over the next few weeks, Kreedon and I spent a lot of time exploring what it would be like for him to live a normal and productive life. His parents were in shock to hear that the voices were still completely gone. But he still had work to do in order to figure out his new life's plan. What does one do when lifelong dysfunctions suddenly vanish?

As unbelievable as this story might sound, I assure you it is real. After the entities had cleared out, Kreedon and I did five more hypnosis sessions. These sessions became increasingly interesting when some of his deceased loved ones started to make appearances encouraging him. Kreedon even had his deceased grandfather appear to him and tell him that he was lucky to have found and worked with me. His grandfather went on to explain that he had spent his entire life haunted by the same gift, but had never learned how to silence the dark voices! What this really shows is that Kreedon had an inherited gift in his bloodline that allowed him to hear and see things beyond this worldly veil. And now, his gift was being used for inspiring peace instead of chaos.

Some Parting Thoughts From Kreedon's Own Pen

When I read Mike's words recalling our experiences together, it brought me to tears. That is truly my life! It is really difficult to wrap my head around the reality that my life has changed so dramatically over the past two years. I am still emotional looking back because of these dramatic changes that have come to my life. Over the past year, it feels like a light bulb has turned on inside of me and gotten brighter and brighter. I feel like I am glowing in a spiritual way. It is really hard for me to explain, but the light has basically replaced the darkness, and I feel it shining inside of me. I have lost fear. I have also gained intuition where I question things. I am making better decisions and am much wiser. All of my friends and coworkers love how I am a brand new sketch pad to work with in life. They are encouraging me to do better all of the time. If it wouldn't have been for my work with Mike, I know I would not be where I am today.

The first year after working with Mike, I felt a little lost and in shock. It really took me a year for the shock of the voices being gone to sink in. But in the past year, I rose to a new level — a new spiritual level. I would have never been able to do this without hypnotherapy.

Before I found Mike, I visited a Psychologist who encouraged me to check myself into a three-week program where we would experiment with several different types of medications in a locked-down facility to see what would work best for me. I walked out of that meeting very frustrated. The answer was No. Friends of mine had tried places like this with no success. My parents stayed committed to looking for solutions, and it was shortly after this that they found Mike Simpson and his wellness center. I had hope that I could change, but based on my research I felt like I was going to be a lost cause for the rest of my life. Suicide seemed like the only option for me, and I contemplated that often as my life grew more and more chaotic. I could see no way out of this until my first conversation with Mike. After our first meeting, I felt the lid come off and I believed everything he told me. He literally set me free from a life of constant chaos and hell. I testify to you that these words are true, and if you suffer from anything similar to what I have been through, I want you to know there is really hope. This really works. You don't need to medicate away the symptoms. Just clean out the darkness and the light will already be there.

My transformation started with a small spark of faith. And my belief and faith grew once we kicked out those spirits and the hypnosis was working. It was really changing me, and it was easier than I ever could have imagined. Why wasn't anyone else out there offering help like this? I just can't explain how free I feel to not have to constantly fight against the darkness. Words can never convey the freedom and peace I have claimed.

Blue Skies Forever

"Gray and Black Shadows Glide In Their Flight
Flowing Thick Blackness, Obscuring The Light
A Quick Crack Of Lightning, The Rollings Of Thunder
A Chilled Mist Of Vapor, Proceeding From Under

That Dark Winter's Eve Glories In Season
But Soon Will Be Bound, When Spring Will Have Risen

A Sharp Piercing Ray Slices The Darkness
That Sunbeam Of Hope Shatters The Mist
A Rainbow Is Formed From Light On High
The Assurance Of Spring, The Light Is Nigh

Blue Skies Forever, Hold Fast, Hold Tight"

— Mike Simpson

God Is A Prayer Away

This chapter has shed light on how evil can wreak havoc by hiding in plain sight. By increasing our awareness and our faith, we can manage evil no differently than managing cold weather. We are not helpless after all. Most importantly, God stands at the head of this creation and is always a prayer away — standing at the ready to release us from the grip of darkness. Faith confuses evil. Let these stories build and strengthen your faith and confidence and go out there and do some good. You are on the winning team!

CHAPTER FIFTEEN

The Bridge

I have gone through meticulous effort to explain and share the very formula I have discovered and used to facilitate miraculous healings. This formula of Let Go and Let God Heal builds a healing bridge between two very different paradigms, Heaven and Earth. Death is not required for us to understand and cross The Miracle Bridge. Not only my own suffering, but the suffering of many others whom I have helped along the way, has been the great catalyst for these healing revelations to be born. These truths were often born in crisis, perhaps no differently than labor pains leading to a new birth. And it is my hope that this collective wisdom accrued through suffering has paved the path to this bridge of healing. I often joke that it would have been nice to be able to talk to "this version of me" back when I was suffering and stuck in my old cave of unbelief. But regardless of how I got here, the bridge is now passable, and the ogre is not happy about it. Fear not. Faith confuses him. He is losing captives to The Bridge.

The Needle

"And again I say unto you, It is easier for a camel to go through the eye of a needle, than for a rich man to enter into the kingdom of God." (Matthew 19:24, KJV)

Most people assume this scripture proves that a wealthy man cannot enter heaven. But, as always, Christ's teachings go much deeper than the surface. When Christ walked Jerusalem, the eye of the needle was *actually* a small gate into the city shaped like a keyhole. At night the main gate was closed and city access was only possible through the needle. For a camel to move through the eye of this needle, all baggage had to be removed from its back and it literally had to crawl through the small opening on its knees. This profound teaching is very pertinent to the healing principles I have outlined in this book. Perhaps we can rephrase this scripture and adapt it to this new paradigm of healing.

And again I say unto you, It is easier for a camel to go through the eye of a needle, than **a bitter** *man to enter into the kingdom of God.*

Whether bitter from suffering or prideful from wealth, it is the same. To cross this bridge into this new paradigm of healing, we must ask the Lord to remove our emotional baggage from our backs so that we can reverently drop to our knees and crawl to safety.

While writing this book, I really struggled to come up with a title. This changed instantly the day I worked with my new client, and now close friend, Bruce. It is his story I would like to share with you here. Bruce has an amazing spiritual ability to view into the spiritual realm at will. I didn't fully understand his gift yet in our second meeting where I taught him what Let Go and Let God means, and also *how* to do it. Prior to this session with Bruce, he had struggled mightily with a dark cloud directly over his heart. This cloud was making him miserable and sabotaging his spiritual gifts. While exploring the origins of this darkness, Bruce simply looked and observed how it was shrouding his heart. This darkness had accrued throughout a painful childhood and was *still* actively haunting him as an adult. He could even observe how that darkness reacted when I moved my hand towards it. It recoiled in anger and fear. That very darkness would often create the sensation of Bruce drowning anytime his gift of sight was activated. In fact, it kept happening as I was working with him. Bruce equated this drowning sensation to nearly drowning as a child. Somehow this darkness was using this trauma from Bruce's past to disrupt his inborn, God-given abilities. I showed Bruce how we could push the darkness away from him and let God take it. Bruce hesitated. I needed to know why. We were now on the precipice of discovering a limiting belief that kept him a willing captive in the dark cave.

Ask and ye shall receive!

I asked Bruce a probing question designed to expose his belief systems about the darkness. I asked, "What would you *risk* if you lost the darkness?" The answer was surprising. After waiting a few moments, he responded, "I'd lose my life if I released the darkness." Bingo. Bruce *believed* that he must retain the darkness so that he could remain in this world to help people. Helping others is extremely important to Bruce. He feared his life would be over if he released the darkness and figured this out. I told Bruce that my life was a contradiction to his belief. He was listening. I explained that I have released my darkness and figured life out, but I'm *still* here on Earth helping people. He gave me a quizzical look. I strategically suggested to Bruce that I doubted he was strong enough to push the darkness away. He's really strong! The instant defiance in Bruce's face was hilarious. This was a challenge I *knew* Bruce would polarize. The darkness was an imposter that had been deceiving him by using his integrity against him. The nerve! Bruce *instantly* shoved the darkness up and away and watched it separate from him like a layer of oil floating to the top of water. Bruce then suddenly saw a myriad of angels rushing to his aid, grabbing the darkness, and literally holding it away from him. He was amused and enthralled.

It was here that I explained to Bruce that it was now up to him to ask God to take the darkness. The angels literally cheered and celebrated that I was teaching this principle to Bruce. They had been trying to get through to him for a long time. Bruce explained it was difficult for them to be quiet while I spoke. But they were frantically urging him to listen carefully to what I was saying while they kept interrupting. Perhaps there were too many cooks in the kitchen! While the angels held the darkness at bay, Bruce did as I suggested and simply asked God to take it. Whoosh! Gone! Bruce literally recoiled in dismay as he watched the hand of God come down and snatch the darkness. He stated, "I suppose that was the hand of God!" This was an absolute miracle that happened right in front of our eyes. I find Bruce's experience compelling because he was actually able to witness this process *without* hypnosis! I usually use hypnosis because it allows us to *bypass* the layer of doubts and fears in the conscious mind that typically prevent the healing miracle from happening. Bruce's spiritual sight was now wide open for the first time in his life. He could see clearly through the lens without the darkness distorting his perspective. The angels were gathered together in the background, cheering. Think of the munchkins from the Wizard of Oz singing and dancing because the witch is dead.

False Beliefs Cluster Together Like Cockroaches

Another limiting belief we found in Bruce's perception was the idea that he had to suffer in order to be a good person. This belief encouraged Bruce to create and maintain suffering so that others would feel comfortable around him. He was willing to be less so others could be more. He didn't want to appear arrogant to others, so sick and miserable was his facade of choice. This belief system was programmed into Bruce as a neglected young man who found purpose and value *only* when helping others at his own expense. I explained to Bruce that this mentality of perpetually denying himself is actually called false humility and based on a faulty principle. His suffering state is not what helps other people, although I believe it reinforced his genuine goodness. His suffering had certainly made him better instead of bitter. But what if Bruce AND the people he is helping can all be free of darkness? I asked him if he had sought me out for help because he *hoped* that I was buried in darkness, mediocre, and miserable. He chuckled. I suggested to Bruce that embracing his gift *and* standing taller by pushing away the darkness would be the very catalyst that would take him to a higher rung on Jacob's ladder. Bruce crossed the bridge without dying. Is it possible to be amazing *and* humble at the same time? If you think the answer to this question is No then you better rethink how amazing the Savior was as he humbly walked the Earth.

Wonder Twin Powers...

Bruce is now a very close friend of mine and has partnered up with me in a joint effort with group workshops to dramatically accelerate the healing process with large groups of people. He joked with me that together, we are like the Wonder Twins, but begged me not to make him be the bucket of water. He explained to me that his older sister always made him the bucket of water while *she* got to be the lightning bolt. The audacity! Bruce is definitely the lightning bolt! In these workshops, Bruce can see quickly what sometimes takes me multiple one-on-one sessions to find in someone. And that takes *way too long* because there are far too many people searching for The Bridge. I am able to use group hypnosis and NLP to open people's minds to discover their own limiting beliefs and attitudes that are preventing God from taking the darkness. And Bruce is able to observe and assist from his perch like a sentinel. Together with our collective efforts, (including services from the anonymous man discussed in chapter 15) we are uniting our gifts to help large groups experience Let Go and Let God Heal. These group workshops are a radical change of paradigm and have been orchestrated by none other than God. It has required an entire lifetime of searching to arrive at this juncture. And timing is of the essence, because we are running out of time.

As the world grows darker, God matches the darkness with equal but opposite force — His Light. A day of Pentecost and *radical* and *revolutionary* healing is returning in preparation for the return of our great King. He will be greeted by an army of Mighty Hunters, standing at the ready.

I wrote the metaphor Eagles Gathering to demonstrate the great principle of emerging victorious from the Refiner's Fire. Before I share this metaphor with you, I would like to share with you the circumstances and back-story that led to my inspiration.

A Metaphor from Heaven

One day when I was counseling a suffering soul about his troubling, newly discovered character flaw, I had a metaphor come into my mind of how lake water will *always* find a crack in the canoe, even if it is microscopic. I took this metaphor a little further and talked about how the water represents the dark forces of the adversary in this world. And if there is any flaw or compromise in the bottom of the canoe, the water will **always** find it in hopes of sinking you. Being in the middle of the lake is not the time you want to discover the problem. The experience of desperately turning around and paddling back to shore with a hole in your canoe is terrifying and counterproductive. In fact, you spend more energy bailing water out of the canoe than you do paddling back to shore. And, of course, this flaw in the canoe prevents you from getting to your destination. Eagles Gathering is a metaphor that elaborates upon character flaws becoming the catalyst for discovery and improvement.

Many of us believe that pain is bad, and we do our best to avoid it. However, I have come to learn that pain *can* be a catalyst for change. Notice that I did *not* say pain *will* be the catalyst for change. It depends on you. Is it possible to suffer endlessly in vicious cycles without learning the message that God is trying to send to us? Yes. The *amount* of suffering we have endured does not necessarily equate to a level of righteousness. Think back to the perpetual martyr. Instead of a lifetime of suffering in misery, these sometimes painful lessons of accountability can be short in duration *and* be the catalyst for a divine character upgrade if we leverage God's Grace.

I was once told that life is like a university. And if we fail a class, we have to keep retaking it until we pass. This is the law of karma, where painful cycles keep *repeating* until we figure them out! So pain *can* be the catalyst for change if we use it to our advantage. This means that if we humble ourselves and ask the Lord to show us the weakness in our character, usually exposed in crisis, these trials can then be released because we have found accountability. The Lord will step in and convert this weakness of our character into a strength by his grace *if* we let him. There are many debates over the definition of God's grace and how we access it. I have come to understand that grace is *not* something we are entitled to, but rather it is something that we can *qualify* for, through humility and faith. As previously mentioned, we acknowledge that the Lord's *dynamite of crisis* is the very upheaval necessary to open the *mine of discovery* in our hearts. And, within, we often encounter those boulders or character flaws that are far too big for us to remove without the Lord's grace and help. And it is this process that takes us deep into the mine of our character, where we discover and claim the gold buried deeply within. It is this highly treasured gold that we take with us from this life.

Eagles Gathering

The Indian Chief, Eagles Gathering, had a son, Zion, who had reached the age of accountability. The time had arrived for Zion to receive his rite of passage from boy to man. He was now to begin the mighty process of eventually claiming his new name of Mighty Hunter. Eagles Gathering came to Zion in the early hours of the morning of awakening, and took him to the place of fire and discovery. Many times, they had met at this sacred place to speak and learn about the distant and future things that would most certainly lead to destiny.

The day had finally arrived where Eagles Gathering would present the long-awaited sacred details of Zion's passage from boy to man. Father explained to him that the time had come for him to build his own canoe with his own hands, and that one day it would be used in the great crossing of the mighty sea. Eagles

Gathering explained that this canoe was to be built from the forbidden wood of TOKOGAE that was extremely common but extremely difficult to tame and master. Father explained there were many knots and imperfections in his chosen tree, but that these imperfections would be identified and confronted with the ax and saw where hard work and struggle would be required. Eagles Gathering explained with concern and caution that many sons had failed at this mission, and faith and diligence would be the only way to see this through.

The construction of this canoe would begin with the descent into the The Valley of Death. Eagles Gathering revealed to Zion a sketch of the canoe, and he explained he would lead him to a place where he would be provided the necessary tools to begin the mighty battle of felling TOKOGAE. Father explained with a sparkle in his eye that he built his own canoe as a boy, and that he went through the very same rite of passage to become a man, a warrior. This is where Eagles Gathering earned his headdress and his first Eagle's feather.

When Eagles Gathering took Zion to the mighty TOKOGAE, Zion fell back dismayed. How would it be possible to cut down such a mighty tree? Eagles Gathering gestured to the ax and explained it begins with the first swing. He instructed Zion that this ax would work with him and even sometimes against him. The more he was to wield this mighty ax, the stronger he would become. It was to be the dismantling of TOKOGAE, and father explained that TOKOGAE was designed to be battled and would not yield easily. The knots and thorns would fight against Zion every step of this mighty felling. Then the next stage would begin

— cutting TOKOGAE into beams, and then from beams to vessel.

Eagles Gathering oversaw Zion's diligent work. They would meet at the place of fire often to report and review the fall of TOKOGAE. Father was proud, and Zion was determined. Zion would end each day with pure exhaustion, and would return with bruises and cuts. But each morning, he would awake and return to the work of demolition, renewed and determined.

TOKOGAE finally came down in a mighty crash and was followed up with a small celebration with a select few at the place of fire. Next, arrived the daunting process of the dismantling of TOKOGAE. Eagles Gathering provided the jagged saw, lathe, and other interesting and curious tools for Zion to begin developing other muscles that the ax hadn't yet developed. The next stage of TOKOGAE's undoing began.

The cutting continued. Cutting. Chopping. Sawing. And then one day, finally, the day of construction began! Zion stood strong in front of the pile of wood and readied himself to move to the next stage of construction that would require a different type of strength and vision. More thought and perspective would be required to start piecing together the mighty vessel.

Many meetings at the place of fire provided intricate details of the canoe's design. Each meeting was an opportunity to discuss only one piece to be constructed. Zion had to trust Eagles Gathering as he worked on each single piece of the complex puzzle. Father would not allow assembly of the canoe until each and every piece was crafted, shaped, and completed. Somehow Zion had to trust that these pieces would fit together into the canoe of destiny. But the design of many parts were so confusing by themselves. Eagles Gathering suggested that Zion work diligently and trust in the process that he was not yet quite able to understand. Zion needed to have faith. He needed to have vision.

The day finally arrived when the final piece of the vessel was shaved, whittled, and completed. In front of Zion were many odd-shaped pieces of wood. Father beamed with joy as the time of assembly had finally arrived. It was exciting work to see this puzzle come together in unexpected and exciting ways! Each piece perfectly fit into the next. Zion continued following father's daily instruction from the place of fire until the canoe was fully assembled.

There was a great celebration in the village the very day the canoe was finally built. Zion had worked diligently, and after such a season of toil and struggle, Zion stood by the fire as the canoe was presented to the villagers where Zion received his partial new name of Hunter. This celebration was grand, but mother was concealing a concerned look in her eyes. Hunter could see that this celebration was to lead to the next part of the test that was now upon him. The celebration ended with tears and joy. Hunter was now to begin the next stage of the journey to claim his own headdress and to complete his new name that was to become Mighty Hunter.

The following morning father met again with Hunter at the place of fire. Father told him that the rainy season was soon to begin, but before it came, he needed to take the canoe into the calm sea each day to learn to navigate. With enjoyment and fulfillment, Hunter learned the craft of navigation and travel, with arms growing stronger with each day of rowing. As anticipated, the rainy season began and Hunter expected he had now found a season of rest from his toil. But the next morning at the meeting of fire, Hunter was told that his vessel was built for the rainy season and it was now time to start taking the canoe into the stormy sea each morning.

Hunter would return each evening with frustrations and sorrow as he continued to discover glaring weaknesses in his canoe while facing extreme cold and raging seas. He would often cry out into the stormy skies, "I have done all that was asked, and yet this is my reward? Failure?" Each weakness was exposed in the failing canoe by the thrashing seas. The faulty wood of TOKOGAE could not withstand the rainy season and would daily rot and break away only to leave dangerous holes in the canoe. Each return from sea required Hunter to use of the bucket to keep the canoe from sinking while paddling into shore. Hunter would return each evening dejected and frustrated, but he kept the many flaws a secret from his father because he felt so inadequate and unworthy. He did not want to disappoint father. Each night Hunter did his best to repair the glaring flaws with the leftover wood of TOKOGAE. But each storm confirmed Hunter's biggest fears of being inadequate and unworthy. "I've done all that was asked and more! Is this whole thing a deception? Or am I simply too weak to to be a warrior? It is time for me to quit lying to myself."

Finally, after many disappointments in the stormy seas, Hunter finally conceded failure and came to his father dejected. "I can not go on father. I have failed you and must accept my complete loss. My efforts and work have failed me and you." Hunter turned his face away from his father to hide his tears. Eagles Gathering placed his hand on Hunter's shoulder and said softly, "I understand my son. I've been waiting for this day with great anticipation." Hunter quickly turned around and gasped, "You knew I failed you?" Father smiled and said, "Yes, my son, I knew about the canoe. I wrestled with my own faulty vessel just as you have done. You see, the wood of TOKOGAE is not enough. It was never enough. It is now time that we take your broken vessel to The Master Carpenter who will replace each flaw with the sacred wood of Life that we alone are unworthy to approach. Let us both together take this broken vessel of your own works and present it to The Master." It was explained to Hunter that his encounter with The Master was not to be discussed with the others because it was sacred and that every warrior would eventually have to also seek Him. And they would tell The Master after they learned their own work with TOKOGAE would never be enough to save them, but that it was mysteriously required for the vessel's construction.

Hunter's vessel was returned from The Carpenter with care and without flaw. It was a new vessel. Hunter's next day in the stormy sea yielded no flaws. Day after day, storm after storm, Hunter's vessel remained whole. Finally, Eagles Gathering offered Hunter a mighty congratulations that his vessel was now perfect, or complete. Eagles Gathering declared it was now time for the Ceremony of Life at the place of fire to present the new vessel before the village.

The mighty ceremony began with a fire that danced and raged higher than Hunter had ever witnessed! The entire village who had at least one headdress feather were present around the fire. Eagles Gathering clapped his hands and directed everyone's attention to Hunter who was standing next to the fire with his war paint freshly applied. My son, tonight you pass through the flaming sword! The fire actually reacted to the clap! Four braves carried Hunter's completed canoe into the middle of the circle and set it down next to Hunter. The warriors grew quiet as Eagles Gathering started to speak.

He turned to Hunter and declared, "My son, this vessel is now worthy. Sea Worthy. Worthy to make the great journey across the mighty waters. It has been thrashed and broken in the full rainy season where your skills and courage have risen to match the most dangerous of seas. The Master has accepted your work. You began as a boy but are now a man, and worthy. Sea-worthy. Behold my brave son, your new name is Mighty Hunter and you are a part of these Eagles that have gathered. I will now explain the process by which you became worthy. This entire vessel you built with your own hands has been *rebuilt* by The Carpenter from the sacred wood taken from THE TREE OF LIFE. TOKOGAE, The Tree of Knowledge of Good and Evil, has been rooted out from this vessel and from your soul. You must know my son, that TOKOGAE must be defeated by every warrior who will stand and fight in the great battle ahead. You see, my son, YOU are the new vessel! And my son, while you were constructing the canoe, The Master was constructing you!"

In Summary

"Be ye therefore perfect, even as your father in heaven is perfect." (Matthew 5:28, KJV)

The word 'perfect' derives from the Latin word perficere, which breaks down into per ("completely") and facere ("do"). Be ye therefore *complete*. As Eagles Gathering illustrates, it is not possible to make yourself complete. Without the Master Carpenter, your efforts are in vain. But He does require your efforts in order to strengthen and develop you for the great battle that lies ahead.

"Be ye therefore **complete**, even as your father in heaven is **complete**." (Matthew 5:28, KJV)

Let Go *of your blindness* and Let God *show you*

Let Go *of your failures* and Let God *raise you*

Let Go *of your bitterness* and Let God *fill you with peace*

Let Go *of your anger* and Let God *love you*

Let Go *of your blame* and Let God *forgive you*

Let Go *of your reasons* and Let God *guide you*

Let Go *of your entitlement* and Let God *fill you full with gratitude*

Let Go *of your resentment* and Let God *release you*

Let Let Go *of your pity* and Let God *fill you with compassion*

Let Go *of your pride* and Let God *soften you*

Let Go *of your story* and Let God *rewrite you*

Let Go *of your regret* and Let God *cleanse you*

Let Go *of your pain* and Let God *soothe you*

Let Go *of your shame* and Let God USE YOU

Let Go *of your darkness* and Let God HEAL YOU

Let Go *of your stony heart* and Let God *give you a new spirit and a heart of flesh*

"A new heart also will I give you, and a new spirit will I put within you: and I will take away the stony heart out of your flesh, and I will give you an heart of flesh." (Ezekiel 36:26, KJV)

"Therefore if any man be in Christ, he is a new creature: old things are passed away; behold, all things are become new." (2 Corinthians 5:17, KJV)

Let Go and Let God,

Amen and Amen

Appendix

I have extensively used and witnessed the powerful effects of Audio Visual Entrainment (AVE), Cranial Electrotherapy Stimulation (CES), Pulsed Electromagnetic Frequency (PEMF), and many other exciting technologies that we are combining with hypnosis and NLP. This powerful combination is transforming lives. Real science with real results!

For more information about our proven technologies and life-changing group workshops, I invite you to learn more at: **MikeSimpson.live**.

Made in the USA
Monee, IL
25 August 2021